TALKING STRAIGHT

TALKING STRAIGHT

RONALD B. ADLER

Holt, Rinehart and Winston
New York   Chicago   San Francisco   Atlanta
Dallas   Montreal   Toronto   London   Sydney

Art by Sheila Morrell

Library of Congress Cataloging in Publication Data
Adler, Ronald B
  Talking straight.

  Bibliography: p.
  Includes index.
  1. Assertiveness (Psychology) 2. Interpersonal communication. I. Title.
BF575.A85A3   158'.1   79-9575
ISBN 0-03-023021-7

For my parents—my first and most important assertiveness trainers.

Contents

Part Three: SPECIFIC APPLICATIONS

Appendixes

Introduction

One look at the shelves of any bookstore will show you that the "how to" market is a booming one. You can find advice on how to repair your car, make a killing in the stock market, grow houseplants, raise children, and even how to arrange a trouble-free funeral, among other subjects.

Frankly, I'm a sucker for books like these. I'm not perfect at any of the above areas, and I always hope that I can pick up a few pointers which will help me do a better job. Usually I'm disappointed. Most books do a vivid job of describing what's wrong with my present situation, and they usually paint a rosy picture of how I ought to run my life. The problem is that few of them tell me clearly and simply how to get from where I am to where I want to be.

My goal in writing *Talking Straight* is to provide a book which is a "how-to" manual in the best sense. As you'll soon see, the following pages are filled with detailed instructions and activities which will help you move in a step-by-step manner toward expressing yourself more skillfully and confidently with the people who matter in your life. While you'll certainly profit from simply reading the text and instructions, you can expect the most dramatic results if you take time to actually complete the activities, either writing your responses in the spaces provided in the book or using separate sheets of paper. These activities are the key to change. They'll give you a chance to think about and practice the communication skills in this book on your own before you are faced with trying them out in the real world.

Talking Straight is a revision of a book I recently authored, titled *Confidence in Communication*. There are several reasons why I chose to modify the original book and issue it in this format. First, *Talking Straight* is adapted to better meet the needs and interests of non-academic readers. The information in this book is designed for readers who want to communicate more effectively in their personal and professional lives, and who don't have the time or inclination to seek help in a regular course of study. The examples which follow come from a wide variety of cases, and it's likely that you will recognize many similarities between yourself and the communicators described in this book.

A second reason for issuing *Talking Straight* is that it has given me a chance to improve on the information offered in earlier incarnations of this book. Authors rarely are able to modify their original work so quickly, and both you as reader and I as writer are fortunate to have this opportunity. The most significant changes I've made are found in Chapter 5, which contains new and extremely helpful material on reducing anxiety by disputing irrational thoughts.

My final reason for offering this separate edition of *Talking Straight* is to give you a chance to receive expert advice and feedback as you try out skills introduced in the book. Readers seldom have the chance to ask questions or receive comments about their understanding of a book, and I'm pleased to say that you will have such an opportunity. It's likely that at one point or another in your reading you will have a question about whether you have approached a communication problem in the best way. For cases like these the publisher has provided a means of receiving an answer. You will find duplicated copies of most activities in this book on perforated pages following the index. You are invited to fill out the activities in question along with any other comments you have and mail them to *Talking Straight* Feedback; Holt, Rinehart and Winston; 383 Madison Avenue; New York, NY 10017. Your material will be forwarded to a trained communication consultant, who will review it, add remarks and suggestions, and return it to you.

My hope and expectation is that if you carefully read the material which follows, complete the activities, and clear up any questions by writing to the address above, you will soon find yourself communicating in a more assertive and satisfying manner.

R.B.A.
Santa Barbara, California

TALKING STRAIGHT

Part One

BACKGROUND ON ASSERTION

What is assertiveness? Why is it important? How do people come to have communication problems, and how can they begin to change their old, unsatisfying habits? These are the questions that Part One of Talking Straight will answer. By the time you have finished Chapters 1 and 2, you will have a clear idea of the need for assertive communication in your life and of how this book can help fill that need.

1
Assertiveness: What and Why

What kind of people want to become more assertive? Here are the stories of several participants in recent communication workshops and classes. See if their goals sound familiar to you.

—June wanted to run for a position on the local school board, but was frightened at the thought of debating her opponent before audiences of voters. "I know that what I have to say is important," she stated, "but the idea of speaking before a group terrifies me."

—Mike was regional sales manager for a national corporation. Although he was acknowledged as bright and talented by everyone in the organization, in a recent performance evaluation virtually all of his subordinates and many colleagues complained about his aggressive manner. "Not willing to listen", "Too demanding—almost hostile", the reports read. Mike knew that his future in the organization depended on his becoming better at communicating his instructions and ideas in a direct but less aggressive way.

—Beth often felt uncomfortable saying "no," and because of this found herself accepting many social invitations that sounded (and usually were) boring. These dull events left her less time to spend with her friends and family, who did matter to her.

—Leslie found it difficult to carry on a conversation with anyone but her closest friends and family. She said, "At parties I run out of things to say after a few minutes and then spend the rest of the time making small talk and feeling like an idiot. It's gotten to the point that I don't go out much anymore so I won't have to feel uncomfortable."

—Frank was a happily married father of three. He deeply loved his wife and children, yet found it impossible to tell them just how much he cared. "They probably know anyhow," he said, "but sometimes I want to tell them how much they mean to me, and I can't get out the words."

—Jerry was married to Susan, a gregarious woman who dominated every conversation with her stories and jokes. Whenever Jerry would join in, Sue would interrupt to correct him or change the subject. This left Jerry feeling like a spectator, angry at being cut off. He wanted to share his feelings with Sue but didn't know how to do so without making her defensive and starting another round of criticism.

ASSUMPTIONS OF THIS BOOK

These accounts represent literally hundreds of stories that concerned men and women have shared with my colleagues and me in an effort to improve the quality of their communication. Over the past few decades social scientists have developed a number of methods designed to help people handle themselves in situations like these. This group of techniques goes by several names: Social skills training, social effectiveness training, personal effectiveness training, expressive training, and the term used in this book, assertiveness training.

Assertiveness training is based on the idea that verbal and nonverbal self-expression are *skills*, similar in many ways to other skills, such as playing a musical instrument, participating in a sport, or writing a clear sentence. Like these other skills, the ability to communicate can be learned. This is good news, for it means that effective self-expression is not a trait possessed by only a few fortunate people, rather, it is a set of behaviors that can be learned by any person who is willing to invest sufficient time and effort. Helping you to define and then to master these behaviors is the major goal of this book. As you read it and carry out the exercises, you'll not only learn a great deal of information about effective communication—you should actually start to *behave* in new, more satisfying ways.

The path to assertive communication is based on three assumptions, each of which is supported by extensive research. Because these assumptions are basic to everything that follows, it is important to state them here.

1. You Can Change This statement may sound obvious, but many people fail to accept it, and thus commit themselves to a lifetime of unsatisfying relationships. The tendency to explain unassertiveness by saying "That's the way I am" is common, as the case of Margaret illustrates. Margaret was an intelligent, attractive woman whose life was made miserable by a domineering great-aunt who had filled the role of a mother since Margaret's parents were killed in an automobile crash when she was a child. The aunt was a critical woman who found fault with most everything her niece did, in spite of the fact that Margaret had almost single-handedly raised three well adjusted sons since a divorce several years earlier. The aunt's complaints ranged from small to large: The boys' hair was too long. The house always (in her estimation) needed cleaning. Margaret was not a decent provider. She owed it to her sons to remarry in order to give them a father. And so it went almost endlessly, according to Margaret's account. When asked why she put up with such constant negativity Margaret replied that asserting herself was out of the question. The aunt was such a strong woman that there was no chance of standing up to her. Besides, the aunt had always helped out financially during hard times, and it would be ungrateful to bite the hand that sometimes fed her family. And finally, the aunt had known and raised her for years, so perhaps her criticisms were right. A course in assertiveness training convinced Margaret that what looked like a lifetime sentence of deference and quiet resentment was not the only alternative open to her. After instruction and practice in the principles that follow, Margaret reported an astonishing change in her relationship with the aunt. Where she had meekly accepted and even agreed with her aunt's remarks, she now expressed her own reasons for living as she did. And as she grew more confident in the validity of these reasons and more skillful in expressing them, the aunt's complaints fell off sharply. "I suppose I could have stood up for myself all along," Margaret confessed, "but I always figured that she was she and I was I and that's the way it always would be."

The lesson in Margaret's story is that change *is* possible, even in situations that seem hopeless. Each of the accounts that opened this chapter had successful endings, and the chances are good that most communication difficulties of this type can also be resolved.

2. Change Can Be Relatively Quick and Permanent As the previous account illustrates, it's not necessary to spend the entire second half of one's life unlearning the unassertive behaviors developed during the first half. People often assume that any worthwhile change takes an extended time—perhaps measurable in years. While this may sometimes be the case, when it comes to improving communication and other social skills it is not necessarily so. You will find that many of the principles of assertive communication are surprisingly simple to learn and to put into action. Most readers will begin to notice changes in their behavior by the time they have finished Chapter 3.

On the other hand, the fact that you can expect to *begin* changing quickly does not mean that this or any book can guarantee instant attainment of your goals. As you will read over and over again, the principle of change stressed in this book is that of gradual but steady progress. As you define each goal, the methods outlined will show you how to begin adding that way of behaving to your life. The advantage to this steady progress is that the changes which result usually last. Unlike New Years' resolutions, which are rarely permanent, the assertive behaviors you develop here will become genuine parts of your personality, so that after an initial period of concentration and practice, they will occur naturally and effortlessly.

3. Change Comes From Doing As its name implies, assertiveness *training* is an active process. While you might learn a great deal intellectually just from reading this book, such an approach is unlikely to help change the way you act toward others. In order actually to bring about a difference in the way you communicate it will be necessary for you to actively practice the concepts introduced here. To help you with this practice, there are a number of exercises scattered through the following pages. It is absolutely essential that you carry out each exercise as you come to it. In doing so you will begin to put into practice the concepts that will improve your assertive skills. While the exercises may sometimes seem artificial, they will help bridge the gap between your present unfamiliarity with assertive behavior and the moment when you will actually use these skills in the everyday world. Just as a pianist must run through scales before performing in concert, it will be necessary for you to practice the assertive exercises. Remember: *No exercises, no change.*

ASSERTIVENESS DEFINED

There are almost as many definitions of assertiveness as there are assertiveness trainers. The term is always used as a kind of shorthand for a group of desirable communication behaviors, but while there are many similarities between the various definitions of assertion, it is a good idea to ask for details upon hearing the word rather than assume it means the same thing to everyone.

As used in this book, *assertiveness is the ability to communicate the full range of your thoughts and emotions with confidence and skill*. There are several words in this definition that need explanation.

The *ability* to express yourself means that you can choose the appropriate way to act in a situation rather than being limited to only one response. For instance, suppose you have been looking forward to a quiet evening at home, only to find that your neighbors have chosen this night for their annual wild party, complete with live band and kegs of beer. An unassertive person might only think of phoning the police to complain (a behavior more aggressive than assertive) or passively sitting home and fuming. On the other hand, an assertive person would be able to choose from a number of other alternatives, such as speaking directly to the neighbors and asking that the noise be lowered, asking to join the fun, or deciding that the issue isn't really important and simply let the neighbors have a good time. Each of these alternatives might be best under different circumstances and for different people, but whatever the ultimate choice is in such cases, the important thing to realize is that an assertive people have a repertoire of behaviors that enable them to act in the most appropriate, satisfying way. Sometimes the choice may be to speak up and sometimes not, but in any case effective communicators are able to select the course of action that is best for them.

The second part of the above definition states that the assertive person communicates a *full range* of messages. Most people are what Alberti and Emmons call "situationally unassertive." They express themselves well most of the time, but lack skill or confidence with certain people or in certain situations. For example, some people have no trouble expressing anger or displeasure but have a hard time sharing affectionate feelings. Others communicate easily with people of the same sex but freeze up with members of the opposite sex. Still others communicate skillfully at home and with friends but are unable to stand up for their rights at work. One goal of this book is to help you identify *all* the situations where you want to be more assertive and to help you do so to the best of your ability.

How well do you express your thoughts and feelings? You can begin to answer this question by taking a few minutes to try the following exercises. Be sure to do so before reading on.

Find a quiet spot where you will not be interrupted. Now picture yourself talking with an important person in your life. Imagine yourself sharing

a. The two things you most appreciate or admire about that person
b. Two ways in which you would like the person to change

Would you have difficulty communicating any of these messages? Would you like to send any of them better? If so, turn now to page 18 and record them there. Do this before reading on.

The preceding definition also states that assertive people are able to communicate their *thoughts*. These include opinions, such as why a certain candidate should be elected or whether a book is worth reading; requests, such as how a jacket should be pressed at the cleaners or one's reasons for wanting to borrow some money; or explanations for various actions, such as why you plan to change jobs or move to another place. Assertive people are also good at communicating *emotions* such as anger, affection, appreciation, hurt, or pride. As assertive person is able to express the *full range* of these feelings, rather than just a few.

An assertive person has *self-confidence*. This does not mean being totally free of anxiety, a state that is probably impossible to reach and might not even be desirable. Even after successfully learning the assertive behaviors in this book, you will probably still find yourself feeling anxious as you practice some of them. Perhaps the fear will come from expressing a legitimate gripe to your boss, standing up for an unpopular idea in which you believe, or saying "I like you" before knowing how the other person feels about the relationship. It is important to realize that confidence does not always mean the lack of fear. In fact, often it is the *courage* to accept your fear, manage it, and to go on, trusting yourself enough to believe you have done the right thing.

Finally, assertive communication is a *skill*. Sometimes sincerity and confidence alone won't help you express yourself well. Just as a tone-deaf singer can be sure of his lyrics while warbling off key, a well-intentioned but ineffective communicator will often fail to get the message across effectively. Meeting strangers is a skill that can be learned. So are making requests, saying "no," and all the other behaviors that make up an assertive personality. Some people are lucky enough to learn good communication skills like these early and easily, but others need to unlearn bad habits and to master new ones. The chapters that follow are written in a how-to form, suggesting the kinds of behavior you might want to learn and showing you ways to make them part of your repertoire.

One final note: Don't expect that after reading this book all your efforts at assertiveness will meet with success. Since you can't control the reactions of others, even the most skillful message won't always bring a satisfying result. Probably the best way to think of your assertive skill is the way baseball players regard their batting averages. Knowing it's unrealistic to expect a base hit on every trip to the plate, they are satisfied to succeed in a reasonable percentage of their efforts. In the same manner, you ought to be content with the knowledge that whatever the results in a particular instance, you're expressing yourself in the best way under the circumstances. Such knowledge will pay off in two ways. First, your overall rate of success will certainly increase; second, even in the instances that don't work out, you'll gain self-respect by knowing that you expressed yourself with honesty and dignity.

ASSERTION IS NOT AGGRESSION

Although this matter will be treated in more detail in Chapter 9, before going any further it's important to clear up a common misconception by distinguishing between assertion and aggression.

For many, the term "assertion" conjures up images of loud, overbearing, argumentative, and on the whole obnoxious people who get their way by intimidating others. This image includes caricatures such as the hostile "women's lib" advocate, the loud-mouthed, back-slapping life-of-the-party type, or the compulsive talker. In light of these stereotypes, it's easy to understand why many people might react to the idea of your undertaking a program of assertiveness training with dismay.

Because of these common reactions it may be necessary for you to do a bit of teaching yourself by pointing out that assertion is *not* aggression; in fact, in many ways it's quite the opposite. Unlike the aggressors, assertive individuals respect the rights of others as well as their own. When problems arise, they seek solutions in which both parties have their needs met. They are friendly and outgoing, but they don't impose themselves on others.

In other words, the object of this book isn't to turn you into an aggressive, demanding boor any more than a physical fitness course aims at producing a lumbering, musclebound hulk. As you'll learn by reading the many examples and case studies that follow, an assertive person is generally a pleasure to be with—a definite contrast to his distant relative, the aggressive communicator.

ASSERTIVENESS INVENTORY

This exercise will help you define some important areas in which you want to improve your communication with others. Below is a list of 30 scenes, each of which could be handled in a number of ways.

As you read each description, try to imagine yourself in the situation. Get a clear mental picture of the events. Picture who else is present: See how they look, talk, and act. Visualize the setting in which the conversation occurs: Where it is, the time of day, the sounds you hear, and so on. Finally, imagine how you would respond in the scene: How you would feel, move, and speak. Even if you have never found yourself in precisely the situation described, it's possible to imagine how you probably would behave.

After taking a few moments to visualize a scene, indicate in the space next to the statement how satisfied you feel about your probable action, according to the following scale. After you have responded to all 30 scenes, turn to the directions at the end of the exercise.

5 = Completely satisfied with your probable action.
4 = Generally, though not totally satisfied with your probable action.
3 = About equally satisfied and dissatisfied with your probable action.
2 = Generally, though not totally dissatisfied with your probable action.
1 = Totally dissatisfied with your probable action.

____ 1. One evening you drop by a friend's house to find a party in progress. You don't know anyone present except your host, who invites you to join the group and then disappears. You have the time to spare and the guests look interesting.

____ 2. You are taking a four-hour plane trip by yourself. You are seated next to a person who seems friendly. This traveler strikes up a conversation by asking where you are from.

____ 3. While eating with a friend in a restaurant, an employer, instructor, or some other person you respect approaches your table and says hello. This person seems to feel like talking briefly with you. He/she has not met your companion.

_____ 4. You are attending the annual Christmas party at the place where you or someone you know works. Although you have very little in common with the others, you do want to be sociable.

_____ 5. A week ago you noticed that an interesting-looking person moved into a house down the street from yours. You would like to meet this person. Now you are walking down the street and notice him/her coming toward you.

_____ 6. You are attending a series of lectures or meetings and notice several people you would like to have for friends. You arrive at the room early and find them in conversation. As you approach, they look up.

_____ 7. A good friend shows you a painting he/she has just finished and asks for your honest opinion. You don't like the painting at all.

_____ 8. While on vacation you are taking a group lesson in a new sport (skiing, rock climbing, etc.) After the instructor has lectured on the basic principles, everyone in the group seems to have caught onto the idea and is anxious to get started. You, however, are still confused about several points.

_____ 9. A neighbor you have grown close to is moving to a distant city, and it is unlikely that you will see each other for a long time, if ever again. You have never directly told this person how you feel about him/her. You are spending a last social evening together.

_____10. A friend compliments you on your appearance. The remark seems sincere.

_____11. You recently had an argument with a friend. After thinking about it, you realize that you were wrong and acted foolishly. You think you owe the other person an apology.

_____12. You have been feeling depressed lately, but haven't mentioned it to anyone. Now a friend asks if anything is wrong.

_____13. A close friend has seemed upset lately and you ask if anything is wrong. He/she responds by demanding that you quit being so nosy and mind your own business.

_____14. Before going out for a social evening, you ask your companion for an opinion of how you look. The other person replies, "If you really want to know the truth, that outfit looks terrible," and begins to elaborate on this remark.

_____15. At your job or school your teacher or boss reacts to your work by commenting, "I know you could do better if you wanted to."

_____16. You have been extremely busy lately. Now you run into an old acquaintance who accuses you of not caring about your friends anymore.

_____17. While engaged in a political discussion, your companion accuses you of not knowing what you're talking about.

_____18. You've just turned down a door-to-door solicitor who is selling magazines for a cause you don't care to support. He/she responds to your refusal by saying "Don't you even care about needy____?"

____19. For some time you have felt more and more distant from a previously close friend or family member. You haven't mentioned this feeling yet, hoping it would pass away. However, the feeling hasn't disappeared, and you see your close relationship dissolving.

____20. You made a dental appointment for 10:00 A.M., specifically telling the receptionist that you have only an hour to spare and receiving assurances that this would be enough time. You arrived a few minutes ahead of time and have now been in the waiting room for 35 minutes. Several patients who arrived after you have been ushered in for treatment.

____21. While attending a movie you are annoyed by loud talking from two people seated near you.

____22. You have been waiting to be served in a crowded store. The clerk asks, "Who's next?" A person who came in after you says, "I am."

____23. While at a party some guests begin making racial and ethnic comments that offend you. The speakers are getting increasingly vocal, and although you think other people must also be bothered, nobody has spoken out yet.

____24. Shortly after moving into a new neighborhood you find that the people next door are rock music fans. They play loud music four or five nights a week until past midnight. The noise is interfering with your sleep.

____25. Several months ago a neighbor borrowed one of your books, which he/she returned with several pages torn and stained. Now the same person has asked to borrow two of your favorite record albums.

____26. An acquaintance has invited you to his/her house twice for social evenings, and you did not enjoy yourself either time. Now the same person has invited you to a party several weeks in advance "so you'll be sure to keep the date free."

____27. Several friends have asked you to join them on a trip that will require your missing one day of the semester or work. You know you will have to talk about this with your instructor or boss.

____28. You want to move several large, heavy pieces of furniture into your house and need a neighbor's assistance. The job should take an hour or two. The neighbor has offered before in a general way to "lend a hand whenever you need it."

____29. You are visiting a new city for a few days and want to make the most of your trip by visiting spots tourists don't usually see. While in a coffee shop you overhear two couples talking about a place you would like to learn more about and possibly visit.

____30. You have recently been given a job that involves assigning work to other people. Today is the first time you have to tell them what to do, and it's important that you get them to do the job well without sounding bossy.

Evaluating Your Answers

The questions you just answered are divided into five groups, each corresponding to a chapter or part of a chapter in Part Three.

Questions 1–6 . . . . Conversation skills (Chapter 7)
Questions 7–12 . . . . Expressing feelings and thoughts
                         (Chapter 8)
Questions 13–18 . . . . Coping with criticism (Chapter 8)
Questions 19–24 . . . . Managing conflicts (Chapter 9)
Questions 25–30 . . . . Making requests and saying no
                         (Chapter 9)

You can use the results in two ways. By looking at each question, you can see how satisfied you are with your behavior in that specific situation. Thus, a response of 1 or 2 on any single question is an obvious signal that you can profit from working on that situation as you read through the book. (A quick look at the Contents and Index will direct you to the appropriate pages.) Before reading on, decide which responses you felt were unsatisfactory or important enough to list on page 18 as possible areas to work on in later chapters.

By totaling your numerical responses for each of the five categories above you can gain an idea of how satisfied you are with your assertiveness in that area. A score of 17 or below suggests that you should concentrate on this area, while a total approaching 30 indicates a "no problem" area.

Totaling your responses for the entire test and dividing by 30 would give an indication of your overall satisfaction with your assertiveness, but such a measure isn't very helpful in changing the way you communicate. As you will shortly learn, most people are assertive in some situations and unassertive in others. Since this is so, the way to change is to focus on those specific situations or areas that need improvement.

THE EXTENT OF NONASSERTION: A SAMPLING

This assertiveness inventory has probably made you aware of several areas in which you don't assert yourself to the degree that you would like to. As a result it would be easy to feel that such unassertiveness is an abnormally great problem for you but a brief look at communication research shows that this is not the case.

Philip Zimbardo and his colleagues at Stanford University spent several years studying shyness, a common type of nonassertion. Their research showed, first, that shyness is a widespread problem: Of over 800 university and high school students surveyed, 82 percent described themselves as having shy dispositions, either presently or at some time in the past. Another 17 percent reported being situationally shy—reacting with shyness in certain situations. Only 1 percent reported themselves as never having experienced shyness. As the researchers point out, these figures are surprising considering the image of brashness and protest that has characterized American youth. The characteristics the Stanford researchers found to be common among their shy respondents paint such a vivid picture of a nonassertive personality that they deserve to be quoted at length:

> He or she is almost always silent, especially in the company of strangers, members of the opposite sex, and other threats. He frequently avoids eye contact and often tries to avoid other people completely taking refuge, perhaps in books, nature or some other private project. He avoids taking action and speaks in a quiet voice when he speaks at all.

> While this sort of nonbehavior is going on externally, the inner world of shyness is filled with self-consciousness; thoughts about the unpleasantness of the situation; and various other thoughts and distractions aimed at averting all of the above. The dominant physiological reactions reported are increased pulse, blushing, perspiration, butterflies in the stomach, and a pounding heart. Motionless on the outside, a chaos within. It's easy to understand why shyness can be so painful.

The Stanford research reinforces the statement that assertiveness is not an either-or phenomenon, but covers a wide range of intensity. At one end of the spectrum are people whose shyness is voluntary. They avoid others because they prefer solitude and often would rather work with things than with people. They will join others or express themselves when necessary, but given the choice, they prefer to be alone. In the middle of the shyness spectrum are people who want to interact with others more but who lack the necessary social skills, such as asking for dates or making conversation. Because of their ineptness in some situations these moderately shy people—who can be labeled *situationally unassertive*—are reluctant to approach others, even when they want to. This is the category into which most people fall, and this is the audience for whom this book is written. Subjects in the extremely shy category are what can be termed *generally nonassertive*. Their fear of communicating with others is so great that it keeps them from the kinds of contact they desire most. As the researchers point out, this extreme shyness is "a form of imprisonment in which the person plays both prisoner and guard." Whatever the labels, it is clear that most people don't enjoy being shy; more than half of the students surveyed stated that they could profit by therapeutic help for their problem and would go to a "shyness clinic" if one existed. (Of course, this book and ones like it partially fill this need.)

In addition to shyness, another characteristic of nonassertion is the inability to stand up for one's personal rights. The number of passive victims in our society is astounding, judging by a series of experiments by

Thomas Moriarty. He recruited male college psychology students to take a difficult 20-minute test in which they had to unscramble letters to form words. The test-takers were seated back to back in a small room. Unknown to one subject, the other was an accomplice of the experimenter. Shortly after the test began, the confederate turned on a portable tape recorder at top volume. Unless the subject protested, a 17-minute rock music concert followed. Some subjects covered their ears and others turned to stare at the violator, but 80 percent made no verbal objections at all. Fifteen percent made mild requests of the accomplice, who was instructed not to turn off the machine until he was asked three times, in order to test the persistence of the subjects. One student handled the situation aggressively by leaping up as soon as the music began and aggressively demanding that it be turned off, so upsetting the accomplice that he complied. When the subjects were told about the nature of the experiment and asked why they didn't stand up for their right to take the test in silence, they responded by claiming that the test wasn't important enough to justify complaining about. Most claimed that if the test had been an important one, they would have spoken out. A followup experiment disproved this contention, however. In this second test new subjects were told that the person with the higher score would be rewarded, while the low scorer would be punished with mild electric shocks. Again, 80 percent said nothing at all about the music, and only one persisted with three demands for silence. As in the first experiment, the subjects later denied the importance of the test. When reminded about the consequences of being a low scorer, some replied "You said *mild* shocks, didn't you?"

Moriarty reports similar results in other settings. When 40 readers in a library were subjected to loud seven-minute conversations, only one asked the subjects to be quiet, while nine got up and left. The remaining 30 readers said nothing. In a similar experiment in a movie theater only 35 percent of the subjects complained when two experimenters carried on a loud, extended conversation. At this point Moriarty speculated that the victims might have behaved in moderation on the assumption that the violators' impolite behavior had been unintentional. So in his final series of tests the behavior of the accomplices was designed to be clearly deliberate. The experiments took place in a phone booth at Grand Central Station in New York City, a place known for its aggressive citizens. The subjects this time were 20 men, most of whom looked like businessmen. As each finished his call, he was approached by an experimenter, who claimed to have left a ring in the booth and asked if the subject had seen it. Of course, all subjects answered no. At this point the experimenter said, "I've got to find it. Are you sure you didn't see it? Sometimes people pick up things without thinking about it." After another denial, the experimenter asked the subject to empty his pockets. Even in this clear accusation of thievery, only 4 of 20 subjects refused to comply. The remaining 16 (80 percent) emptied their pockets.

Assuming that the subjects described here are representative of most people, the average citizen in our society emerges as a shy person who is unwilling to stand up for even the simplest of personal rights. As other research measures different expressive skills, we can predict that the need for assertiveness training of some sort will become even clearer.

Recall a recent instance in which you felt shy or failed to stand up for your rights. If you would like to change your behavior in such situations, record your description of this problem on page 18.

The Consequences of Unassertiveness If unassertiveness simply inhibited communication, it would be bad enough, but the problem is greater than this, as another look at the work of Zimbardo and his associates at Stanford shows.

Nonasserters pay for not expressing themselves in several ways. The most obvious costs are social ones. Shy people make few new acquaintances and have a hard time building friendships with those people they do meet. They often wind up feeling isolated, even in a crowd, and thus become victims of the unhappy social disease of loneliness. Even when they do mingle with others, nonexpressive people are often misunderstood. It's easy to misinterpret the silence of shyness and discomfort for boredom, hostility, or snobbishness. As Zimbardo points out, this is even true for attractive people, who others figure must be standoffish out of choice, since "they have everything going for them."

Because nonasserters are so often silent, it is hard to learn about their appealing qualities, such as intelligence, common interests, sense of humor, and sensitivities. To make things worse, this lack of information keeps others from responding to the nonasserter, thus making conversation even more difficult and starting a vicious circle of silence. Because shy people are reluctant to stand up for themselves, they often remain silent as others attack their cherished beliefs. And even when they do try to defend their opinions, nonasserters are often so nervous and unsure of themselves that their thoughts come out in a confused way.

Besides the social consequences, nonassertiveness takes a psychological toll on its victims. In their book, *Creative Aggression*, Bach and Goldberg describe three attitudes that often develop in people who are not able to express the full range of their feelings. Some simply withdraw from any kind of meaningful contact with others, taking refuge in impersonal activities: watching TV for hours at a time, lavishing all their affection on such inanimate objects as cars or motorcycles, becoming preoccupied with earning money, or distracting themselves with liquor or other drugs.

Other people deal with their inept communications by becoming cynics, claiming that people aren't worth caring about anyway. Bill was a sad example of this category. He claimed that the best thing about being 18 was his freedom to move away from his parents, whom he shrugged off as "jerks," yet he listened intently in class when other students talked with pride about their families. In different cases cynics cope with their despair by turning to objects unworthy of respect and therefore worthless enough to manipulate with no hesitation. Communicators with this attitude often become the aggressors we mentioned earlier: They take an "I'm O.K., you're not O.K." attitude, yet often feel just the opposite.

A third group of nonasserters reacts to their condition with despair at themselves and what they see as the human condition. They claim that people are disgusting creatures and that life in this imperfect world is not worth living. As Bach and Goldberg point out, the results of this attitude can be depression, emotional breakdown, or even suicide in the most extreme cases.

Besides social and psychological consequences, nonassertion also can have its physiological costs, often in the form of psychosomatic illnesses. We are not talking about hypondochondria, in which people believe they are ill but aren't, or malingering, in which they pretend to be sick. Psychosomatic disease is real: It differs in no physical way from an organically caused one. The characteristic that distinguishes a psychosomatic illness is that while the pain comes from a condition in the person's body, the problem has its origins in some aspect of the person's psychological adaptation to his surroundings. Psychosomatic problems can grow out of the chronic anxiety that asserters feel over their inability to express their thoughts and feelings. To understand this anxiety, it is helpful to think of a prehistoric man being attacked by a saber-toothed tiger. His body automatically responds in several ways to this threat: His heartbeat speeds up, his blood pressure rises, his body produces hormones that give him full energy by speeding sugar to his muscles and brain. The pupils of his eyes dilate, thus improving his vision. His digestion stops, in order to reroute the energy used there toward meeting his enemy. His red blood cell count increases in order to deliver more oxygen to his cells and to carry away carbon dioxide. Mobilized in all these ways, the caveman is ready to handle the threat by either fighting or fleeing.

Today our bodies react the same way to stress-producing situations: defending yourself when someone attacks a cherished belief or one of your personal rights, considering the risk of sharing a deeply held feeling, standing before a group to give a speech, or deciding whether or not to say no to an unwelcome request.

Often in situations such as these which call for an assertive response, fears and inhibitions keep us from using all this mobilized energy to resolve the crisis at hand. And over a period of time the failure to act on these impulses leads to a constant state of physiological tension that damages the digestive tract, lungs, circulatory system, muscles, joints, and the body's ability to resist infections. It even hastens the process of aging.

At first these claims might sound preposterous, but a growing body of medical evidence points to their truth. For instance, in 30 years of research Wolf (1965) found that the mucous lining that protects the inside of the stomach responds minute by minute to both conscious and unconscious emotions. When a person becomes angry, the lining becomes enflamed, producing excessive amounts of acids and gastric juices. In fact, ulcers have been produced experimentally in animals by subjecting them to stress. People who develop ulcers have stomachs that are almost constantly in this state of agitation, and often this condition is caused by a failure to express their feelings fully.

Hypertension, or high blood pressure, and heart trouble also often have their roots in chronic stress. Over a five-year period Flanders Dunbar studied a random sample of 1,600 cardiovascular patients at Columbia Presbyterian Medical Center in New York City. She found that four of five patients shared common emotional characteristics, many of which are representative of either nonassertive or aggressive communicators. For instance, most of her patients were argumentative, had trouble expressing their feelings, and kept people at a distance. McQuade and Aikman describe other characteristics of cardiovascular sufferers—easily upset but unable to handle upsetting situations, anxious to please but longing to rebel, alternately passive and irritable.

Besides suffering from these conditions in disproportionate numbers, there is evidence that nonasserters sometimes face another physical problem. The immunological system, which protects the body against infection, seems to function less effectively when a person in under stress. Sometimes the body doesn't respond quickly enough to infection; at other times it responds incorrectly, as in the case of allergic reactions. Stress has even been diagnosed as one cause of the common cold. It is important to realize that stress or anxiety alone are not sufficient to cause these disorders. There must also be a source of infection present. But as research by Swiss physiologist Hans Selye suggests, persons subjected to stress have an increased chance of contracting infectious diseases. As Selye states, "If a microbe is in or around us all the time and yet causes no disease until we are exposed to stress, what is the cause of our illness, the microbe or the stress?" Medical researchers now suspect that cancers are caused by a malfunction in the body's system of immunities, and thus may also be linked to stress.

All this talk about psychosomatic illness is not to suggest that a life of nonassertion automatically leads to ulcers, heart trouble, and cancer. Obviously, many shy or aggressive people never suffer from such ailments and many assertive people do. And just as clearly there are many other sources of stress in our society besides nonassertion: financial pressures, the problems of people we care for, the unsatisfying features of urban life such as pollution and crime, and the nagging threat of war, to name a few. Nonetheless, an increasing amount of evidence suggests that the person who is unwilling or unable to be fully expressive stands increased risk of developing physical disabilities. Just as nonsmokers are less likely to contract lung cancer than their pack-a-day counterparts, relaxed and skillfull communicators have a better chance of living a healthy life.

The major goal of Talking Straight is to help you to become a more skillful, self-assured communicator. In order to do so, you will be working on a self-modification project as you read through this book. Each chapter will help you move closer to your personally chosen goals, so that when you have finished the last one, you will find yourself behaving in new, more satisfying, assertive ways.

The first step in changing your behavior is to define a problem clearly. Throughout Chapter 1 you have described several situations in which you would like to express yourself more assertively. Look over these responses now, see if you need to add any other important ones, and then pick the five situations that seem most important to you. List them here.

1. _____
   _____
   _____

2. _____
   _____
   _____

3. _____
   _____
   _____

4. _____
   _____
   _____

5. _____
   _____
   _____

SUMMARY

Chapter 1 has introduced you to the fundamental assumptions of this book: Relatively quick and lasting change is possible for any person who is willing to understand and practice the steps outlined. Assertiveness has been defined as the ability to express the full range of one's thoughts and feelings with confidence and skill. This mode of communication has been contrasted with aggression, which is often mistakenly equated with assertion. The characteristics of the nonassertive personality have been outlined, and the psychological, social, and physical consequences of unassertiveness have been detailed. Finally, you should have taken the first step in moving toward more assertive communication in your own life by completing the exercises throughout the chapter and summarizing the results on page 18. If you have not already completed these exercises and hope to improve the quality of your communication by using this book, finish them before going on to Chapter 2.

Shy people often feel isolated.

2
Assertiveness Can Be Learned

Four summers ago Robin was born. She seemed to spend the first months of life in her own world, oblivious to the family and friends who had awaited her arrival so eagerly. Like all infants, her life was governed mostly by basic physical needs and instincts: She cried incessantly until her demand of the moment was satisfied by feeding, a blanket, or a dry diaper, and no training was necessary to teach her the purpose of her mother's breast. At this early stage nobody was foolish enough to try to teach Robin how to behave. In fact, in those early weeks the tables were reversed: she ran the family, and those around her gradually learned how to please her.

After a few months Robin began to change. The first sign was a very definite toothless grin directed at her mother and dad—clearly different from the earlier, fleeting grimaces Dr. Spock described as symptoms of gas. Of course, this event was greeted with much jubilation: hugs and kisses between all concerned. And with that first smile a lifelong dialogue began between Robin and those around her; for as her smiles continued to be followed by excitement and approval, Robin began to realize (though certainly not consciously) that she had some *control* over her environment. Later she learned more behavior that resulted in recognition. Certain sounds brought forth parental approval: "Mama," "Daddy," "kitty" . . . while others had no payoff. Certain actions were also followed by verbal and nonverbal praise: tossing a ball, eating with a spoon, and keeping her diapers dry. Other behavior met with unpleasant consequences: picking up kitty by the neck, throwing food, running into the street were followed by harsh reprimands, occasionally slaps on the wrist and bottom, and sometimes banishment to her bedroom for a two-minute sentence of solitary confinement.

Of course, while Robin's parents were guiding her, she also shaped their behavior. They now know that a plate of beans or tuna fish will be ignored or pushed aside, and so they choose other foods that meet with greater approval. They know that the finest blanket is no substitute for her tattered piece of lamb's wool, and so they diligently search for the Fuzzy before each bedtime. Robin and her parents are constantly influencing each other, just as everyone shapes and is shaped by those around them.

This kind of influence is what psychologists mean by the term *learning: any relatively permanent change in behavior that results from an individual's interaction with the environment.* This definition makes it clear that learning goes on in many places besides school. Whether we intend it or not, our actions affect the behavior of others, and we in turn are affected by their actions. Each of us learns to speak from observing and trying out the behaviors of those around us. We learn the social standards of our culture by the examples of our contemporaries and the results we get as we act in various ways. The same holds true for our morals, pastimes, fashions, aesthetic tastes, and virtually all our behavior and attitudes: All are products of our experience.

Most behavior is learned. This tremendously important fact forms the cornerstone of this book, for it means that just as you can learn writing or mathematics or tennis, it is also possible to learn assertiveness. Further, it means that unassertiveness is not caused by a person's shortcomings or a character defect, but rather poor learning experiences.

This chapter will briefly describe how people learn. The information here is based on decades of careful experimentation and observation by psychologists and other students of behavior. Once you understand these principles you should gain a clearer picture of why you behave as you do, and how you can change. You will see that the types of unassertiveness you described at the end of Chapter 1 are very likely a product of your past learning, and that you can use the principles here to retrain yourself to be a more skillful, confident communicator.

THE ROOTS OF UNASSERTIVE BEHAVIOR

Our discussion of learning begins with a description of how people come to be unassertive. On page 18 you made a list of communication traits that you would like to change. As is true with almost all unsatisfying behaviors, you probably act in these ways for one of three reasons:

You May Act Unassertively Because You Were Never Exposed to Better Alternatives Two important ways to learn social skills are by observing models and receiving advice. Many people—especially overly shy or aggressive communicators—have not been lucky enough to benefit from either way of learning, as they come from backgrounds where no one expressed their thoughts and feelings openly. As the saying goes, we are victims of our own parents, who in turn are victims themselves. Thus, unassertiveness often appears to run through generations like a hereditary trait.

Sandy was the oldest of four sisters and grew up with almost no male playmates. Through the sixth grade her only contacts with boys were at school, where the children mostly stayed with members of their own sex. When junior high school brought the beginnings of dating, Sandy simply had no idea how to behave. "Boys were like Martians to me," she recalled. "I didn't know what to say to them or even how to look them in the eye. After I messed up the first few chances I did have, I suppose I got the reputation of being a dull date. Since kids in my school hung around in groups, I wound up with nondating friends, and so in high school I never did learn how to act with boys. It wasn't until I went off to college and got a fresh start that my social life improved."

Some people have had good advice and a chance to observe good models and still aren't able to express themselves very well. Unassertiveness in such cases can still be a result of poor learning, as Todd's story illustrates: Todd grew up in a house full of gregarious brothers, sisters, and parents. In college he belonged to the varsity football team, whose members gave him plenty of social advice. In spite of this large number of models Todd still found himself shy around people he didn't know well. The following conversation suggests why.

INSTRUCTOR: "Todd, you say you're depressed because you're uncomfortable with strangers even though you've had plenty of models."

TODD: "Yeah. You said in class that all you have to do to communicate better is to watch people who are good at it and get their advice."

INSTRUCTOR: "Not exactly. Some people are lucky enough to pick up skills just by casual observation or advice, but others need detailed training and practice. I notice you're in the starting lineup this year, yet last year you didn't even make the team."

TODD: "Yeah. Football doesn't come that easy to me. It took a lot of hard work over the summer and some extra time with the coach for me to make it."

INSTRUCTOR: "Well, it's exactly the same with being assertive. Having models isn't always enough. At times you need to get some special coaching and practice. Most people wouldn't expect to become an expert skier or painter or musician just by watching others or getting casual advice; and expressing thoughts and feelings is at least as complicated as those skills. So often, the way to break out of a style of communication is to study the more desirable alternatives in a systematic way, with plenty of expert advice and coaching. When you combine these with a desire to communicate better, you'll usually get results."

You May Act Unassertively Because You Have Been Reinforced for Doing So *Reinforcement is any consequence that increases the likelihood of a behavior occurring in the future.* If you tell a joke that gets a laugh, you will probably try that and other jokes in the future because the positive recognition of laughter is desirable, and thus reinforcing. If your protestations about poor merchandise in a store are rewarded with a refund, the refund is the reinforcer that will encourage you to stand up for your rights again in similar circumstances. Chapter 6 describes several types of reinforcers and how to use them, but for now it is enough to realize that a reinforcer is the "payoff" for a behavior that makes a person more likely to act a certain way in the future.

Many parents unintentionally teach their children to be passive, manipulative, or aggressive by reinforcing those behaviors. Almost everybody has seen the following drama take place in a supermarket: Mother is in the checkout line with two-year-old Junior in the basket. Suddenly Junior spots the display of chocolate bars just beyond his reach and demands, "Candy, Mama!" Mother says no, at which point Junior throws a temper tantrum. After a minute or two of his screaming, the mother feels as if all the shoppers are staring at her, and so she breaks down and shoves a candy bar at her son, pleading, "Just be quiet!" The lesson here is not lost on the toddler: Any time you want a candy bar, just throw a fit. Aggressive behavior is reinforced.

Our society abounds with positive, reinforcing terms for unassertive behavior. Being labeled as "nice" or "friendly" is a compliment, even when a boring or offensive situation makes these behaviors inappropriate. An informal survey of households with young children will show that politeness is more frequently stressed and rewarded than is candor. "It's better to create a good impression than to express your true feelings," seems to be the message there.

In the same way nonassertiveness seems to be the ideal in the adult world. This is especially true for the role women have traditionally been expected to play. "She's a sweet person," "She never has a bad word to say about anyone," "She doesn't have an angry bone in her body," or "She's always in a good mood" are all meant as compliments. With reinforcement like this it is easy to see why it pays to behave unassertively.

You May Act Unassertively Because You Have Been Punished for Being Assertive Some kinds of punishment are physically unpleasant, such as spankings or denial of food. Other kinds are social—for example, being ridiculed, criticized, or ignored. In all cases we can say that *punishment is any unpleasant consequence that reduces the frequency of a behavior's future occurrence.*

Many people have learned through unpleasant experiences that assertiveness does not pay. The teenager who is ridiculed for not going along with the crowd, the child who is reprimanded for questioning parental orders, and the beginning public address student whose first attempt at speechmaking meets with derisive laughter—all will find it harder to assert themselves in the future. After only a few repetitions of the social disapproval or parental criticism or the ridicule of classmates, these people will probably stop behaving in the way that brought on the punishment. Thus, assertive behavior is weakened through unpleasant consequences.

Chuck's story illustrates the way in which assertion is sometimes punished. After graduating from college with a degree in engineering, Chuck felt lucky to find a job as a designer for a large aerospace company. After a few months on the job he began to notice several inefficient procedures in his department, and on his own time worked out new methods that he was sure would save the company money while improving quality. After rechecking his calculations to be sure they were correct, Chuck excitedly brought them to his supervisor, expecting praise or even an early promotion. Instead, he was surprised to find his boss unenthusiastically promise to look into the idea when he got a chance. Several months went by, during which Chuck pushed for some reaction to his plan and his boss became more and more hostile. Finally, a long-time employee gave Chuck a piece of advice: The boss did not appreciate anyone rocking the boat; things went smoothly in the department just as they were, and nobody was interested in changing the system. In this operation "the way to get along was to go along." If Chuck valued his future with the company, he had to play the game. At this point Chuck was faced with a choice. Either he could drop his innovative ideas and advance slowly but surely in the company (possibly someday reaching a position where he could bring about changes), or he could continue openly asserting himself and face the prospect of losing his job. Because of a tight employment market and the fact that the job was generally a satisfying one, Chuck decided to keep quiet and stay on. However, he had received a real-life lesson in learning nonassertiveness through the threat of punishment.

Even the *anticipation* of punishment can stifle assertion. Many times people will behave passively in order to avoid punishment that has not occurred yet, but which they expect will follow their act of assertion. This was the case for Pat, the man in Chapter 1 who was afraid to ask questions in class. A talk about his history in school revealed that he had no trouble speaking up in class until the sixth grade. For some reason, his teacher that year seemed to dislike Pat and criticized practically all his questions and contributions. A year of having every comment punished taught Pat a lesson: Keep quiet and avoid trouble. In fact, Pat grew to fear criticism so much during this year that any situation calling for a contribution left him feeling uncontrollably anxious and fearful, even when he knew the answer and there was no cause for worry.

All through high school and into college Pat's fear of criticism outweighed his curiosity and kept him quiet, even though his teachers probably would have welcomed his contributions. Pat remained silent all those years in anticipation of a punishment that would never come, and in so doing illustrated the principle of *avoidance behavior*, which is the plague of many nonasserters. As its name suggests, people engaging in avoidance behavior are trying to evade situations they expect will result in punishing consequences. In Pat's case, the behavior was speaking up in class. In order to avoid this unpleasant act, he developed several strategies—sitting in the back of the room, avoiding eye contact with his instructor, and taking courses that called for a minimum of student participation. In these ways he would be less likely to have to speak up . . . a behavior he expected would result in criticism or ridicule.

Of course, Pat's fear of such punishment was unnecessary, but because he never did speak out, he never discovered this fact. This story illustrates the biggest problem involved with avoidance behaviors: they persist long after their value is gone. In cases like this it is the fear of an *imagined* punishment rather than the existence of real unpleasant consequences that keeps people acting unassertively.

You May Be Unassertive Because You Believe in One or More Irrational Myths Almost from the time they learn to speak, children are taught to accept the belief system of their society. Many of the beliefs that compose this system are useful ones: for example, the idea that physical violence is not an acceptable way of resolving conflicts or the principle that a healthy body complements a healthy mind. On the other hand, there are a number of irrational beliefs—called "myths" here—that actually inhibit effective social functioning. We shall discuss five myths that stifle assertiveness.

The Myth of Perfection. People who accept this myth believe that a worthwhile communicator should be able to handle any situation with complete confidence and skill. While such a standard of perfection might serve as a target and source of inspiration (rather like making a hole in one for a golfer), it's totally unrealistic to expect that one can reach or maintain such a level of behavior: people simply aren't perfect. Perhaps the myth of the perfect communicator comes from believing too strongly in novels, television, or films. In these places we are treated to descriptions of such characters as the perfect mate or child, the totally controlled and gregarious host, and the incredibly competent professional. While these images are certainly appealing, it's inevitable that we will come up short when compared to them.

Once you accept the belief that it's desirable and possible to be a perfect communicator, the thought follows that people won't appreciate you if you are imperfect. Admitting one's mistakes, saying "I don't know," or sharing feelings of uncertainty or discomfort become social defects when viewed in this manner. Given the desire to be valued and appreciated, it is a temptation to try at least to *appear* perfect. Thus, many people assemble a variety of social masks, hoping that if they can fool others into thinking that they are perfect, perhaps they'll find acceptance. The costs of such deception are high. If others ever detect that this veneer of confidence is a false one, then the actor is seen as a phony, and regarded accordingly. Even if the unassertive actor's role of confidence does go undetected, such a performance uses up a great deal of psychological energy and thus makes the rewards of approval less enjoyable.

The alternative way of behaving for persons who succumb to the myth of perfection and fail to measure up to the impossible standard they have set for themselves is to withdraw from interaction with others—in effect, to state that "If I can't communicate well, I won't do it at all." Needless to say, these sad individuals suffer as much as do their insecure, pretending cousins who claim to be perfect.

The irony for these communicators who fruitlessly strive for acceptance through perfection is that their efforts are unnecessary. Research and common sense both suggest that the people we regard most favorably are those who are competent but not perfect (Aronson, 1972). It is easy to speculate on why this is so. First, many people see the acts of others as the desperate struggle that they are. In these cases it's obviously easier to like someone who is not trying to deceive you than one who is. Second, most of us become uncomfortable around someone we regard as perfect. Knowing we don't measure up to these standards, the temptation may be to admire this superhuman, but from a distance.

Not only can subscribing to the myth of perfection keep others from liking you, it also acts as a force to diminish your own self-esteem. How can you like yourself when you don't measure up to the way you ought to be? How liberated you become when you can comfortably accept the idea that you are not perfect, that:

—like everyone else, you sometimes have a hard time expressing yourself;
—like everyone else, you make mistakes from time to time, and there is no reason to hide this;
—you are honestly doing the best you can to realize your potential, to become the best person you can be.

The Myth of Acceptance. The myth of acceptance states that the way to judge the worth of one's actions is by the approval they bring. Communicators who subscribe to this belief go to incredible lengths to seek acceptance from people who are significant to them, even when they must sacrifice their own principles and happiness to do so. Adherence to this irrational myth can lead to some ludicrous situations:

—remaining silent in a theater when others are disturbing the show for fear of "creating a scene";

—buying unwanted articles so that the salespeople won't think you have wasted their time or think you are cheap;

—ridiculing individuals or ideas merely to gain stature as "one of the group"

—greatly inconveniencing yourself by running errands, lending money, and the like, not because you genuinely want to, but so that others will think you are nice.

In addition to the obvious dissatisfaction that comes from denying your own principles and needs, the myth of acceptance is irrational because it implies that others will respect and like you more if you go out of your way to please them. Often this simply isn't true. How is it possible to respect people who have compromised important values only to gain acceptance? How is it possible to think highly of people who repeatedly deny their own needs as a means of buying approval? While others may find it tempting to use these individuals to suit their ends or amusing to be around them, genuine affection and respect are hardly due such characters.

In addition, striving for universal acceptance is irrational because it is simply not possible. Sooner or later a conflict of expectations is bound to occur: one person will approve if you behave only in a certain way, while another will only accept the opposite course of action. What are you to do then?

Don't misunderstand: eschewing the myth of approval does not mean living a life of selfishness. It's still important to consider the needs of others and to meet them whenever possible. It's also pleasant—one might even say necessary—to strive for the respect of those people we value. The point here is that when you must abandon your own needs and principles in order to seek these goals, the price is too high.

The Myth of Causation. People who live their lives in accordance with this myth believe that it is their duty to do nothing that might possibly hurt or in any way inconvenience others. This attitude leads to behaviors such as:

—visiting one's friends or family out of a sense of obligation rather than a genuine desire to see them;

—keeping to yourself an objection to another person's behavior that is in some way troublesome to you;

—pretending to be attentive to a speaker when you are already late for
another engagement or are feeling ill;

—praising and reassuring others who ask for your opinion, even when
your honest response is a negative one.

A reluctance to speak out in situations like these is often based on the assumption that you are the cause of others' feelings: that you hurt, confuse,
or anger them. Actually, such a position is not correct. You don't *cause* feelings in others; rather, they *respond* to your behavior with feelings of their
own. To recognize the truth of this statement, consider how strange it
sounds to suggest that we make others fall in love with us. Such a statement
simply doesn't make sense. It would be more correct to say that we act in
one way or another, and that some people might fall in love with us as a result of these actions, while others wouldn't. In the same way, it's incorrect
to say that we *make* others angry, upset, sad—or happy, for that matter.
Behavior that upsets or pleases one person might not bring any reaction
from another. It's more accurate to state that others' responses are as much
or more a function of their own psychological makeup as they are determined by our own behavior.

Restricting your communication because of the myth of causation can result in three types of damaging consequences. First, as a result of your caution you often will fail to have your own needs met; there's little likelihood
that others will change their behavior unless they know that it's affecting
you in a negative way.

A second consequence of keeping silent is that you are likely to begin re-
senting the person whose behavior you find bothersome. Obviously this
reaction is illogical, since you never have made your feelings known, but
logic doesn't change the fact that keeping your problem buried usually
leads to a buildup of hostility.

Even when your withholding of feelings is based on the best of intentions, it often damages relationships in a third way; for once others find out
about your deceptive nature, they will find it difficult ever to know when
you really are upset with them. Even your most fervent assurances that
everything is fine become suspect, since the thought is always present that
you may be covering up for resentments you are unwilling to express.
Thus, in many respects, taking responsibility for others' feelings is not only
irrational—it is also counterproductive.

The Myth of Helplessness.   This irrational idea suggests that satisfaction
in life is determined by forces beyond your control. People who continu-
ously see themselves as victims make statements such as:

—"There's no way a woman can get ahead in this society. It's a man's
world, and the best thing I can do is to accept it."

—"I was born with a shy personality. I'd like to be more outgoing, but
there's nothing I can do about that."

—"I can't tell my boss that she is putting too many demands on me. If I did, I might lose my job"

The error in statements like these becomes apparent when you recall the point made in the introduction of this book: there are very few things you can't do if you really want to. Most "can't" statements can more correctly be rephrased in one of two ways.

The first of these ways is to say that you *won't* act in a certain way, that you *choose not* to do so. For instance, you may choose not to stand up for your rights or not to say no to unwanted requests, but it is probably inaccurate to claim that some outside force keeps you from doing do. The second phrase that can often more accurately replace "can't" is the assertion that you *don't know how* to do something. Examples of this sort of situation include not knowing how to state a complaint in a way that reduces defensiveness or being unaware of how best to carry on a conversation. Like these two problems, many difficulties that you might claim can't be solved do have solutions: the task is to find out what those solutions are and to work diligently and learn how to apply them.

When viewed in this light, it's apparent that many "can'ts" are really rationalizations to justify one's not wanting to change. Once you've persuaded yourself that there's no hope for you, it's easy to give up trying. On the other hand, acknowledging that there is a way to change—even though it may be difficult—puts the responsibility for your predicament on your shoulders. Knowing that you can move closer to your goals makes it difficult to complain about your present situation. You *can* become a better communicator—this book is one step in your movement toward that goal. Don't give up or sell yourself short!

The Myth of Catastrophic Failure.   Communicators who subscribe to this irrational belief operate on the assumption that if something bad can possibly happen, it will happen. Typical catastrophic fantasies include:

—"If I invite them to the party, they probably won't want to come."
—"If I speak up in order to try and resolve a conflict, things will probably get worse."
—"If I apply for the job I want, I probably won't be hired."
—"If I tell them how I really feel, they'll probably think I'm a fool."

While it's undoubtedly naïve to blithely assume that all of your interactions with others will meet with success, it's equally damaging to assume you will fail. The first consequence of such an attitude is that you'll be less likely even to attempt to express yourself at important times. This is a clear illustration of the avoidance behavior described in the previous section: by behaving in a manner that reduces the possibility of anticipated punishment, you never discover whether your expectations of catastrophe are, in fact, realistic. To see the folly of such an attitude, simply carry the concept of avoidance behavior to its logical extreme. Imagine people who fear *everything:* how would they live their lives? They couldn't step outside in the morning to see what kind of day it is for fear they would be struck by lightning or a falling airplane. They couldn't drive in a car for fear of a collision. They couldn't engage in any exercise for fear the strain might cause a heart attack. If this example seems ridiculous, consider whether you have ever withdrawn from communicating because you were afraid of consequences that weren't likely to occur. A certain amount of prudence is wise, but carrying caution too far can lead to a life of lost opportunities.

Even when one acts in spite of catastrophic fantasies, problems occur. In many cases the fact that you expect to fail can make that failure more likely. The principle behind this fact has been termed the "self-fulfilling prophecy," and it will be discussed in detail in a few pages. For now, realize that you may be sabotaging your own chances of success simply by expecting that you won't succeed.

One way to escape from the myth of catastrophic failure is to reassess the consequences that would follow even if you don't succeed in your efforts to communicate successfully. Keeping in mind the folly of trying to be perfect and of living only for the approval of others, realize that failing in a given instance usually isn't as bad as it might seem. What if people do laugh at you? Suppose you don't get the job? What if others do get angry at your remarks? Are these matters really *that* serious?

▶ No one is born unassertive. Once you realize that your present style of communication is a result of past learning, you will see that it is possible to learn more rewarding ways of self-expression.

Turn to the list of unassertive behaviors you recorded on page 18. Pick the three items there that seem to be the biggest problems for you now. Complete the spaces below for each.

EXAMPLE: a) The behavior   When angry with my family or friends, I either keep the feeling to myself or express it indirectly by hinting, grumbling, or sulking.

b) How it was learned and perpetuated
☒ I have never learned better alternatives
☒ I have been rewarded for behaving unassertively
☐ I have been punished for behaving assertively
☐ I have believed in irrational myths

c) Explanation   I grew up in a household where nobody seemed to share angry feelings directly. Some of my friends did come from families where anger was outwardly expressed, but in extremely aggressive ways which I found unappealing. Therefore, I have had no close models for being assertive. Also, now when I do sulk, hint, or grumble, I often get my way, so this indirect aggression has been reinforced.

1. a) The behavior _____

_____

_____

_____

b) How it was learned and perpetuated
  ☐ I have never learned better alternatives
  ☐ I have been rewarded for behaving unassertively
  ☐ I have been punished for behaving assertively
  ☐ I have believed in irrational myths

c) Explanation _____

_____

_____

_____

_____

_____

_____

2. a) The behavior _____

_____

_____

b) How it was learned and perpetuated
  ☐ I have never learned better alternatives
  ☐ I have been rewarded for behaving unassertively
  ☐ I have been punished for behaving assertively
  ☐ I have believed in irrational myths

c) Explanation _____

_____

_____

_____

_____

3. a) The behavior _____

_____

_____

b) How it was learned and perpetuated
  ☐ I have never learned better alternatives
  ☐ I have been rewarded for behaving unassertively

(continued)

☐ I have been punished for behaving assertively
☐ I have believed in irrational myths

c) Explanation _____

_____

_____

_____

_____

_____

_____

ASSERTIVENESS IS ALSO LEARNED

To the degree that you have learned or failed to learn social behaviors, you are not at fault for the unsatisfying ways you communicate. Just as a person with limited experience around water is not to blame for an inability to swim, you are not at fault for having difficulty in some types of self-expression. Just as a child who was once attacked by a large dog generalized that fear to all other dogs, you may have an aversion to communication settings with unpleasant associations. In these cases your tendency to behave unassertively is understandable. This fact that behavior is shaped by experiences frees you from the common error of blaming yourself for past communication problems which have stemmed from inadequate learning. In this sense you have been as much a victim of your misfortune as an agent of it.

A word of warning: Although you may not be responsible for many of your past communication difficulties, do not accept the myth of helplessness and claim that a poor learning history is an excuse for *future* unassertiveness. The temptation to rationalize unassertiveness as beyond your control is tempting, but it is a rationalization nonetheless. As you read and practice the skills in this book, you can take advantage of the same principles by which you learned unsatisfying communication habits to teach yourself new, more satisfying ways to behave. Where you were once unable to find desirable models, you can now learn to search out and study them. Where before you may have been at a loss for alternatives to passive or aggressive behaviors, you will now have a repertoire of assertive responses available to you. Where you were once reinforced for behaving unassertively, you can now increase the chances that you will be rewarded for speaking in a straightforward manner. While these promises may sound overstated, you should realize that they are not based on any "miracle cure," but rather on the same principles by which you learned your present style of communicating. The difference is that now you will use those principles deliberately to reach goals of your own choosing.

THE SELF-FULFILLING PROPHECY

In addition to learning, there is another factor that affects the success of your attempts at communicating. To see what it is, consider the sports world for a moment. Any player will testify that attitude as much as ability often makes the difference between winning and losing. Athletes who expect to perform well generally do so, while those who anticipate failure usually are defeated. In this sense the competitor with a losing attitude probably does more to defeat himself than does his opponent, and the player who "knows" he is number one will succeed to a degree beyond what his physical talents suggest. This same principle applies to other kinds of endeavor. Students who expect to do poorly in spite of studying long and hard for a test lose confidence upon walking into the classroom and score below their potential. A speaker, actor, or other performer who expects to do poorly usually finds the prediction to be accurate—but only because the catastrophic expectation becme so strong that it assured failure.

Each of these cases illustrates the *self-fulfilling prophecy,* in which the expectation of success or failure actually assures that very outcome. While predicting events such as the first snow of winter have no effect on whether or not those events take place, occurrences such as those listed above happen precisely because people expect them to.

To understand how the self-fulfilling prophecy affects communication, consider the case of Nancy, a college instructor who was highly regarded by both her colleagues and students. Nancy learned of an opening in a university where she had always hoped to work. The job description fit her qualifications well, and a survey of the competition showed that she was at least as well qualified as any other applicant. Initially Nancy felt confident about her chances of landing the job, but as the time of her interview came closer, she began to feel more and more doubtful. "It's too good to be true," she reported thinking. "Even though I know I'm qualified, the interview committee will never learn about my real personality in the hour I'll be facing them." On and on went her catastrophic monologue, and although she could sense what was happening, Nancy came to believe her gloomy predictions about how the interview would go. When the day finally came, Nancy put on her best smile and faced the committee. "I said all the right words," she said, "but somehow things just didn't click. I had a bad attitude, and I'm convinced to this day that that's why I didn't land the job."

It is impossible to overstress the dangers of a negative self-fulfilling prophecy. The major lesson in this book is that people change; the fact that you were unassertive in the past does not *have* to predict your future behavior.

While a pessimistic self-fulfilling prophecy can hinder your growth as a communicator, approaching a situation with positive expectations can help the desired outcome occur. Imagine the difference in Nancy's employment interview is she had felt confident about herself. In the same way, picture the difference that positive expectations can make in a variety of other situations: striking up conversations with interesting people, requesting help when confused, performing before a group, defending your rights as a consumer, and many other instances. Of course, positive expectations alone usually are not enough. They need to be based on a foundation of expressive skills. You will learn how to increase your assertive repertoire in future chapters. The important fact to realize now is that *you can* be a more confident and skillful communicator.

▶ What role does the self-fulfilling prophecy play in shaping your communication? Turn to the list of communication problems you've made on page 18 and recall any instances in which you thought about yourself in a manner that made these events occur when they might otherwise not have happened; in other words, where you behaved in accordance with the self-fulfilling prophecy. List three such instances here, indicating for each one a description of how you behaved, the other person or people involved, and the circumstances in which the behavior occurred.

EXAMPLE: I was recently invited to a party at which I didn't know anyone but the host. I went, even though I was sure I'd have a terrible time. Because of my expectation, I didn't try to meet anyone. Looking back, I can see that I may have created my own miserable situation.

1. _____

_____

_____

2. _____

_____

_____

3. _____

_____

_____

SUMMARY

There are four types of learning experiences that can lead to unsatisfying communication: never having been exposed to assertive behavior; having been punished for past assertions; having been rewarded for being unassertive; and believing in irrational myths. Among these irrational ideas are the myths of perfection, acceptance, causation, helplessness, and catastrophic failure. Fortunately, just as these principles have led to unproductive styles of communicating in the past, by conscientiously reapplying them you can master new and more effective expressive skills in the future.

The self-fulfilling prophecy is another factor that affects communication. Often one's success in communicating is determined more by the expectation of success or failure than by skills. For this reason it is essential to approach communication situations with a realistic attitude rather than selling oneself short.

Any time you want a candy bar, just throw a fit.

Part Two

FUNDAMENTALS OF ASSERTION

By reading this far you've seen how people learn to behave unassertively or aggressively, and you've found that it's possible to change these unproductive styles.

The information in the next four chapters will give you detailed directions for becoming more skillful and confident at communicating in situations that are most important to you. You'll discover how to set personal goals, prepare to use them in real-life situations, and reduce the anxiety that sometimes comes with self-assertion. Finally, you'll learn a method for mastering the types of communication which are most complicated and difficult for you.

If you follow the directions in these pages faithfully, you will almost certainly find yourself quickly becoming a more self-assured and assertive communicator.

3

Identifying Problems and Setting Goals

Dave was a good-looking 26-year-old veteran who couldn't seem to approach attractive women. He first mentioned his problem to an instructor with a sudden confession. "I've got to do something about myself. I'm just no good around women," he declared after a class discussion on sex roles. When questioned further, he went on, "I'm a complete washout with girls. I don't know how to behave around them."

By following the steps Dave took in solving his problem you will get a clearer idea of how to work on your goals. You'll discover that often being able to define a problem and describe how you want to behave is the biggest step in achieving your aim.

MOST ASSERTIVE PROBLEMS ARE SITUATIONAL

The first point to realize when defining a communication problem is that you may be exaggerating its size. Very few people are totally unassertive. Rather, most of us have difficulties in certain situations. Though it is common—and understandable—in a moment of depression to think, as

Dave did, that you are a total failure, a bit of reflection usually shows that such a belief is overstated. Statements like "I'm a shy person," "I can't speak in groups," or "I can't stand up for myself" may seem accurate, but they usually paint a gloomier picture of one's behavior than the facts indicate. (Nevertheless, frequent repetition of such negative statements may ensure that the unhappy condition does become more·and more frequently true, according to the self-fulfilling prophecy.)

For an example of one problem that proved in fact to be situational, rather than general, we can return to Dave.

"You say you're a complete failure with women," Dave's instructor declared. "Let me ask you a few questions so we can see just where you stand. Some of them will sound facetious or silly, but believe me, they're not. First, are you a flop when you communicate with your mother?"

"Of course not," Dave replied.

"Do you have any sisters?" the instructor asked, and on receiving an affirmative reply, she went on. "Do you feel O.K. about the way you handle yourself with them?"

"Sure."

The instructor went on. "Well, then, what about me? I'm a woman. Are you unhappy with the way we get along?"

"No. But that's not what I mean. I'm talking about people around my age—say between 19 and 30."

"Well, that's definitely a more helpful definition of the problem. But I still don't think it's completely accurate. I've noticed you talking quite often with Nancy and Connie in this class."

"That's true. But I really don't have any problems with them." When asked why not, Dave replied that he had known Nancy for years, and she didn't seem any different from his male friends as far as conversation went.

"But that still doesn't account for Connie," insisted the teacher.

"This may sound cruel, but I don't find her very interesting or attractive, and so it's easy for me to talk to her."

The instructor summarized. "So you have no trouble talking to women who are in your family, who are older than you, who are friends, or whom you don't find interesting and attractive. Is that it?"

At this point a look of comprehension crossed Dave's face. "That's right. You know, I'm really not a flop with *all* women—just ones I'd like to take out! Putting it that way really doesn't help me with my dating, but for some reason it does seem to make a difference."

Let's examine what has happened with Dave up to this point. First, he has discovered that whatever difficulties he has with women are limited to one specific group. This realization has left him feeling better, for it shows that instead of being a total social failure, he is a relatively competent person who needs to work on just one phase of his communication. Second, Dave now at least knows specifically who he must deal with to bring about any changes. In these two ways, instead of having no idea of even how to begin to solve his problem, simply narrowing the problem down has helped Dave move closer to a solution.

Like Dave, most communicators do quite well in the majority of settings and have problems only in certain situations. You might be quite comfortable accepting praise about your talents, intelligence, and work, but be uneasy when complimented on your appearance. It might be easy for you to say "I'm sorry" or "I was wrong" except with a particular person. You might be skillful at expressing affection in a joking way but find it difficult to do so directly. Each of these cases illustrates that most people are generally assertive, but have communication problems in certain circumstances. By discovering just what these circumstances are you will have taken a big step toward communicating more effectively.

There are three types of situations in which you might find assertion particularly difficult. (1) Sometimes, as in Dave's case, they revolve around *a certain person or people.* Examples of such person-centered difficulties are the student who becomes flustered when called on by a certain teacher, the employee who can object to offensive language from everyone except the boss, or the person who feels uncomfortable with people from different racial or ethnic backgrounds. (2) In other cases assertive behavior becomes difficult in discussing certain *topics.* For instance, a husband or wife might have a hard time discussing sex or discipline of their children, while finding it easy to share other thoughts. Other topic-related difficulties include asking for financial assistance, expressing confusion about the future, or accepting justified criticism of some work. (3) Another factor that often influences assertiveness is the *setting* in which communication takes place. For instance, some people are comfortable socializing in small groups but become ill at ease at large parties. Others can dismiss unwanted door-to-door solicitors with aplomb, but have a hard time turning down requests for contributions or products when approached on the street.

In the following pages you will discover which of these problems apply to you. Whatever the problem, however, the same basic point applies: Unsatisfying behaviors are usually limited to certain situations, and defining the specific instances in which they occur can make the problem less threatening and easier to remedy.

▶   This exercise will help you to identify the situational nature of your communication and to define your personal assertive goals more clearly. Review the list of personal unassertive behaviors you made on page 18. From that information choose three important areas of communication from your life and describe your strengths and weaknesses in each area. Since recording the problems on page 18, you may have become aware of some other ways in which you would like to behave more assertively. If this is so, you may substitute such problems for one or more of the items on page 18.

REMEMBER, IF YOU SERIOUSLY WANT TO IMPROVE YOUR OWN COMMUNICATION, YOU MUST DO EACH EXERCISE IN THIS BOOK BEFORE READING ON.

EXAMPLE: a. Type of communication Expressing anger

b. My strengths in this area When it's really important, I express my anger directly to my friends and family instead of holding it inside or being indirectly or directly aggressive.

c. My weaknesses in this area I often get angry at poor service in stores, restaurants, and government offices. When this happens, I don't say anything and wind up with an upset stomach.

1. a. Type of communication _____

b. My strengths in this area _____

c. My weaknesses in this area _____

2. a. Type of communication _____

b. My strengths in this area _____

c. My weaknesses in this area _____

3. a. Type of communication _____

b. My strengths in this area _____

_____

_____

c. My weaknesses in this area _____

_____

_____

_____

DEFINING THE PROBLEM BEHAVIORALLY

The previous exercise has given you a general description of some situations in which you want to behave more assertively. Though this is a good start, you will need to define your problem areas even more clearly before any change can occur. You can accomplish this step by learning to write *behavioral definitions.* It would be hard to overstate the importance of this skill, for without it the chances of improving your communication are drastically reduced. At the outset of a journey travelers need to know where they are and where they want to go in order to arrive at their destination quickly and safely. In the same way you need to pinpoint how you presently behave and how you would like to express yourself in order to have the best chance of reaching your goal. Behavioral definitions will help you in this process. Three steps are necessary in constructing any behavioral definition.

1. Who Does the Problem Involve? Dave had already accomplished this step in the discussion earlier in this chapter. It was clear that he had difficulty communicating with women whom he wanted to take out. He got along comfortably with those who were considerably older or younger and with those he did not find interesting or attractive. He also had no problem with good-looking women who were appealing but who were already married or dating other men steadily. He froze up only when he was faced with a prospective date.

Sometimes identifying the core of a problem is this simple, but at other times it takes more time and effort. This was the case with a woman who complained about her inability to turn down people requesting money for charitable causes. Although her statement of the problem seemed to be a clear one, further questioning showed that she already was able to decline the sales pitch of many solicitors, such as door-to-door evangelists offering religious pamphlets. She also had no difficulty turning down telephone salespeople offering products she did not want. After further discussion the woman narrowed down the class of solicitors in question to those who aroused her sympathy: disabled veterans, those with physical handicaps, and young children (she recalled the ordeal of selling Girl Scout cookies herself as a child). But even at this point something was wrong with her description. A friend asked why, if she felt sorry for such people, she was reluctant to donate money to their causes. Further, if the cause was legitimate enough to earn her sympathy, why was she mad at herself for contributing a few dollars? The woman responded that she felt fine contributing to some people for whom she felt sorry, but that she felt like a fool after donating money at other times.

What was the difference? Recollections of her experiences finally brought out that she felt victimized when the solicitor's sales pitch involved a gift of some obviously worthless token in exchange for the contribution. Though she might gladly have donated her cash with no reward beyond feeling good, a few ounces of candy or a shoddy keychain given in return for several dollars left her feeling duped. After defining her problem this clearly, the solution was obvious. Whenever the woman was approached by a solicitor who offered tokens in exchange for contributions to a worthwhile cause, she would simply give an amount she felt was appropriate and decline any gifts or products offered in return. In this way she knew that all of her money was going to the cause in question, and she never needed to feel that she had "bought" an inferior product.

When defining your communication problem, make the description of the people involved as specific as possible. Ask yourself whether the difficulty involves an entire category of people (women, salespeople, strangers), a subclass of the group (attractive women, rude salespeople, strangers you'd like to meet), or a specific person (Jane Doe, the clerk at a particular store, a new person in your neighborhood). The more specific you can be while fully describing your problem, the greater will be your chances of success.

2. In What Circumstances Does Your Problem Occur? When Dave was first asked this question, he replied that he was uncomfortable with potential dates whenever and wherever he was near them. Further questioning by his instructor, however, proved this to be inaccurate.

"Dave, you say you're no good at communicating with women in any circumstances. Let's explore a few situations and see. I know you work in an auto repair shop. You must run into pretty, eligible girls with a job like that. Do you do all right then?"

"Well, that depends. As long as I'm talking about their car or cars in general, there's no problem. I have plenty of things to say, and they usually seem interested. Also, since I do know what I'm talking about, I think I do pretty well in those situations. But even at work when the subject changes away from cars, that's when I get nervous."

"So at work as long as the subject sticks to business, you're O.K. How about school? Are there any times there when you handle yourself well?"

"Only one I can think of. In my chemistry class I have a fantastic girl for a lab partner. Usually I just stand around her like an idiot, but last week we really got involved in an experiment, and for a while we were both talking and laughing with no problem. It was great! But as soon as the lab was over, I was just as quiet and nervous as before."

"I'm starting to see a pattern," noted the instructor. "It seems as if you're situationally unassertive with women you find attractive. As long as there's a structured subject that you know about and can discuss, you're fine. It's just when you have to pick a topic on your own that you have problems."

Once Dave and his instructor had agreed to this definition of the problem, a partial solution suggested itself. Dave learned that one way to increase his successful conversations with women was to approach them in settings where there was clearly a subject to talk about. There turned out to be several such situations available: discussing schoolwork with girls in his class, asking female sales clerks about their products, and asking strangers for directions, to name a few. By starting conversations in these environments he could talk comfortably until enough common interests had developed for him to carry on in any situation without fear.

There are several questions to ask yourself in order to define the circumstances surrounding a problem behavior. In what places does the problem occur? Does it occur at particular times? When you are discussing particular subjects? Is there anything special about you when it occurs: Are you tired, embarrassed, angry, confused? Do you feel good or bad about your physical appearance? Is there any common trait shared by the other person or people involved? Are they friendly or hostile, straightforward or manipulative, nervous or confident, in a hurry, bored? In other words, you must discover what circumstances set apart your problem situation from ones in which you have no difficulty.

3. What Specific Behaviors Do You Find Unsatisfying? Of the three questions you must ask yourself to identify a problem, this one usually requires the most thought. A further look at Dave's talk with his instructor illustrates the process involved in defining problem behaviors.

"O.K., Dave," the instructor continued, "so far we've nailed down at least part of your problem: it involves attractive young women whom you'd like to date, and it takes place wherever there is no structured situation that gives you a familiar topic to discuss. Now it's time to find out just how you act in these situations that's so unsatisfying."

Dave replied quickly. "That's easy. I don't have anything to say."

"But how do you act?" the instructor persisted. "What do you *do* when you have nothing to say?"

"I already told you. I stand around looking like a fool. The girl must know that I'm a nervous wreck."

"Dave, this still isn't a clear description of your behavior in the situation. Maybe we can approach the problem differently. Imagine that you were describing your actions to someone from another planet. This creature doesn't know what a "fool" is or how one behaves. To make the alien understand what you mean, you'll have to describe only the *observable* actions that relate to your problem. For instance, do you bite your fingernails while talking to these eligible girls, or do you shift from foot to foot when you're nervous?"

"No, but I see what you're getting at."

After a few moments of thought Dave confessed that he really didn't know exactly what he did in his problem circumstances—only that he felt like a fool while doing it. To help Dave become aware of his specific behaviors the instructor suggested that he keep a diary of his attempted conversations with women in unstructured situations for a week. Each time he was faced with a situation that fitted into this category he was to note how he acted and to write a detailed account of his situation as soon as possible.

Seven days of self-observation revealed to Dave a number of details about his behavior. First, he learned something about the circumstances in which it took place: Out of twelve entries in his diary recording situations in which he felt uncomfortable with attractive women, seven involved what he characterized as "party" situations—times when a group of men and women were together purely for social purposes. Three other entries recorded events at school: two while waiting in lines at the bookstore and student union and one when an attractive student sat down at his table in the library's crowded informal lounge. Of the remaining two incidents, one occurred when Dave dropped by a friend's house and met his cousin from out of town, while the other happened while he was waiting for service in a line at a quick-service hamburger place. Based on this week's sample, which Dave reported as fairly typical, he was able to redefine his statement of the problem circumstances from "unstructured situations" to "at parties and in public places."

Two specific behaviors that constituted the problem emerged from Dave's diary. As he suspected, the first one was what he labeled "long silences." These were times when neither Dave nor the female spoke for periods of perhaps 20 seconds or more. A second difficulty occurred when Dave tried to converse in the anxiety-provoking situation. He often failed to complete sentences he did start. These "trail-offs," as he termed them, gave the appearance of a man tongue-tied from nervousness and obviously did nothing to improve his social image.

As you record your own unsatisfying behaviors, you should keep several thoughts in mind. First, the behaviors you record should be *observable*. While feelings such as anxiety, anger, happiness, or affection may be important elements of the situation, merely describing them in such terms will not give you enough information to make change possible. You must also include an account of the behaviors that can be observed by both you and others. Recall the suggestion of Dave's instructor and imagine yourself describing the problem behavior to someone who has no knowledge of human emotions and thus must have each trait described in terms of its observable elements.

Your description of the problem behavior should also be *complete*. That is, it should include all the significant actions that make up your problem. To be sure you have described all the ingredients of your problem you should study the chapters in Part Three of this book that apply to you. In addition, you can also get a complete picture of your behavior by seeking feedback from others and by recording your own actions in the type of diary described above.

Besides being observable and complete, your description of the problem should be *specific*. Record each behavior in precise terms. Instead of characterizing yourself as a "pushover on the job," state how you act: do you agree to last-minute requests to work late, or do you take on work that others should be doing? Rather than saying that you use "aggressive language," note the specific words or phrases and state the tone of voice in which you say them.

ELEMENTS OF ASSERTIVE COMMUNICATION

Sometimes it's difficult to pin down the exact, observable behaviors that can show you how to express yourself more effectively. These pages will help you by describing the traits an assertive communicator ought to possess in most situations. Review this list before recording your assertive goals, and see which items you ought to include.

Visual Elements "Actions speak louder than words" may be an overworn phrase, but it's still true. If you mean what you say, your nonverbal behavior will back up your statements. On the other hand, the most assertive words will lose their impact if expressed in a hesitant, indirect manner. In which of the following dimensions can you act more assertively?

Eye Contact. Inadequate eye contact is usually interpreted in a negative way as anxiety, dishonesty, shame, boredom, or embarrassment. Even when they are not aware of a person's insufficient eye contact, others will often react unconsciously to it by either avoiding or taking advantage of the person exhibiting it. Don't go overboard and begin to stare down everyone you meet—this will be just as distracting as the other extreme—but do be sure to keep your gaze direct.

If it is necessary, you can gradually begin to increase your eye contact by first directing your glances toward different parts of the other person's face, such as the forehead, mouth, or chin. From a distance of four feet or so it's impossible to tell whether this kind of behavior is any different from an actual eye-to-eye look.

Distance.   Choosing the correct distance between yourself and another person is an important ingredient of assertion. Anthropologist Edward Hall (1959, 1969) has outlined four distinct distances used by Americans in differing situations. *Intimate distance* ranges from the surface of the skin to about 18 inches. As its name implies, it is appropriately used for private purposes: expressions of affection, protection, and anger. *Personal distance* runs from 18 inches to approximately four feet, and is used with people we know well and feel relaxed with. As Hall states, this is the range at which we keep someone "at arm's length," suggesting that while there is relatively high involvement here, the immediacy is not as great as that which occurs within intimate distance. *Social distance* ranges from four to 12 feet, and is generally appropriate in less personal settings: meeting strangers, engaging in impersonal business transactions, and so on. This is the range at which job interviews are often conducted, customers approached by salespeople, or newcomers introduced to us by a third party. We often accuse someone who ought to be using social distance but instead moves into our personal space of being "pushy." Finally, Hall labels as *public distance* the space extending outward from 12 feet. As its name implies, public distance is used in highly impersonal settings and occasions involving larger numbers of people: classrooms, public performances, and so on. Be sure you are using the appropriate range for the messages you want to express.

Facial Expression.   In the typical assertiveness training group one or two participants will express confusion as to why they have such trouble being taken seriously. They claim to use the appropriate language, keep eye contact, stand at the proper distance, and so on. When asked to demonstrate how they usually express themselves, the problem often becomes apparent: Their facial expression is totally inappropriate to the message. Many communicators, for example, verbally express their dissatisfaction while smiling as if nothing were wrong. Others claim to share approval or appreciation while wearing expressions more appropriate for viewing a corpse. After one student demonstrated his behavior in job interviews, the reason for his lack of success became obvious. Although he claimed to feel confident about his abilities, his clenched jaw and miserable expression advertised a tense job candidate. The problem in each of these examples is the same: in order for you to be taken seriously your facial expression should match the other parts of your message.

Gestures and Posture.   Like facial expressions, your movements and body positioning can either contribute to or detract from the immediacy of a message. Fidgeting hands, nervous shifting from one foot to another, or slumped shoulders will reduce or even contradict the impact of an assertive message. On the other hand, gestures that are appropriate to the words being spoken and a posture that suggests involvement in the subject will serve to reinforce your words. Watch an effective storyteller, interviewer, actor, or other model and note the added emphasis they give to a message.

Recognizing the importance of these actions doesn't mean that you should begin to act in an exaggerated way to make your point. The ridiculous sight of a person with waving arms or a jabbing finger can be just as distracting as a zombielike pose. The point here is to loosen up enough to let your gestures suit the words they accompany.

Body Orientation.   Another way of expressing your attitude is through the positioning of your body in relation to another person. Facing someone head on communicates a much higher degree of immediacy than does a less direct positioning. In fact, a directly confronting stance in which the face, shoulders, hips, and feet squarely face the other is likely to be interpreted as indicating an aggressive attitude. (To verify this impression, think of the stance used by a baseball player who is furious with an umpire's decision or a Marine drill instructor facing a recruit). Observation for assertive models will show that the most successful body orientation for most settings is a modified frontal one, in which the communicators are slightly angled away from a direct confrontation—perhaps 10 to 30 degrees. This position clearly suggests a high degree of involvement, yet allows the occasional freedom from total eye contact, which you have already learned is not to be desired.

Vocal Elements   The items in this section do not focus on *what* you say, but rather on *how you say it*. To understand how the voice conveys messages, recall a time when you have overheard a muffled conversation going on behind a wall or a closed door. You almost certainly had a good idea of the type of feelings being exchanged even though you could not understand the words being spoken or see the visual behavior of the communicators. Let's take a look at four ways that your voice can convey assertiveness.

Loudness.   The volume of your voice says a great deal about your feelings at the moment. There are two ways in which loudness affects the immediacy of your communication. First is the basic volume you use—the way you speak most of the time. You may, for instance, have the habit of talking so softly that others find it hard to understand you. Whatever the reasons for such a quiet tone, the impression it often creates is one of timidity and uncertainty. On the other hand, you might talk so loudly that other listeners become uncomfortable around you. Excessive volume usually suggests aggressiveness, anger, or boorishness, even when you have no such feelings.

Unlike the people who always express themselves at an inappropriate volume, others speak too loudly or softly only at certain critical times. For instance, you might find your normally pleasant voice change into a shout when you are angry. Or you might almost entirely lose your voice when you are upset. Needless to say, either of these extremes will usually diminish the effectiveness of your message.

Rate. Some speakers talk too rapidly and others too slowly. A speedy delivery often conveys a sense of nervousness or aggression, while an overly hesitant manner often appears to indicate uncertainty.

The average rate of speech is between 100 and 120 words per minute, thus providing a gauge against which you can measure your own speed. Simply find a written passage of that length and clock the time it takes you to read it in a conversational manner. By practicing this passage and other types of statements over and over, you will develop a feeling of the proper rate you should use in each situation.

Fluency. In addition to speaking at a proper rate and volume, another important vocal factor is the absence of disfluencies: unnecessary sounds such as "um," "er," "ya know," as well as other distracting vocal mannerisms such as repetitious and long pauses. You might already be aware of using certain disfluencies in your speech. If not, try asking others who know you well whether you use any. As a teacher of courses in speech, I was surprised to learn from a class discussion of fluency that I tended to overuse "O.K." in my lectures and discussions. The class pointed out the ways I used this "word" almost constantly: "O.K., now let's talk about defensiveness," "We'll work on nonverbal communication next Tuesday, O.K.?" and so on. Once a self-appointed student reporter counted 109 "O.K.s" in an 80-minute class period! After I became aware of this habit, it was easy enough to eliminate it with a self-modification project (see Chapter 6), but it took feedback from another source to bring this habit to my attention.

Affect. The affective ingredients of your voice include both your tone and inflection. These elements are major tools for expressing your feelings. Think of the number of messages you could convey with a single sentence such as "I hope you will call me," just by changing the tone. These simple words could communicate excitement, hopefulness, affection, sarcasm, anger, or disinterest, depending on the variations in pitch chosen by the speaker.

In addition to varying the tone, notice how many more shades of meaning could come from stressing different words:

"*I* hope you will call me." (*They* don't want you to call, but I do.)
"I *hope* you will call me." (I doubt that you will, but I'd like it.)
"I hope *you* will call me." (I don't care about anybody's call but yours.)
"I hope you *will* call me." (I know you're able, but I hope you'll choose to.)
"I hope you will *call* me." (Don't just send a postcard, but phone me!)
"I hope you will call *me*." (Don't call anyone but me.)

You can probably think of additional meanings for this sentence by combining tone and emphasis in other ways.

Many communicators reduce the immediacy of their messages by underplaying the affective dimension. Speaking in a monotone will soon bore almost anyone. Using the same pattern of inflection to express every thought can be irritating. Try to become aware of the tones and inflections you use and see whether they get your message across most effectively.

Verbal Elements   Now that you understand how much of an assertive image depends on your actions and voice, we are ready to consider the importance of the language you choose to deliver your message. This section won't describe the exact words to use in order to be more assertive; Chapters 7, 8, and 9 will give you specific thoughts on expressing yourself in different settings. The following pages describe several ingredients that ought to go into *any* assertive message, regardless of the subject.

Complete Sentences.   One of the surest ways to appear uncomfortable or confused is to speak in disjointed or complete sentences. In contrast, a speaker who can express ideas in complete, coherent thoughts is much more likely to be understood and taken seriously. The sentences you speak needn't be complex or make use of an extensive vocabulary. The point is simply to express your thoughts in a manner that suggests you have thought them out in advance and are presenting them with confidence.

If you have difficulty completing sentences in your everyday speech, you can begin correcting the problem in two ways. First, speak in shorter sentences. You'll find that a series of brief thoughts will express your ideas just as clearly as one long, complex sentence. Second, try as much as possible to mentally review your thoughts before speaking. Don't rehearse a script, but be sure of exactly what you want to say before speaking out and notice how much more clearly you will express yourself.

Develop a Core Statement.   One of the first principles of effective communication is that a good speaker should have a single, controlling thought on which all other remarks are based. The core statement of this book, for instance, is that you can learn a set of skills that will allow you to communicate confidently and successfully in your everyday relationships. Every idea you read here supports this main point. In the same way, the meaning of any subject will become clearer when you express it concisely. If a piece of merchandise proves unsatisfactory and you want your money refunded, say so—don't beat around the bush. If you are confused and need help from others, let them know in plain terms. If you appreciate the friendship of someone, make your feelings clear. When you state your thoughts in a brief, clear core statement, you will be rewarded in two ways. First, you'll be misunderstood less often; second, people will be more likely to take you seriously.

There are at least two common reasons for failing to make a clear core statement. The most common one is embarrassment. Many times you might be reluctant to express just what is on your mind for fear it won't be appreciated or accepted. People often fail to complain about poor service for fear of being judged "touchy." Others fail to express appreciation or affection because it might not be reciprocated. Sometimes you might be reluctant to express an opinion for fear someone would disagree. Rather than speaking out in situations like these, the usual alternative is to send the message indirectly. As you will read in Chapter 9, the results of indirectly stated messages are usually unsatisfying: anger, resentment, hurt, or feelings of being manipulated.

A second reason for failing to make a clear core statement is that we often don't know ourselves exactly what is on our minds. Precisely what bothers you about a neighbor's behavior? Exactly what is wrong with the merchandise you have recently bought, and what do you want to do about it? Just what do you appreciate about another person? What are your opinions, and how did you reach them, and how do they differ from the other ideas you have heard expressed?

▶ Whether your problems in stating a core idea clearly are due to embarrassment or hazy thinking, the point is the same. An assertive message must be brief and to the point. Take a few minutes to organize your thoughts and feelings on each of the following subjects into one concise sentence.

a. Describe one dissatisfaction you presently have with the behavior of a friend or acquaintance. _____

_____

_____

b. List one personal belief that you suspect others might dispute.

_____

_____

_____

c. Write one expression of gratitude or appreciation you feel toward another person, including your reasons for feeling as you do. _____

_____

_____

Don't Overqualify Statements.   Often we are apprehensive about how a message will be received, and in order to soften its impact we qualify our thoughts or feelings. Qualifiers are words or phrases that discount the immediacy of a message:

—"You probably will think I'm being touchy, but . . ."
—"I hope you don't mind, but . . ."

—"I hope I'm not bothering you, but . . ."
—"I may be wrong, but . . ."

The common element in all these qualifiers is the word "but;" which serves to discredit everything in the sentence that precedes it. In fact, when used often enough, the mere sound of "but" serves as a warning that the forthcoming thought will totally contradict what has already been said: "John, I've really enjoyed going out with you, but I want to have a change." "We've found your work here quite satisfactory, but our budget forces us to let you go." "The paper you wrote in this course had several good ideas, but I graded it as a D for the following reasons . . ."

Other qualifiers include:

—*just* (as in "I just wanted to talk to you for a few minutes," or "There's just one problem . . .")
—*kind of*, *sort* of (as in "I was kind of unhappy about what you said about me," or "I sort of hope you can keep the noise down.")
—*little* (as in "There's a little problem I need to talk about," or "I wish you could try a little harder to be on time.")
—*any type of apology* (such as "I'm sorry to bring this up," or "I hate to ask this favor.")

You can see from these few examples that in overusing qualifiers you become your own worst enemy, discounting everything you've said before the other person even responds.

Don't succumb to the myths described in Chapter 2. Remember: You have the right to appear foolish, to be unsure of yourself, to express your feelings, and to act independently of the approval of others. Don't apologize for yourself: There's nothing wrong with your thoughts! Take yourself seriously, and others will start to do the same thing.

This suggestion doesn't mean that you should totally remove qualifiers from your language. Of couse there are times when you ought to apologize for your actions or express your uncertainty, but don't overdo it or your image will suffer, both in your own eyes and in the eyes of others.

CHECKLIST OF ASSERTIVE ELEMENTS

Use this checklist to evaluate the assertive impact of any message. Apply it to yourself in order to see which areas you might improve. You can also use the list to help others evaluate their assertiveness.

Visual Elements

—appropriate eye contact.
—distance suits the occasion
—facial expression matches the words being spoken

—gestures are suitable—no fidgeting or other distracting mannerisms
—posture indicates alertness without tension
—body orientation is direct without being confrontive

Vocal Elements

—loudness suits the circumstances
—rate of speech not too fast or slow
—good fluency: absence of distracting vocal habits ("um," "uh," "er," etc.)
—tone reinforces the verbal message
—inflection appropriate for verbal message

Verbal Elements

—message expressed in complete sentences
—idea clearly expressed in core statement
—no qualifiers discount message

▶ Write behavioral definitions for three communication problems; either ones you listed on page 18 or ones you discovered as a result of the checklist immediately above. If you have any difficulty defining the problem behaviorally, begin a diary in which you record your behavior in the situations you have specified. When you are ready, answer the questions below.

REMEMBER, IT IS IMPORTANT THAT YOU COMPLETE THIS ACTIVITY BEFORE PRO-
CEEDING.

EXAMPLE: a) The people involved in my problem Guests visiting my home.
b) The circumstances in which my problem occurs When I am tired or have something more important to do than keep talking with my guest.
c) The problem behavior I continue to talk to the guests as if I had nothing else to
do. I respond to their statements, and deny that I'd like them to go when they suggest that it may be time to leave.

1. a) The people involved in my problem _____

_____

b) The circumstances in which my problem occurs _____

_____

_____

_____

c) The problem behavior _____

_____

_____

_____

2. a) The people involved in my problem _____

_____

   b) The circumstances in which my problem occurs _____

_____

_____

_____

   c) The problem behavior _____

_____

_____

_____

3. a) The people involved in my problem _____

_____

   b) The circumstances in which my problem occurs _____

_____

_____

_____

   c) The problem behavior _____

_____

_____

_____

SPECIFYING TARGET BEHAVIORS

Having now defined several assertive problems, you are ready to decide on new, more desirable ways of communicating. Like the problem statements you have just written above, your goals should be expressed in behavioral terms. Actually, most of your work is already done, since each of your target behaviors will include two of the elements you have already defined there: who your ideal behavior will involve and the circumstances in which it will occur. To complete a behavioral goal you need to add one final ingredient to these elements: a definition of *the precise behaviors you hope to achieve*.

In describing these desirable behaviors it might be helpful to recall the many folk tales in which a character is granted one wish (or two or three, depending on the story). In most accounts the greedy master hastily insists on a gift that is not exactly what he intended. As a result of this carelessness, instead of gaining happiness, the unfortunate victim winds up worse off than before. Probably the best example of such a tale is the story of King Midas, who asked that everything he touched turn to gold and wound up with a 24-carat son!

It is a good idea to remember the moral of tales such as this as you define your personal assertive goal. Thoughtfully constructing this target will leave you a happier communicator, while failing to specify precisely how you want to behave can at best result in frustration and at worst in disaster, as the story of Henry illustrates.

Henry had just begun a potentially successful career as a sales representative for a large industrial supplier. The only problem was that he was nervous in making presentations to important customers. He described the behavioral components of this nervousness as a pounding heart, sweaty palms, and flushed complexion. As you will learn in Chapters 5 and 6, there are methods to deal with such anxiety, and Henry was wise to choose them as a means of reaching his goal. He completed a self-modification project and reported feeling relaxed throughout his next few conferences, confident that his new behavior would result in increased sales.

In truth, just the opposite happened: Instead of winning new customers, he actually received fewer orders. Reconsideration of his plans showed why. Henry had not stated his *total* goal. In addition to being relaxed, an effective salesman needs to exhibit other behaviors, one of which is the ability to organize his presentation in a logical sequence. Henry had succeeded so well at being relaxed that he ignored this equally important skill. As a result, the customers were treated to a casual but disorganized approach. Like King Midas, Henry got exactly what he asked for, but found the consequences to be different from what he expected.

Now that you realize how important it is to specify the precise results you hope to accomplish, you are ready to write your own goals. While such targets might seem obvious in light of the problem statements you constructed on pages 54 and 55, you can be sure to get the best results by asking the following questions about each of your goals.[1]

1. Is It Specific? As you will read again and again in this book, your greatest chance of success will come when you can define the new ways you want to communicate in the clearest possible terms. Your goal statement should describe each of the discrete behaviors you hope to master in a

---

[1] This list is adapted in part from Jack Canfield and Harold Wells, *100 Ways to Enhance Self-Concept in the Classroom,* Englewood Cliffs, N.J.: Prentice-Hall, 1976.

given situation. The best way to compile such a list is to visualize yourself behaving in the desirable manner and then to note all the significant elements of that picture. There are instructions for such visualization later in this chapter.

2. Is It Realistic? You must believe that you can reach the target you set for yourself. This does not suggest that your long-term goals should be modest ones; on the contrary, as you learn the skills described in this book, you will probably find that you can accomplish much more than you expected. However, it would be unwise to expect your efforts to result in perfection or spectacular change in a short time. For instance, it makes more sense to aim for the target of responding to an instructor's questions than expecting always to come up with a flawless answer.

3. Is It Positive? Whenever possible, try to construct a target that involves increasing the frequency of a desired behavior rather than reducing the frequency of an unwanted one. For example, instead of stating "I want to stop avoiding a certain person," say "I want to approach that person more often." Rather than stating "I want to be less shy about accepting compliments," say "I want to accept compliments with a smile and a 'thank you.'" Such positive goals will help you in two ways. First, they will tell you exactly what you must do to express yourself better instead of merely describing present unproductive actions. You can understand the desirability of positive goals by comparing the vague parental order, "Stop being so messy," with the more positive request, "Put your toys in the closet." The first instruction merely states what the child is doing wrong, while the second offers a solution. Another reason for stating goals positively will become apparent in Chapter 6. When you begin counting the frequency of your target behaviors, it is much easier to count the presence of positive actions than the absence of negative ones.

4. Does It Deal with Frequent Behaviors? While it might be desirable to improve your communication with a relative you see only once a year or to behave more confidently in an important job interview, it would be wise to direct your first attempts at increasing assertiveness during some events that occur more often. The reason is simple: Practice is a key to improvement, and events that occur regularly and often give you more chances to develop your skill. As you master techniques for self-change that appear in later chapters, your chances for success will be greater with more frequent practice.

5. Is It Important? While you obviously won't choose undesirable goals for an assertive project, there is a danger of picking goals that are not important enough to demand the attention and effort necessary for success. As you have already seen, even the process of defining some targets takes much time and thought; the steps involved in reaching those targets require the same amount of rigor. For this reason you should take care to choose goals that you seriously want to achieve and are willing to work for.

6. Is It Controllable? Many assertive goals involve other people. In such cases you should be sure to focus only on modifying your own behavior, not on changing theirs. Expressing dissatisfaction about poor service to those responsible for it is a better target than expecting your remarks to always meet with success. Attempting to express feelings of affection more openly is preferable to expecting that such statements will always be reciprocated. Remember, just because you act assertively, there is no guarantee that others will always respond favorably.

7. Is It Measurable? You should be able to count how often you engage in the target behaviors over a given period. For instance, instead of stating that you want to meet more strangers, say that you aim to meet at least five (or some other number) new people in the next week. In the same way, your intention to decline 80 percent of the undesired invitations you receive in a month is better than merely trying to say no more often to such requests. (Chapter 6 covers the subject of measurement in detail.)

8. Is It Humanitarian? As a matter of principle, personal goals should never be destructive to yourself or to others. Though a target of humiliating anyone who disagrees with you would be achievable, you should seriously question whether such an aggressive behavior is desirable. Instead, you might better aim at mastering a style of behaving that maintains both your dignity and that of others.

WHEN YOU HAVE DIFFICULTY SPECIFYING A GOAL

So far this discussion has assumed that you already have an assertive goal in mind and that you are looking for instructions on how to reach it. Unfortunately, this is not always the case. Sometimes the difficulty is precisely that you cannot think of any alternatives to your present unsatisfying way of communicating. For example, you might become embarrassed when complimented on your appearance, work, or some other trait, and be unable to respond comfortably and gracefully. You might find yourself behaving argumentatively whenever criticized even mildly about your judgments, yet not know how else to act. In such cases there are three methods you can use to define an assertive goal.

1. Modeling Often simply observing a model—a communicator who acts in ways you admire—can be a source of ideas about more desirable ways to express yourself. This point becomes clear by taking another look at Dave, who found this to be so in his project of conversing more skillfully with attractive, eligible women at parties and while in lines. At the suggestion of his instructor he observed the way friends acted in such situations. Dave learned that several men achieved success in ways he would never feel comfortable using: for instance, making jocular insults and loudly claiming to be infatuated with the women in question. Dave did, however, make one observation that was useful. He noted that all of the successful models maintained frequent eye contact while talking with women in whom they were interested. Upon reflection Dave could see that this nonverbal behavior communicated interest much more effectively than the occasional furtive glances he shot while speaking. Thus, "maintaining eye contact while speaking and listening" joined "speaking in complete sentences" and "limiting silences to 20 seconds or less" as Dave's behavioral goals.

You can learn from models in a number of ways. *Live* subjects whom you can observe in person are one source of ideas. Like Dave, you may be able to find people who behave in ways you would like to master. On the other hand, sometimes no such live models may be available, in which case *symbolic* models are equally valuable. Symbolic models include characters in books or films, as well as public figures you might admire. If Dave had been unable to find suitable live models, he might have decided to emulate some fictional character he had once read about. Of course, in selecting either a live or symbolic model you should be sure the character is someone you can realistically expect to imitate. Though is might be desirable to be as strong as Paul Bunyan or as witty as the character on your favorite television comedy, striving for such unattainable goals can only lead to frustration.

THE PROCESS OF DEFINING A GOAL BEHAVIORALLY

I'm no good with women.

↓

I'm no good with attractive, eligible women I'd like to date.

↓

I'm no good with attractive, eligible women I'd like to date when I meet them at parties and in public places.

↓

I remain silent for long periods of time and don't complete my sentences with attractive, eligible women I'd like to date when I meet them at parties and in public places.

↓

I want to carry on conversations with no silences longer than 20 seconds, finish all sentences I start, and maintain eye contact with attractive, eligible women I'd like to date when I meet them at parties and in public places.

In addition to learning how to behave from models, you can also benefit from observing the rewards that follow from their actions. Dave noticed how the direct eye contact of his friends resulted in friendly responses from the women they approached. Thus, he had a greater incentive to change himself. In the same way you can note how the live or symbolic models you choose benefit from their actions, and in so doing gain reinforcement for trying the new behaviors yourself.

When introduced to the idea of learning from models, some people object to behaving in what they consider to be a phony, unauthentic way. "I want to be myself," they insist, "not an imitation of someone else." This resistance is understandable, but it is based on a misconception. The behaviors you observe, practice, and eventually master will never be carbon copies of someone else's, for as you take them on they will become uniquely yours. Consider the many skills you have already learned by modeling and you will see that they have not threatened your individuality or authenticity. You learned to speak from models, yet the way you use language is unlike anyone else's. The same holds true for your writing style, sense of humor, and a host of other traits. You are unique, and gaining new ideas about how to communicate from a model will not threaten that uniqueness. On the contrary, you will still be yourself, but with more skills than you previously had.

▶ Take a moment now to think of models who skillfully handle each of the situations you described on pages 54–55. The models you choose can be either real or symbolic. For each problem, note the name of the model you have selected and describe the specific behaviors this person exhibits that you would like to master.

EXAMPLE:

The model My friend Cecily

The behaviors your model exhibits that you would like to master When she is tired or busy and guests seem to be staying, she explains without apologizing why she needs to do something else. Usually she doesn't have to say anything more: people understand and leave.

Model 1

The model _____

The behaviors your model exhibits that you would like to master _____

_____

_____

_____

Model 2

The model _____

The behaviors your model exhibits that you would like to master _____

_____

_____

_____

Model 3

The model _____

The behaviors you model exhibits that you would like to master _____

_____

_____

_____

2. Advice Sometimes no models are available to provide ideas on target behaviors. In other cases you might observe competent models, yet be unable to determine exactly what they do that makes them effective. At such times it is worthwhile to seek advice.

Advice can come from several sources. Often friends or family members can offer useful suggestions about how you might change. People who are familiar with the way you behave can often spot an alternative that might never have occurred to you. In addition, such acquaintances can often modify your perception of the original problem. For instance, they might on one hand insist that you are exaggerating the seriousness of your dilemma, or on the other suggest that you are underestimating the extent to which you need to change.

Advice can also come from consultation with such professionals as teachers, physicians, counselors, therapists, and ministers. Dave received such help from his instructor with beneficial results. Often it is not necessary to receive constant guidance from a professional. Simply obtaining suggestions about suitable goals might be all you need; after that you can manage the process of changing on your own.

A third source of advice can come from publications such as this book. As you attempt to formulate your goals in this section it might be helpful to explore the chapters in Part Three that apply directly to your own concerns. A survey of the Contents, the Index, and the list of assertive goals in Appendix I offers clues to the pages that may be useful to you. Besides *Confidence in Communication* there are many other publications that can help you define a target. A number of these are listed at the end of each chapter in this book, and the bibliography contains additional sources.

3. Idealized Self-Image Psychologist Dorothy Suskind has developed a third source from which you can generate ideas for assertive goals. She often advises her clients to visualize themselves as possessing all the traits they find desirable. Such a fantasy often produces a long list of images, which can then be translated into specific behaviors. This technique often works well for people who cannot discover any models or sources of advice. When instructed to imagine themselves suddenly transformed into skillful communicators in a problem situation, a clear picture often presents itself.

This was the case for Jan, a student who had become so nervous giving presentations in a public address class that she resorted to drinking two martinis before delivering each speech. After being instructed to visualize an idealized self-image of herself addressing the class, she described an informal style of delivery that sounded extremely effective. With her professor's help Jan translated her visualization into a list of specific behaviors: relaxed posture, smiling facial expression, pleasant tone of voice, and anecdotal pattern of organization. She was then told to plan a speech that included all these elements and to rehearse it, keeping the successful image in mind. When the day came to deliver her next assignment, Jan and her professor were pleased to find that the image had served to provide goals that were easily reached (with no martinis!). "My problem was just that I always saw myself as failing," Jan explained. "As soon as I got a picture of myself doing O.K., I knew I could deliver the speech just fine, and I did."

Take a moment and visualize an Idealized Self-Image for each of the problem behaviors you listed on pages 54 and 55. To be most effective, this visualization should take place while you are sitting in a relaxed position with closed eyes in a place free of distractions. Picture yourself in a specific scene and imagine the dialogue and nonverbal behaviors that you use to express yourself. If you note any parts of this image that you would like to work on in your real life, record them in Appendix II.

CHECKLIST FOR WRITING BEHAVIORAL DEFINITIONS

A. Who does the problem involve?
  1. What person or group of people do you communicate with in the specific situation?
B. In what circumstances does the behavior occur?
  1. At what *times* does it occur?
  2. In what *places* does it occur?
  3. What is *unique about you* when it occurs?
  4. What is *unique about the other*(s) when it occurs?
C. Which of your present behaviors constitutes the problem?
  1. Is the behavior *specific*?
  2. Is it *observable*?
  3. Is your description *complete*?
D. Have you stated your target behavior clearly?

1. Is it *specific?*
2. Is it *realistic?*
3. Is it *positive?*
4. Does it deal with *frequent behaviors?*
5. Is it *important?*
6. Is it *controllable?*
7. Is it *measurable?*
8. Is it *growth-facilitating?*

Now it is time to begin defining your assertive goals. Appendix II offers a place where you can describe some ways in which you would like to improve your communication. Turn there now, and using the problems you outlined on pages 54–55 (as well as any others that now seem important), describe precisely how you would like to behave in the future. If you are still unclear about possible goals, refer to the list of assertive targets in Appendix I.

As more goals occur to you, continue to record them in Appendix II. The remaining chapters in this book offer a number of methods by which you can reach these goals.

RESULTS OF SETTING BEHAVIORAL GOALS

By now you can see that clear behavioral goals are quite different from the vague ones you originally stated. Although the process of writing such targets can take considerable thought and time, your efforts should be rewarded in several ways:

1. When goals are stated behaviorally, specifying the limited context in which most communication problems occur, you'll more clearly realize that you are almost certainly situationally, not generally, unassertive. As you read earlier, the relatively limited nature of your difficulties should be encouraging, for it should show that you are probably more competent at expressing yourself than you might previously have thought.

2. When goals are stated behaviorally, some problems solve themselves, as Dave's story illustrates. After realizing that one personal aim was to complete every sentence he started, Dave found that doing so became easy. The problem was simple enough that his new awareness and concentration proved sufficient to bring about the desired change. In the same way many other undesirable communication traits disappear once they are brought into the open. A newspaper reporter conducted more successful interviews once she realized the necessity for increasing eye contact and smiles with her subjects. A shy consumer learned to say "I'm not interested" to aggressive sales clerks after realizing that it is not pleasant or necessary to oblige unwanted offers of assistance. Once they learn to define their own problems behaviorally, a high percentage of readers utter virtually the same words: "As soon as I realized the problem, it disappeared."

Of course, not all types of unassertiveness disappear so easily. Sometimes new communication skills take time to learn, and in other cases the anxiety that accompanies difficult situations needs to be reduced. Even in these instances behavioral goals are valuable first steps in the process of improving self-expression. Their usefulness comes from setting a clear target toward which you can work and against which your progress can be measured. Dave's desire to reduce the number of long silences fitted this pattern. Though simply realizing that he wanted to reach this target was not sufficient to bring about the desired change, his clear target statement did help. Keeping it in mind, Dave was able to observe models who were good conversationalists and attempt to adapt their conversational techniques to fit his own style. He also was able to gather tips from Chapter 7 on ways to keep conversations going and to use this information in the self-modification project described in Chapter 6. Following the steps there produced good results. After two months of steady progress, Dave expressed satisfaction with the results. While he still experienced occasional difficulties in some conversations, such instances were infrequent enough to be unimportant to him. Dave also reported feeling much more confident around attractive women and much better about himself.

SUMMARY

In Chapter 3 you have learned how to identify problems and to write goals in behavioral terms. You have seen that most communicators are situationally unassertive, having difficulties in some areas of their lives while being basically competent in most others. You have seen that the first step in solving a problem is to define it behaviorally by stating who is involved, in what circumstances the difficulty occurs, and the specific unsatisfying behaviors you hope to eliminate. After defining your problem, you should set personal goals by describing in similar detail the precise behaviors you hope to exhibit in the situation you have already described. If you have difficulty defining target behaviors, you can observe the behavior of either live or symbolic models, seek advice in this book and elsewhere, and visualize an idealized self-image of desirable communication. If you follow these steps carefully, you should be rewarded by a new appreciation of your present skill as a communicator, as well as taking a first step toward solving whatever problems you do experience in your assertive skills.

4

Behavior Rehearsal: The Value of Practice

After reading this far you've probably noticed an increase in your own communication skill. Often simply defining a problem and setting a clear goal will bring about the desired change. There are probably still instances, however, where you have a hard time behaving assertively, even though you know what you *ought* to be doing.

For example, Susan reported problems with a neighbor whose hobby was collecting and repairing old junked cars, one or two of which usually filled the space in front of her house for several weeks at a time. Susan had always had a hard time complaining to others whose behavior affected her, and to make matters even more difficult, this neighbor had a reputation for being stubborn and uncooperative. Faced with this challenge, Susan set her goal as "approaching the neighbor and requesting that he leave space for me to park in front of my house." Not stopping here, Susan further clarified how she wanted to approach the neighbor: to look him in the eye, speak loudly and clearly, and to avoid apologizing for the request, which she believed was within her rights.

In spite of this thoughtful preparation the results were unsuccessful. "I told him what I wanted," Susan described, "but it was a disaster. I started out just fine, but when the guy said that it was a public street and that I had no right to complain, I didn't know what to say. When I tried to claim that parking by my house was a reasonable request, he said I shouldn't start sounding like a 'women's libber,' talking about my rights so much. Well, that really upset me, and I guess I came unglued and sulked away."

How could Susan have improved her chances for succeeding with this reasonable request? She needed to add two elements to her efforts: a *gradual approach* to her challenging target, and the opportunity to *practice* her encounter before it actually took place. In other words, just as an athlete needs to practice for a big event or a student can benefit from taking increasingly challenging sample examinations, you can improve your real-life communication by rehearsing difficult situations in gradual steps.

In this chapter we'll look at a method for increasing your personal assertiveness that includes these features. It's based on two principles: "One step at a time" and "practice makes perfect." As you read the following pages, don't be fooled by the apparent simplicity of these elements, for along with the method of goal setting described in Chapter 3, they're probably the most important and useful tools for increasing assertiveness that you can learn.

SHAPING

Shaping is the process of approaching your target in gradual steps. You can understand how shaping works by looking at how it can be applied to a physical skill, such as skiing. Picture yourself arriving at a mountain resort, never having been on skis before. You look around at the towering peaks and watch other vacationers gracefully gliding down the steep slopes. At this point it seems impossible that you could ever master this sport, but you try to swallow your doubts as you mount the chair lift and ride to the top of the most difficult run. On your way up you visualize one catastrophic accident after another; you picture yourself suffering from broken bones and torn ligaments, covered with heavy plaster casts. By the time you arrive at the top of the mountain you are calling yourself a fool for ever thinking you could possibly ski. But at this point you have no choice, so with knees shaking, off you go. . . .

Clearly this one-step approach to a challenging sport isn't the wisest one to take. The reason why is obvious: Skiing is too complicated a skill to learn all at once. A much smarter approach would be to begin practicing long before reaching the snow by doing exercises to get your muscles in shape. Perhaps you could read a few books and see some films on the subject in order to pick up a few pointers. You would also be wise to talk to some good skiers and learn their suggestions about how to start and what to expect, perhaps even enrolling in a professional skiing school. Then upon arriving at the resort, you would begin by trying the gradual inclines of the beginners' slope until you developed a feel for the skis. After you felt comfortable there, you would gradually move on to more and more challenging runs, until you finally were ready to take on the most difficult one.

Learning to communicate more assertively isn't too different from learning to ski. It's definitely not wise to try an overnight transformation from a relatively shy, unassertive speaker into a self-confident one who can handle any situation. While you *might* succeed with this bold approach, your chances for failure are greater; and once you have failed, it's much more difficult to pick yourself up and try again.

The foolishness of this all-at-once approach explains why New Year's resolutions about assertiveness (or most other subjects) usually end in failure: it's unrealistic to expect yourself to change a long-seated habit overnight. How many of these resolutions have you kept lately? Do you even bother making them anymore? There must be a better way to change. Fortunately, shaping does provide that alternative. This process calls for you to set up an ultimate goal and approach it gradually, in a series of small, attainable steps. Let's take a look at an example of how shaping works.

Mary wanted to feel more comfortable expressing herself to people she saw as authority figures when her opinions disagreed with theirs. Through the process of behavioral goal setting she defined "authority figures" as her college instructors, minister, and boss. Rather than suddenly speaking her mind every time she disagreed with these people, she wisely decided to begin to change by asking a few questions of one instructor who seemed especially open-minded and willing to encourage discussion. After feeling comfortable with him, she moved on to sharing her thoughts in a second and then a third class. Her successes in these areas bolstered her confidence enough that she now was ready to express disagreements with her minister, who proved surprisingly receptive to Mary's newfound assertiveness. Finally she was prepared to face her boss, who at first was not as agreeable to hearing her ideas as the other people had been. "He listened to what I had to say and then went right ahead and did it his way," Mary reported. "A few months ago his reaction would have crushed me, but since I knew it was my right to express my thoughts as long as I didn't get too aggressive about it, I just agreed with him when he said that I'd never doubted his opinions before and tried to explain why I spoke up. A few days later my boss actually accepted my suggestion and complemented me for coming up with it! I never would have had the confidence to stick to my guns unless I'd already been successful with my instructors and the minister."

MARY'S SHAPING HIERARCHY

Goal: Express my opinions fully to authority figures when they disagree
with me.

Subgoals: 1. Question one or two comments of Professor A.
2. Express disagreement with Professor B.
3. Express disagreement with Professor C.
4. Express disagreement with Minister.
5. Share my idea of how to change the job with my boss.

There are a number of ways you can move toward your target gradually.
Instead of approaching more and more challenging *people* as Mary did, you
can work on one or two assertive *elements* at a time, perhaps starting with
your posture and vocal tone and then moving on to distance, fluency, and
unqualified statements later. Another approach is to gradually increase the
frequency of your assertions, starting with only one or two per week and
then expressing yourself more often. Another series of shaping steps involves approaching increasingly difficult *situations* involving the same
person or people. You will read more about these approaches in Chapter 6,
but for now the main thing to realize is that your greatest chances for
progress will come from approaching your goal one step at a time, making
sure that your chances of success are good in each case.

▶ From the list of assertive goals you have recorded in Appendix II, pick three that you would
like to work toward. Decide how you could break each one into a series of subgoals, and list
your plans below. Before you begin writing, you might find it useful to discuss possible approaches with a friend or instructor, in addition to previewing the material on shaping in
Chapter 6, if necessary.

EXAMPLE: I want to take the initiative in my social life by inviting friends to activities instead of
waiting for them to make the plans.

step a. Casually invite R. (carpool partner) to drop by my place on our way home
from work.

step b. Invite J. (a neighbor) to go to the nursery shopping for garden supplies.

step c. Invite J. over for lunchtime salad prepared from my garden.

step d. Invite W. over for dinner.

step e. Invite W., V., and S. with their families over for weekend party.

Goal 1. _____

_____

_____

step a. _____

_____

step b. _____

_____

step c. _____

_____

step d. _____

_____

step e. _____

_____

Goal 2. _____

_____

_____

step a. _____

_____

step b. _____

_____

step c. _____

_____

step d. _____

_____

step e. _____

_____

Goal 3. _____

_____

_____

step a. _____

_____

step b. _____

_____

step c. _____

_____

step d. _____

_____

step e. _____

_____

BEHAVIOR REHEARSAL

Now that you've divided your personal goals into a series of easily reachable steps, you're ready to work on reaching them. You can do so through the process of *behavior rehearsal*, a systematic way of practicing and improving a new behavior in a safe environment before trying it in real life.

To understand how behavior rehearsal works, let's look at another sports analogy. Consider a football team preparing for a championship game. You needn't be an expert to know that the weeks before the contest are devoted to diligent practice. The opposing club's probable strategies are analyzed, as are your own team's strengths and weaknesses. During scrimmages certain members take the role of the opponents to simulate actual game conditions. The preparation doesn't involve just talking about how the team should play; instead the goal is actually to experience in advance as much as possible of what will happen. The value of such practice becomes clear once the real game has started. If the sessions have been well planned, the players will feel they have been there before, and to that degree they will know how to act almost instinctively.

What is true for athletes also holds for performers. A concert pianist must practice a piece over and over in order to play it skillfully at a recital. Actors rehearse their lines before a performance so they will carry out their roles in the most convincing manner. Speakers practice their remarks in order to make sure their delivery will be effective.

Since you know by now that assertiveness is a skill, what is true for an athlete, musician, or performer is also valid for you, the communicator. You can learn to communicate more effectively by practicing your target behavior in advance. This doesn't mean that you ought to develop a detailed script for each occasion and follow it no matter what happens; you'd obviously appear artificial and unresponsive if you tried this. Behavior rehearsal can, however, help you experience the *general* situations that you'll encounter later so that you'll get a basic idea of how to handle them comfortably and naturally. Recall our hypothetical football team again. Imagine that in practice they anticipated that their opponents would pass the ball about 60 percent of the time and run it for the rest of their plays.

However, in the actual game it develops that the reverse is true; about two-thirds of the plays are runs and the rest are passes. This change wouldn't seriously bother our team. The behaviors practiced during the week would still be useful; they would simply have to be adjusted to meet the real conditions.

In the same way you'll be able to practice a set of skills on your own and transfer them to your everyday life without losing much effectiveness or spontaneity.

Steps In Behavior Rehearsal   There are six steps in increasing your assertiveness through behavior rehearsal. As you look at them, imagine how they apply to the goals you have listed in Appendix II.

1. Define the Target Behavior.   By following the instructions in Appendix II you have already done this for the goals you listed there. Remember to follow the same process in other cases, too. A clear target behavior should describe the *people* involved in your assertive act, the *circumstances* in which it will occur, and the *specific way* you want to act. If necessary, review the goal-setting checklists on pages 62–63 for a brushup on the other characteristics a good target behavior should possess.

2. Observe a Model of the Target Behavior.   Whenever possible, it's best to watch another person carry out the behavior you hope to learn. Think about your own experience in learning any skill to see how helpful a model can be, whether the subject is cooking, writing poetry, or living what you consider to be a moral life. Whenever you can arrange it, live models are an ideal source of information on how you might act, but don't overlook other types of models: ones described in books such as this, fictional characters you have read about or seen acted out, or even imaginary characters you create yourself. The same purpose will be served by all these models, who will give you a pattern to follow when you practice your target. Remember that the object isn't necessarily to copy the models' actions verbatim, but rather to gain ideas about how you can adapt this behavior to suit your own personal style.

3. Rehearse Your Target Behavior.   Just as our hypothetical football team practices on a friendly field before a game, you can profit by rehearsing the way you want to act before actually approaching the target situation. The rehearsal scene gives you a chance to try out new behaviors in a safe atmosphere. You can make mistakes, change your words and actions, and even make a fool out of yourself (everyone does once in a while!) without risking the consequences that might follow in the real situation.

As you read in the introduction to this book, the ideal setting for behavior rehearsal is in an assertiveness-training group or some other type of communication class or workshop. Here you have a supportive atmosphere, since all the members share your desire to improve. Also, since overt rehearsal requires one or more people to play the others involved in your target situations, the group provides a source of actors. In addition to helping as role players, other group members can give you useful feedback about your strengths in the scene as well as pointing out areas where you could improve. Of course, the leader of an assertiveness-training group is also a useful source of information and advice, as well as being a model of effective communication.

Sometimes you might not be able to rehearse your assertive scene in a group specifically designed for this purpose. This needn't be a major problem, for you can practice a target behavior with anyone who is willing to cooperate and able to represent the other person involved. Other possible settings for rehearsal would be classes, counseling sessions, or simply a get-together with friends.

4. Receive Coaching, Feedback, and More Modeling.   Once you have tried out your target behavior, you can get some reaction to how you appeared. You probably have an idea of how the scene went, but the people who observed you might have some useful perspectives to share. There are three points to remember in giving feedback to a rehearsal scene. First, *be sure to recognize your strengths in a scene before discussing the weaknesses.* Because you're striving for improvement, it's easy to overlook the well-executed parts of a message. Don't let this happen. Remember that the most lasting improvement comes in small steps, and that each of these steps should be recognized. A second point to remember is to *work on only one or two changes at a time.* Again, recall the purpose of shaping. As desirable as it would be to improve everything about your message instantly, it's difficult to handle too many demands at once. Settle for a few changes at a time and you'll reach your ultimate goal soon enough. The third point to keep in mind is that *you are the final* judge of what changes need to be made in your behavior. While others can offer valuable feedback by commenting on how your specific actions look to them and how they think you ought to handle a situation, you're the person who has to bring off any changes; and unless you feel comfortable doing so, all your efforts will only result in an artificial, unsatisfying performance.

5. Practice the Target Behavior Again, Receiving Additional Feedback, Modeling, and Coaching.   Now that you are armed with the advice from Step 4, replay the scene. Remember to focus only on improving the one or two points you just discussed. Keep the strong points you demonstrated in your first run-through. After you have replayed the scene, it is time for another period of feedback in which other members will compliment you on your improvement and suggest other ways that you could profit by further changing your remarks.

Repeat this process of rehearsal and feedback as long as it seems useful, and end it when you feel you are ready to carry out the behaviors you have learned.

6. <u>Try Out the Scene in Real Life</u>. Now you are ready to take advantage of your practice. The next time the situation you have been preparing for occurs, try out the new skills you have learned.

Remember that you needn't feel obligated to handle the real-life scene exactly as you did the rehearsal situation. It's unlikely that any scene will occur precisely as you anticipated. The key to real-life success is to stick with the basic principles you have learned, but adapt your specific actions to fit the situation.

A SAMPLE BEHAVIOR-REHEARSAL SCENE

The following pages describe a typical behavior-rehearsal session from an assertiveness-training group.[1] Notice how the group members apply several points covered so far in this book:

—Visual, verbal, and vocal elements are used to make the target behavior more specific.

—The trainer and other group members reinforce Judy's desirable behaviors as well as suggesting improvements.

—Judy is the final judge of which suggestions for change she feels comfortable with and will incorporate into her plan.

In this scene, Judy, the manager of an apartment complex, has decided to ask her boss, Mr. Brown, for a larger reduction in her rent due to the time her job requires. In this dialogue the trainer (Tr.) has set the scene as realistically as possible, with Judy entering her employer's (E's) office.

Tr: Come in and say what you want and see how it goes. You're not supposed to be perfect, so just give it a try.

E: Come in!

Judy: Hello, uh, Mr. Brown, uh, how are you? It's been a long time since I've uh, met with you.

E: Yes, Judy, what can I do for you?

Judy: Well, uh, I don't know, uh, I know you're very busy and everything, but I wanted to ask you something about my apartment manager's job.

E: Yes, what is it?

Judy: Well, I was wondering if you realized how much time it took to do all the things the job requires?

E: I should think I do, after all it's what I'm paying you for, isn't it!

Tr: OK, let's stop here since it's easier to take the situation a little bit at a time and focus on it closely. What can you all tell Judy that you thought was assertive about what she's said and how she's behaved so far? [Other group participants are labeled "P." Note their *specific, behavioral* comments.]

[1] Reprinted with permission from Arthur Lange and Patricia Jakubowski, *Responsible Assertive Behavior*. Champaign, Ill.: Research Press, 1976.

P_3: Your voice was loud and clear.

P_4: Your tone sounded genuinely interested when you asked how he was doing and yet you were brief.

P_5: You walked right in and sat down facing him directly.

TR: Those were good specific observations of your nonverbal behavior. What else did you like, Judy?

JUDY: I was pleased that I did speak up right away and that I got to the issue quickly.

TR: Those are both true. What would you like to do differently?

JUDY: Well, I'd like to stop saying "uh" when I speak so that my voice flows more smoothly . . . and I didn't like the way I raised the issue of the job. It seemed too indirect and I put too much responsibility on Mr. Brown to continue the issue. [Note that Judy evaluates her own performance]

TR: Those are both excellent points. How would you raise the issue of job time differently so that you are really expressing what you want to say?

JUDY: I would tell him how much time I actually put into the job and express my wanting a greater reduction in rent.

TR: That sounds much more like what you said you wanted to communicate earlier. Try it again and we'll particularly look for your dropping the "uh's" and stating your concerns more directly. [Note limited specific goals.]

E: Come in!

JUDY: Hello Mr. Brown, how are you?

E: Fine, Judy, what can I do for you?

JUDY: Well, I've been concerned for some time now that I have been working about 20 hours a week as apartment manager and I would like you to consider increasing my rent deduction to $200 per month.

TR: OK. Stop. Will people give Judy some specific feedback about what you think she just did that was assertive?

P_3: You definitely dropped the "uh's" and your words flowed much more smoothly.

P_4: I thought you were just as clear and direct as can be in stating your information and making your request. It was great!

P_5: You also eliminated stating your great concern over interrupting his busy day so that your concerns were stated more directly.

JUDY: Yeah, I really liked the way that sounded, too. I also felt that I was more in control of the conversation when I expressed my request directly.

TR: That's great, you did make the changes you wanted. Is there anything else you'd like to do differently?

JUDY: Well, yeah, I was aware that I had a sort of shy or sheepish grin while I was talking and I'd like my face to express my serious concern.

TR: OK. And does anyone else have any changes you might suggest to Judy?

P_6: Yeah, Judy, would you want to make more eye contact with Mr. Brown?

JUDY: Oh, yes, that's a good point; I was looking away a lot.

TR: OK. Try it again and this time focus on your facial expression and eye contact.

Judy then practiced several more interactions. At first the employer was encouraged to be cooperative and support the request. When Judy successfully completed the entire scene to her satisfaction, the trainer then asked her to practice the scene with the employer responding negatively (e.g., anger, threat, indifference, guilt, or whatever "hooks" her). The situation was then practiced until *Judy was satisfied* with how she assertively handled the employer's uncooperative response. Below is an example of such an extended practice.

TR: Judy, when we talked earlier about the catastrophes you worried over before going in to see Mr. Brown, you mentioned that he might get angry with you and yell or berate or accuse you somehow. Would you like to practice an extension of this situation where Mr. Brown is not as cooperative as before?

JUDY: Yes, I really would because that's what ties me up most inside. If I knew I could handle that, I would be more confident.

TR: OK. Tell Bill (the participant role playing Mr. Brown) what he should be like.

JUDY: Well, you would first act real busy and then when I bring up the issue of how much time I spend as manager, you would begin asking me in an accusing manner how I do spend my time, as though you believe I don't really do anything. Then when I talk about getting a greater reduction in rent, you get angry and accuse me of trying to put something over on you.

E: That's really clear. I'll give it a good try.

TR: Try it from the beginning and I'll stop you after a few interactions.
(knock, knock)

E: Come in, come in!

JUDY: Hello Mr. Brown, how are you?

E: All right; what do you want to see me about?

JUDY: Well, I want to talk with you about how much time I'm putting into the apartment manager's job. It's over 20 hours a week, and——

E: Twenty hours a week! What could you possibly do that takes 20 hours a week! Just what are you doing that supposedly takes so much of your time?

JUDY: Well, uh, lately a lot of people are losing their keys and I have to let them in and——

E: Surely, that doesn't take 20 hours now does it?

JUDY: Well, no, I guess you're right. But I have had to check a lot of damage and repair work and make arrangements to have it fixed. That takes a lot of time, right?

TR: OK, let's stop here. Tell Judy what you liked about the way she behaved.

P_4: Your voice was calm and pleasant when you greeted him. And when you began explaining your business, you sounded appropriately serious.

P_6: You had a good eye contact most of the time.

P_7: You got to the point very quickly and clearly.

TR: Those are good points. What did you like, Judy?

JUDY: Well, I liked everything about the way I entered and got to the point. I felt calm. My facial expression and my voice matched my words. I also liked that I was willing to answer his question about how I spend my time even though he cut me off to ask it. At another time I might have been so flustered with his breaking my train of thought that I would not be able to respond at all.

TR: That's an excellent observation, Judy. Really insightful. Is there anything you would like to do differently?

JUDY: Yes, when he interrupted me I was still anxious. What I wanted to do was think a bit so that I might give him a more complete answer. I responded quickly with something that really doesn't take a whole lot of time, although it is an inconvenience, but that's a different issue. So what I'd like to do is pause briefly, collect my thoughts, and answer calmly. I also could hear myself sounding apologetic or defensive like I was talking to a strict parent. So I'd also like to sound more "informational" and less intimidated.

TR: Those are good, clear changes. It does sound like Mr. Brown keeps people off guard by challenging and questioning, which puts him in a sort of judgmental position and pulls for you to be adaptive and seek his approval.

JUDY: Yes, that's the way I see him and how he'd like me to be. And I do have a right to my opinions.

TR: That's an excellent point. Do you have some ideas how you could help yourself to take the time you need to collect your thoughts?

JUDY: Like we discussed before, when I notice my anxiety going up, I could remind myself to take a deep breath and focus on what I want to tell him.

TR: Very good. Let's try it again. Focus on pausing to think and stating your answer in an informational manner without seeking his approval. Let's pick it up where he says, "What do you want?"

E: What are you here to see me about?

JUDY: I want to talk with you about how much time I'm putting into the manager's job. It's over 20 hours a week and I——

E: What? How could you possibly be working 20 hours a week? Are you kidding; just what are you doing that supposedly takes so much of your time?

JUDY: (pauses briefly) Most of that time has gone into checking damage or malfunction reports from tenants and making the appropriate arrangements for repairs. I also have to check each repair job and verify its completion. Then there's the regular administrative work required for rent collection. I also spend several hours a week showing apartments to prospective tenants. As a matter of fact, I have kept a rough record the past three weeks of how much time is spent doing what.

E: OK, so you do put in those hours. You're getting a rent reduction, aren't you?

JUDY: Yes, that's what I want to discuss with you. I would like to have the rent reduction increased to $200 per month which amounts to about $2.50 an hour.

TR: OK. Stop. That was really excellent! Will people tell Judy what you really liked?

P_3: Yeah. You were really hanging right in there; you did pause when he interrupted you and your response was firm and you sure gave him some excellent facts. Your voice changed most of all; you sounded confident.

P_5: I really liked the way you stayed calm and informational instead of falling for his pressure tactics.

P_6: You didn't say "uh" when he interrupted you, like you did last time and your facial expression was serious but not harsh.

JUDY: That's good to hear. It felt really good to me, too. I was in control of my thoughts and although I got a little anxious, I was able to realize what I wanted to say and how I wanted to say it and I did it!

In both of the above examples, the situation was segmented into workable units, considerable reinforcement was given and focused on improvements, participant involvement was solicited for positive feedback and suggestions for change, and Judy was given ample opportunity for self-assessment. The feedback and assessment were behaviorally specific, attending to what Judy said, as well as the way in which she communicated. . . . One last point merits consideration. In the above example, emphasis was placed on evaluating Judy's behavior, rather than on the employer's reactions to her behavior. This was done deliberately since nonassertive persons tend to give less attention to realistically evaluating their own behavior, and instead overly focus on the other person's reactions. Naturally, we do not recommend that participants totally disregard how others respond to them. In some situations, it is important that the other person's reaction is examined, especially if that person holds power or significant reinforcers for the individual. It is important, however, that such an examination involve thinking rationally about the other person's reaction, as opposed to catastrophizing. In these situations, the trainer and group members may help identify ways in which the participant could be assertive and yet minimize the chances of a negative reaction from the other person.

Covert Behavior Rehearsal Sometimes no one is available to act out your target scene with you, making overt behavior rehearsal impossible. In such cases you can use the alternative method of *covert rehearsal* to practice your goal. Covert rehearsal follows the same basic plan you have just learned, the difference being that the practice is carried out privately through visualization. The basic steps discussed above still apply. First, set a specific behavioral goal. Next, seek models to get a clear idea of how you might carry out the behavior. The actual practice of the behavior is done in your mind by picturing yourself behaving in the desired way, and then imagining how the other people involved in the scene would respond.

There is no question that this method works. Covert behavior rehearsal has proved at least as effective as the overt type described above. In perhaps the most interesting application of the technique psychologist Richard Suinn (1976) taught a modification of it (he termed it visuo-motor behavioral rehearsal, or VMBR) to competitive skiers. They mentally practiced racing techniques, competitiveness, and memory in order to cut down on skiing errors and increase competitiveness. The results were impressive: One college team won its league championship, a number of individual contestants improved their performance over previous levels, and after a few sessions of VMBR and other behavioral techniques, the U.S. Olympic Nordic Cross Country Relay skiing team turned in its best performance ever.

The key to success in covert behavior rehearsal is *clear visualization*. In order for the process to work you must be able to vividly picture yourself in the target scene, as if you were actually there. Simply observing yourself as you would a movie actor is not as effective as actually seeing the sights, smelling the odors, and hearing the sounds you would encounter in real life. The effect of clear visualization can be dramatic. Suinn describes the experience of one swimmer who reported that the scene actually changed from black and white to color as she mentally dove into the pool and experienced the cold temperature of the water in her rehearsal scene. The electromyograph responses of a skier as he went through the course in his imagination also indicate the impact of these methods: the needle jumped into activity as the athlete began his race, peaking at points that corresponded to the muscle bursts that occur as the contestant hit his jumps and rough spots on the course. One professional skier actually moved his boots while skiing the course in his mind. In the same way you should be sure that your images are almost as realistic as if you were there in person.

You can increase your ability to visualize clearly by picturing each scene below. Start by seating yourself comfortably in a quiet spot where you won't be interrupted. Read the description of one scene, making sure that you understand exactly where it will take place and what will be going on. After you clearly understand these elements, close your eyes and actually let yourself experience the situation. After a short break repeat the procedure for each of the following scenes. At this point you should be ready to use the same method to rehearse your target behavior covertly.

Practice Scene 1

Picture the place where you live. Start by imagining yourself lying in bed, having just awakened in the morning. How alert or sleepy are you? Are you looking forward to getting up or are you resisting the idea? How much light is in the room? What do you see as you look about? What sounds do you hear? Now feel the sheets and blankets against your skin as you move about in bed. Notice how your skin feels, and become aware of the taste in your mouth. Now get out of bed. Feel your feet as they hit the floor. Is it cold? Go ahead and stretch, exercising the stiffness out of your muscles.

Now walk into the bathroom. What do you see there as you look around? Turn on the water faucet in the sink and listen to the splashing sounds it makes. Now splash cold water over your face—how does it feel? Next, pick up your toothbrush and squeeze some toothpaste onto it. Go ahead and brush your teeth, being aware of how the brush feels in your mouth and the sweet, minty taste you experience.

Now walk back into your bedroom and approach the place where you keep your clothes. Visualize all the articles you see there, one by one. Can you remember than all? Run your hand over a few of them and notice the texture of the cloth. Now pick out what you will wear today, and begin to dress yourself. As you handle each article, experience how it feels as you hold it and put it on. When you are finished, go to your mirror and look at yourself, noticing each detail from head to toe.

Practice Scene 2

You are driving your car on a crowded city freeway. It's midday, and the temperature is in the high eighties. Your windows are open, and you can feel the hot, dirty air blowing around your body. There is a strong smell of exhaust fumes, and the noise of the traffic fills the air around you. The sky overhead is sunny, but there is a brownish tinge of smog around the horizon. Your car radio is tuned to a news broadcast, and the announcer is presently delivering the weather forecast: more sun, heat, and smog.

All around you are autos, trucks, and busses. As they move, the sunlight occasionally reflects off a piece of chrome or paint. You are driving in the fast lane, and the feeling is almost as if you are being swept along by the vehicles around you. At the moment you are being followed by a large truck. Suddenly the driver pulls up to only a few feet behind you and flashes his lights, signaling you to move over or speed up. Because of the heavy traffic you can do neither. Now the truck driver sounds his loud air horn, startling you. You signal with your directional flashers, trying to find space to pull over, but none of the drivers will let you change lanes. As the truck driver behind you continues to honk and tailgate you, the noise, heat, confusion, and pressure lead to a feeling of panic welling up inside you.

Practice Scene 3

You have purchased a shirt or blouse from a local merchant, only to find that the size was incorrectly labeled and that the item is consequently too small. You have just walked into the store to return the item. The door closes behind you, and the sounds of the street are replaced by the noise of the cash register and other customers talking with salespeople. Notice the difference between the artificial indoor light and the bright sun outside. Feel the difference in the air temperature against your skin. Look around the store and notice the racks of clothes. What items do you see on each one? What colors and patterns do you see? Feel the weight and notice the texture of the item in your hand. What color and pattern is it?

Now the salesperson walks toward you. What expression is she wearing? How do you feel? Now you hold the item up and state your problem. Listen to the sound of your voice and hear the exact words you use to explain yourself. What tone of voice do you speak with? Are you talking quickly or slowly? What is your posture and facial expression?

Now the clerk responds. Listen to her exact words, and observe the nonverbal messages she sends. How do you feel now? Go ahead and listen to your response, letting the conversation run its course, paying close attention to exactly what takes place and how you react.

After you have covertly practiced the scene in which you want to behave more assertively, use the same feedback process you would for overt rehearsal. Think about how you performed. See which behaviors you handled especially well, and which one or two could use improvement. After you have an idea of how you could handle yourself better, review the scene mentally again with the added improvements and repeat the evaluation process. Finally, when you are ready, go ahead and carry out the scene in real life.

If this process of covert rehearsal still sounds far-fetched, consider how often we use it in everyday thoughts, though usually for destructive ends. How many times have you failed in some important way—perhaps a job interview, a social occasion, or an athletic contest—by predicting that it would be a disaster. Catastrophic expectations such as these have a way of becoming self-fulfilling prophecies by obsessing you to such a degree that you end up behaving in the horrible way you anticipated. Covert rehearsal uses this same principle to achieve positive ends, helping you to visualize yourself behaving successfully.

SUMMARY

In this chapter you have seen how two methods—shaping and behavior rehearsal—can help you assert yourself more effectively. Shaping is based on the principle that it is easier and more productive to master a skill in small steps than try to tackle it all at once. There are a number of ways to shape a skill: increase the frequency with which you practice it; approach increasingly difficult people involved; attempt more and more challenging situations; and progressively add more elements of the ultimate target. Each of these methods will be explored in further detail in Chapter 6.

Behavior rehearsal is a method for practicing an assertive response in a safe environment before attempting it in real life. There are five steps involved in this process: The first is to define the target behavior clearly. Next, whenever possible you should observe a model carry out that goal. The third step is to rehearse the target behavior yourself. Fourth, receive feedback, coaching, and additional modeling to see which elements of the rehearsal were successful and which needed improvement. The fifth step calls for rehearsing the behavior again, this time taking advantage of the feedback received in the preceding step. Finally, it actually becomes time to try out the newly learned behavior in real life.

Behavior rehearsal can be conducted either overtly or covertly. In the latter case the same procedure described above is used, except that the target scene is reviewed in the communicator's mind instead of being acted out publicly.

5
Communicating with Confidence

Wally wasn't what I would call a good friend, but I knew him well enough
to recognize that he was angry and upset when he entered my office one
afternoon. After a few minutes of polite conversation he came to the point.

"You know I've been singing for some time. A lot of people have said I'm
pretty good, and that I ought to do some professional performing, but I've
always been terrified to stand up in front of strangers. Well, Jeff, a mutual
friend was telling me about the assertiveness training group you're
leading, and I thought the things you teach might help me feel more
confident. I tried everything he said you recommended: I watched good
singers as models and defined clearly how I wanted to behave on stage. I
set up a hierarchy of performances so that I started singing in front of
friends and at parties before I auditioned for a real job. All that worked fine.
I did get hired for a couple of weekends at a small club in town. I even used
covert rehearsal to get ready for my opening night."

Wally went on dejectedly. "Well, my debut was a disaster. The minute I stepped on stage my mind went blank. I couldn't remember which numbers I'd planned to do. My throat closed up. I finally managed to croak out a few tunes and get off stage, but I didn't come back for a second set and I haven't gone near the club since. I've decided to forget the whole idea of ever being a professional singer, but I did want to ask you whether many people are hopeless cases like me."

I tried to answer Wally's question in two steps. First I assured him that there are many, many people who are anxious communicators. Whether their "audience" is a business associate or customer, a new acquaintance, an authority figure, or a hostile stranger, their fear is so great that they're incapable of acting as they know they should. Like Wally, their problem isn't one of lacking communication *skills:* they know precisely how they want to act, and some of them even know how to use the skills described in previous chapters to acquire those talents. In spite of mastering these skills, they still lack the confidence to use their talents in real life.

I went on to correct Wally's mistaken idea that finding himself in such a predicament meant his future as a singer was hopeless. Fortunately there are methods for reducing communication anxiety which have proved to be highly successful in cases just like his. In fact, I suggested that if Wally was interested we could use these methods to help overcome his fear of performing in public. By looking at Wally's case as you read this chapter you can see how these methods will work in your own life.

WHAT THIS CHAPTER CAN DO FOR YOU

Before going on it's important for you to realize that the object of this chapter isn't to make you into a totally calm, anxiety-free communicator. A certain amount of tension (as well as other emotions such as anger) is inescapable, and even useful in human relationships. The rush of excitement and apprehension you experience before speaking to a group, going into a job interview, or expressing an important disagreement with someone who matters to you stimulates your alertness and helps you use all the energy at your disposal. If you were totally calm in situations like these, you probably wouldn't perform as well as you potentially could.

When your feelings of fear or anger become more intense, however, the results are not so beneficial. The physiological changes which accompany strong emotions often can block you from communicating effectively. Racing heart, pounding temples, upset stomach, and shaking limbs are hardly useful behaviors. Also, when you're intensely upset your ability to concentrate is diminished so that you can't keep your mind on what you truly want to say.

Realize, then, that the goal here isn't to turn you into a nerveless machine, but rather to help you develop the ability to recognize your emotions, put them into perspective, and go on to express yourself clearly, honestly, and effectively.

WHEN TO USE THE METHODS IN THIS CHAPTER

The first step in managing communication anxiety is to examine its nature. You can do so by following these instructions.

▶ Describe two communication situations in which you find yourself fearful or anxious.
EXAMPLE: Who the situation involves: Smokers. Mostly strangers, but friends, too.
The circumstances in which it occurs: When the person's smoke is blowing in my face, especially at crowded parties and meetings and when I'm eating.
The way you behave: I feel nauseated and have the urge to either leave or ask the smoker to put his cigarette out. I imagine that if I did either, the smoker and everyone else would think I was obnoxious and rude, so I keep quiet.

SITUATION #1
Who the situation involves: _____

_____

_____

The circumstances in which it occurs: _____

_____

_____

The way you behave: _____

_____

_____

SITUATION #2
Who the situation involves: _____

_____

_____

The circumstances in which it occurs: _____

_____

_____

The way you behave: _____

_____

_____

There are two quite different sources for your anxiety in situations like these. The first is that you simply don't know how to act. If, for example, Wally didn't know how to carry a tune or play his guitar he'd have had a good reason to fear performing. In the same way, if you don't know how to introduce yourself to strangers, organize your thoughts when speaking before a group, or handle yourself in a job interview, you would be justified in feeling anxious. As you've read over and over in these pages, communication is a skill that needs to be learned. Therefore, if your anxiety is caused by lack of knowledge or insufficient practice, you ought to begin by finding the parts of this book that will give you some detailed instructions in these areas. Start by reviewing the elements of assertiveness listed in Chapter 3. Look also at the specific suggestions that deal with building relationships (Chapter 7), expressing feelings (Chapter 8), and managing conflicts (Chapter 9). Don't forget to look for models and seek other advice that can help you learn just how you might act more assertively. Remember to define your goal as clearly as possible in behavioral terms (Chapter 3). Once your goal is set, you can use the behavior rehearsal method described in Chapter 4 or the self-modification technique in Chapter 6 to help you reach your target. Most of the time you'll find that like my fear of driving, your anxieties will clear up once you have defined and learned a skill.

On the other hand, it's likely that you have one or more anxiety problems that can't be resolved by the above-mentioned approaches. Either you already know exactly how you ought to behave but your fear keeps you from bringing if off, or you are too anxious even to learn the necessary skill. It's cases like this that lend themselves to the methods that follow. They'll help you with that fear or discomfort which you know has no reason for being there, but persists nonetheless.

Now look at the communication problems you listed on page 83. If your anxiety in either of them is due to a skill defect, use the other chapters in this book to learn the skills in question. If you already know how to act but still become anxious in these situations, read on.

WHY PEOPLE FEAR SELF-ASSERTION

Before getting to the methods for managing your anxieties, it might be helpful to look at some reasons people feel nervous in the first place. There are at least three such reasons.

Previous Experience The most logical reason for feeling apprehensive about asserting yourself is because of an unpleasant experience or experiences in the past. Sometimes a string of barely noticeable events can be enough to create feelings of anxiety. Mary found it impossible to speak up in any of her classes. She became fearful at even the thought of volunteering her opinions, and she was overcome with anxiety when called on to answer even the simplest of questions. This fear had nothing to do with Mary's intelligence; her grades were well above average, and they would have been even higher if she found a way to participate more in classes. Mary's social life was also quiet. While she felt comfortable with her family, she reported experiencing the same fear when around anyone but them and her closest friends. Because of these fears, Mary wasn't able to respond comfortably to the strangers who approached her, and thus she seemed doomed to an unsatisfying life.

By chance Mary enrolled in an interpersonal communication class that focused on assertive skills. Through her experience there the roots of her unassertiveness became apparent. For the first five years of her life, Mary grew up in Great Britain. Upon moving to the U.S., her accent became something of a curiosity for others and a burden for her. She recalled her teachers and other adults frequently singling her out and commenting on her unusual manner of speaking. Even though their remarks were always favorable, they often led her classmates to tease her. Embarrassed by all the attention, Mary reacted by withdrawing to avoid further discomfort. Upon hearing this story, Mary's classmates insisted that they found her accent charming, but she had a difficult time ridding herself of the anxiety that came from thinking of herself as being different.

Other communicators have found that a single incident leads to fear in later situations of the same type. This was the case for Wally. He had played guitar during most of his teenage years, though never publicly. Around the age of 20 a relative arranged for him to serve as the warmup entertainer for a rather large concert featuring a well known comedian. The experience turned out to be a disaster. The comedian's reputation was such that the audience came to the theatre in a boisterous mood, and were not interested in the soft rock style of music Wally had rehearsed. In their eagerness to hear the entertainer whose reputation had brought them there, many audience members started shouting loudly at Wally, spoiling his composure and leading him to play poorly. From this point on Wally was convinced that he had no talent, and led him to become anxious at the thought of ever performing publicly again.

These accounts illustrate how the past—even when it is no longer relevant—can haunt us. No one but Mary thought she sounded odd, and it's likely that Wally's experience would not repeat itself if he chose his audiences more carefully in the future. Yet the image of past events lingered like a ghost for both of these people, perpetuating fears that no longer had any reason for existing. Of course, the sad thing is that because they believed they had good cause for feeling anxious, they did react nervously as a kind of self-fulfilling prophecy.

Are any of the fears you listed on page 83 based on unpleasant past experiences? Take a look at them now and see. If one or more are, ask yourself whether the events that originally caused you to feel anxious then are likely to occur now. Be realistic and estimate the odds.

Fear-Inducing Models A second reason we become fearful is that we've seen others exhibit anxiety in similar circumstances. The YMCA in our town offers swimming lessons for young children, and for some time we have wanted to enroll our four-year-old daughter, Robin. The lessons are only offered on Tuesday mornings, a time when I'm not free to take her. I suggested that my wife take Robin, but my wife Sherri is reluctant to do so because of her own fear of water. She wisely pointed out that Robin would probably pick up these feelings, thereby learning the new idea that swimming pools and the ocean are frightening places.

In the same way we often learn to be afraid of asserting ourselves by watching others. People from unassertive backgrounds are likely to be unassertive themselves. If we have friends or family who are reluctant to express affection, deal with their anger, or admit that they are wrong, we will learn to feel the same way. For this reason it's important to realize that while some people around you find expressing themselves difficult, this doesn't mean that such feelings are natural for everyone. Seek out others who have the attitudes you would like to posses, and use them for models.

Take another look at your list of fearful situations on page 83 and see if your feelings there have come from watching others in similar circumstances. Ask yourself whether you must necessarily feel this way just because others have. Who have you known that handles themselves well in such situations?

Irrational Attitudes Sometimes a person's fear of self-assertion is based on one of the irrational myths about how one ought to behave that are listed in **Chapter 2**. Let's take another look at some of the most prevalent myths to see if you believe any of them.

One irrational idea that can lead to increased fear is *catastrophic failure*. A person with this attitude fears that if things don't go well, the consequences will be disastrous. A belief in this myth can lead to some bizarre fantasies: "If I don't handle myself well at the party, everyone will think I'm a fool." "They'll probably laugh at me and never have anything to do with me again." "If the boss doesn't agree with my suggestions, she'll probably fire me." "If I ask the people talking in the theater to quiet down, they'll probably make a scene."

While the likelihood of such consequences occurring isn't impossible, consideration of them becomes irrational when you become convinced that such outcomes will occur. While it's true that some people might think you're a fool, they might also think you're sensational. Instead of firing you, the boss might take your suggestion in stride or even give you a raise. The talkers in the theater could respond indignantly, but they just might apologize for creating a disturbance and let you watch the movie in peace. If you realize that your catastrophic fantasy is only one possible outcome of your assertion—and often an unlikely one at that—you will see that many of your fears are groundless.

Another irrational cause of fear is the myth of *acceptance*, it's possible and necessary for others always to like you and to approve of your actions. If you believe this, you will fear expressing your opinion or standing up for yourself whenever there's a possibility that someone might disapprove of your actions. For instance, you might be afraid to return a piece of defective merchandise or to protest poor service because the salesperson will think you are obnoxious or too persistent. Assuming that you have stated your need directly and politely, and assuming that you believe that what you're doing is correct, the choice then becomes who is to be the judge of your behavior, the salesperson or you. In other words, if you let the evaluation of others become more important than expressing your important beliefs, then you have chosen to sacrifice self-respect for approval. And the irony of this sacrifice is that you'll often lose the admiration of others when they see that you don't even respect yourself enough to stand up for your own beliefs.

A third fear-inducing belief is the myth of *perfection,* the idea that you must handle all your relationships faultlessly or you are a failure. With a standard like this it's easy to see why you would be terrified to approach others, to express your feelings, or to stand up for your rights; for it's almost certain that in at least some respects you are going to handle yourself less than perfectly. A far healthier attitude is to realize that while you'll constantly make some mistakes in asserting yourself, you've done a noble deed by the very act of trying. Beyond this, you are probably becoming better and better each time you do express yourself.

A final myth—that of *total confidence*—is another self-defeating attitude. This irrational idea is based on the belief that an effective communicator never feels any apprehensions or misgivings about speaking out. We've already discussed the fact that fear is a natural emotion in many situations that call for an assertive response. The measure of success in such cases is if you can put the fear into perspective rather than indulge in catastrophic fantasies, and then function while recognizing that you *are* anxious.

Because belief in one or more of these irrational myths is so often the cause of excessive communication anxiety, the next pages will offer you a method for reducing such beliefs in your life.

REDUCING FEAR BY DISPUTING IRRATIONAL THOUGHTS

For most people fear—and other emotions as well—seem to have a life of their own. You wish you could feel calm when approaching strangers, yet your voice quivers. You try to appear confident when asking for a raise, yet you feel your eye twitching nervously.

At times like these it's common to say that strangers or your boss *make* you feel nervous just as you would say that a bee sting would *cause* you to feel pain. The apparent similarities between physical and emotional discomfort become clear if you look at them in the following way:*

Activating Event	*causes*	*Consequences*
Being stung by a bee	causes	physical pain
Approaching strangers	causes	nervous feelings

Looking at your emotions in this light makes it appear that you have little control over how you feel. This is how Wally viewed his problem. According to his description, the experience of performing before an audience made him feel uncontrollably nervous.

I explained to Wally that the apparent similarity between physical pain and communication anxiety isn't as great as it seems to be. It is not *events* such as meeting strangers or singing before a group that cause people to become nervous, but rather the *beliefs they hold* or the *interpretations they make* about these events. I told him about a story that psychologist Albert Ellis offers to make this point clear. Imagine yourself walking by a friend's house and seeing your friend stick his head out of a window and call you a string of vile names. Under these circumstances it's likely that you would feel hurt and upset. Now imagine that instead of the house, you were walking by a mental hospital when the same friend, who was a patient there, shouted offensive names at you. In this case your feelings would probably be quite different; most likely sadness and pity. You can see that in this story the activating event of being called offensive names was the same in both cases, yet the emotional consequences were very different. The reason for the different feelings you would experience has to do with the interpretations you would make in each case. In the first instance you would be likely to think that your friend was very angry at you and, further, to imagine that you must have done something very terrible to deserve such a response. In the second case you would assume that your friend had experienced some psychological difficulty and most likely feel sympathetic.

From this example Wally began to see that it is the interpretations people make of an event that determines their feelings. Thus, the model for emotions looks like this:

Activating Event	*Belief or Interpretation*	*Consequences*
being called names	"I've done something wrong"	hurt, upset
being called names	"Friend must be sick"	concern, sympathy

---

* The information in this section is adapted from the writing of Albert Ellis and Gerald Kranzler. For more information about their work, see the bibliography in the back of this book.

I pointed out to Wally that perhaps his problem came from making faulty interpretations of the events surrounding his performance, which led him to feel fearful or nervous for no good reason. "What interpretations do you make about the event of performing before an audience?" I asked him.

"I can tell you what happened to me on stage at the club" he answered. "As soon as I got up there I thought to myself 'I'm doing a lousy job. Everybody's still talking and drinking. They must think I'm really a jerk. It's just like the last time I performed, at the concert. Pretty soon they'll probably start to shout me off the stage. I'm getting out of here!'"

I suggested that we look at these beliefs and see how sensible they were. We began with Wally's thought that he was doing a lousy job because everyone was talking and drinking after he began his performance. A few questions disclosed that the club in question was a neighborhood gathering place. The management provided entertainment to add to the atmosphere. But, Wally agreed, the patrons' main reason for coming was not to pay close attention to music, but to socialize with acquaintances and meet strangers. In light of this I asked him how realistic it was to expect the audience to fall into rapt silence whenever any entertainer began to perform. Wally agreed that perhaps it was unrealistic to expect much attentiveness when he was hired to play what amounted to background music.

We went on to look at Wally's thought that the audience thought he was a jerk. I asked what evidence he had for making that interpretation. Was anyone jeering at him or walking out in protest? His reply to the question was negative. After a few minutes it became apparent to Wally that it was *he* who thought he looked like a jerk, not anyone else. When asked why he felt like this, Wally replied that he had made "all sorts of mistakes" in his playing. When I asked what kind of mistakes, he went on to describe several musical technicalities having to do with chord progression and styles of guitar picking which I didn't understand at all. I agreed that his performance probably wasn't perfect, but asked him whether members of an audience such as the one he was playing for would be likely to notice any of the small faults he had described. Wally decided that they most probably wouldn't recognize them.

Finally Wally and I talked about his third interpretation: the idea that his experience in the club was just like his earlier traumatic performance as warmup for the comedian, and that the audience would soon start to hoot him off the stage. A bit of reflection showed that the two events were not at all similar. Where the earlier one involved an audience impatiently waiting to see a well known star, the patrons of the club were present to enjoy the music provided as a background to their conversation. Where the concertgoers were a hostile group, the club patrons were at worst indifferent and at best receptive.

By this time Wally was feeling much better. "It's crazy" he said. "I really didn't have that much to be afraid of. It's almost as if I was making things hard for myself when they didn't have to be."

Wally had started to see that it is not events themselves that cause unpleasant emotions, but rather the often irrational interpretations of these events. This same principle applies in many other communication situations where you might become fearful. Suppose, for instance, that you were attending a party and knew nobody else who was present. Upon entering the room you look around to see all the other guests involved in conversation. Now consider two possible interpretations and notice the differing emotional consequences which would result from each. You could say to yourself, "These people are perfectly happy talking to each other. They don't need or want to know me. They're probably talking about subjects that I don't know anything about, and they'd be irritated if I was to butt in on them." This interpretation of the event would probably lead to feelings of nervousness and discomfort on your part. Yet how rational or realistic is such an analysis? Imagine instead how differently you would feel if you thought to yourself, "While everybody seems content enough talking, there are probably at least one or two people here whom I would like and who would enjoy talking with me. If I wait here, someone might approach me or they might not. The best way for me to get acquainted is to start talking. Even if I don't find anybody with whom I hit it off, that just means I don't have the same interests or personality as the others here. There's nothing wrong with me or them." With an attitude like this you'd be much more likely to feel confident about approaching others.

Rationally interpreting events in your life can dramatically reduce the level and number of fears you experience. In order for you to start looking at your life more realistically, you can use the following steps as a guide.

Three Steps toward Rational Interpretation This method for elimination of irrational ideas is quite simple, yet very effective.

1. Describe the Activating Event and the Emotional Consequences. The best way to begin putting your fears into perspective is by becoming sensitive to the times when you do become anxious while communicating. Then notice the event which preceeds each such feeling. Do you become nervous when around certain *people* due to factors such as age, background, or status? Are certain *settings* the stimulus for your unpleasant feelings: parties, work, school? Perhaps the *topic* of conversation is the factor which sets off your anxiety, whether it be politics, religion, sex, or some other subject.

2. Record Your Self-Talk in the Problem Situation. A bit of thought will show that we all spend a great deal of time talking to ourselves. (To test this, take 20 seconds now and listen to your own internal voice . . . Did you hear yourself? You probably said something like "What voice? I don't talk to myself!")

You use your internal voice to make interpretations. For example, look at some common but irrational interpretations people often make which lead to communication anxiety.

—Upon meeting someone new: "My God, she (or he) is beautiful, intelligent, and talented. Next to her I look like nothing. I'm sure she isn't interested in the likes of me."

—Before making a speech: "I can never face the audience. I don't know my subject, and I'm sure everybody will think I'm wasting their time. I'll probably get so nervous that I'll choke up. I know I'm going to fail!"

—Preparing for a job interview: "I'm underqualified. They'll probably ask questions which I won't know how to answer. I can remember a million things that I did wrong in my last job. They wouldn't want to hire someone who screws up as much as I do."

After tuning into your self-talk, see if you can recognize any irrational myths described on pages 86–87 which apply to your situation.

3. Dispute Your Irrational Self-Talk. At first you'll need to practice this technique by disputing your irrational thoughts after the event is over, using the format which follows. After you've had practice with this method, however, you will be able to stop yourself from falling into irrational patterns on the spot.

Remember the common irrational myths you need to dispute:

The Myth of Perfection While it's certainly important to do the best job you can and to strive to become more and more competent, nobody is perfect. If you expect yourself to behave faultlessly—even in an area of your expertise—you are bound to wind up disappointed. If you put the demand on yourself to be perfect in all areas, you are dooming yourself to a life of perpetual dissatisfaction.

The Myth of Acceptance While it's pleasant to have the approval and affection of those people you value, you don't *need* these evaluations. Remember that the only way it's remotely possible to gain everyone's approval is to sometimes compromise your own ideals, in which case you may gain the respect of others at the cost of respecting yourself.

Also consider the irrationality of seeking approval from those whose opinions you don't really value when the cost is unhappiness or sacrifice for yourself.

The Myth of Causation Don't fall into the trap of believing that you cause others to feel as they do. Remember, just as you can interpret others' actions in ways that make you happy or unhappy, others have the choice of reacting to you in various ways. If you decline an invitation, the person who invited you can choose to feel rejected for lack of your acceptance, but he or she can also respond with equanimity. You are not responsible for others' feelings!

The Myth of Helplessness When you are feeling unhappy for one reason or another, realize that you have the choice to go on that way or to change. After the initial shock and pain of losing a job, you have the choice of sitting around moping and feeling sorry for yourself or picking yourself up and looking for a new position. If you are jilted by a lover, you can decide whether or not to let that rejection affect your future relationships. If the town you've enjoyed living in is changing in a way that doesn't suit you, you have the choice of either making it fit your tastes or moving. If you decide that the place will change in spite of your efforts, you can still choose either to stay and accept the changes, stay and complain, or move.

It's up to you to decide how you'll let events affect you.

The Myth of Catastrophic Failure It's just as irrational to expect that things will always result in disaster as it is to think they'll work out perfectly. The idea here is to take a realistic look at the future and set your expectations accordingly. Broken deals, friendships, plans for the future, jobs . . . all of them *can* fall through, though they don't always do so. Just as it's foolish to let yourself become obsessed with contracting an incurable disease or being struck by a falling airplane, it's unnecessary to worry about other unpleasant occurrences which *might* happen.

Even if the undesirable does occur, you should ask yourself whether the results must be as catastrophic as you originally feared. Of course you'd be unhappy if you lost a friend, a mate, or a job, but would it be the end of the world? Only if you let it be. It's your choice.

▶ Use the space below to dispute any irrational beliefs which might be causing communication anxiety for you. Begin by applying the form below to the situations you listed on page 83. Or, if you prefer, use it with any other unpleasant emotions associated with your communication.

EXAMPLE: a. The activating event and the emotional consequences which follow <u>The last time we were together my friend T. made the remark that she thought I was a tightwad. For a couple of days since then I've felt depressed and apprehensive about seeing her.</u>

<u>b. Your self-talk concerning the event I guess I interpreted her remark to mean that she didn't like the way I handle my finances with friends, and further that she didn't think much about me as a friend because of the way I've treated her. Since I care about her a great deal, I'm depressed at the loss of her friendship.</u>

<u>c. Dispute any irrational ideas I suppose my interpretation was catastrophic. It's accurate to say that she doesn't approve of the way I handle money, but I don't think that will jeopardize our friendship. She's told me often that she values me a lot, and I know that she'll accept me in spite of what she sees as my tight-fistedness.</u>

Situation 1

a. The activating event and the emotional consequences which follow _____

_____

_____

b. Your self-talk concerning the event _____

_____

_____

_____

_____

_____

c. Dispute any irrational ideas _____

_____

_____

_____

_____

_____

Situation 2

a. The activating event and the emotional consequences which follow _____

_____

_____

_____

b. Your self-talk concerning the event _____

_____

_____

_____

_____

_____

c. Dispute any irrational ideas _____

_____

_____

_____

_____

REDUCING FEAR BY RELAXATION AND DESENSITIZATION

If you think about it for a moment, you'll realize that there are two components to fears about communication—or any other subject, for that matter. The first consists of physiological reactions: rapid pulse, heavy perspiration, nervous stomach, and so on. The second component of any fear is the thoughts which accompany it: catastrophic fantasies, self-criticism, feelings of inadequacy, and so on.

The method of disputing irrational thoughts which you just learned works on the principle that if you can eliminate fear-producing ideas, then the unpleasant physical parts of your anxiety will go away on their own. This approach worked well for Wally in his performing, and it should produce good results for you most of the time.

Occasionally, however, you may be unable to convince yourself that your anxiety is, in fact, irrational. Possibly you'll have trouble because you are so used to accepting one or more irrational myths. On the other hand, from time to time your apprehension may be totally rational and justified.

This was the case for June, who was running for a position on the local school board. Her opponent was a well known attorney, and she knew that in order to defeat him she needed to gain the support of several local organizations. The most crucial of these was the P.T.A. of a large local high school. June and her opponent were scheduled to meet in a debate of the campaign issues before the P.T.A., and the knowledge that her success as a candidate depended on doing well at this meeting left June with feelings of great apprehension as the day of the debate grew nearer.

After meeting with June, it became clear to me that her concern was not irrationally based. A good performance was critical at this meeting. June didn't have much experience in debating, and her opponent was quite skillful in this area. Although June did have fantasies of failing in the debate from time to time, it seemed that her problem was primarily one of staying physically calm enough during the debate to keep her wits about her and express herself most effectively.

In order to help June achieve this calm state, I taught her to use the skills of progressive relaxation and self-desensitization which you will now learn. These techniques take exactly the opposite approach to relaxation as the method of disputing irrational thoughts which you just learned. Instead of reducing physical fear by first learning how to think clearly, in this method you begin by physically relaxing yourself, which in turn enables you to think and act calmly and rationally. The principle upon which relaxation and desensitization operate is termed *reciprocal inhibition*. Simply stated, this theory suggests that since it is impossible to be both tense and relaxed at the same time, by enabling yourself to be physically relaxed in a previously troubling situation you will be able to think and feel confident. Where before you have been conditioned to respond with nervousness, now you'll retrain yourself to act in a relaxed manner.

HIERARCHY BUILDING

The surest way to start the process of reconditioning is to build a hierarchy of fearful situations. As you learned in Chapter 4, one way to learn a new skill is by shaping—breaking down a goal into smaller, more easily attained segments and learning those segments one at a time. The same principle holds for overcoming excessive fears. Although June might have been able to shake off her anxiety by giving the speech she dreaded, the chances are just as great that she would have become more terrified. This failure would have added to her fears, making the prospect of any future talks even more terrifying. We chose a wiser course by having her gradually approach the ultimate goal of talking to the PTA by building a hierarchy of subgoals, so that each small success would move her closer to the ultimate goal of being a confident speaker.

As a rule, effective hierarchy should consist of between 10 and 20 steps, spread evenly enough so that the gap between each one is small enough to be crossed comfortably when the time comes. Let's take a look at the hierarchy June used.

1. Talk with campaign manager about possibility of debating opponent.
2. Solicit topics for debating from friends and supporters.
3. Meet with opponent to plan debate series.
4. Speak before a small group of voters about issues which I'll later debate.
5. Listen to opponent talk before an audience in order to learn his speaking style and themes he stresses.
6. Visualize debating with the opponent: imagine his possible remarks and my responses.
7. Practice debating with campaign manager, who takes role of my opponent.
8. Go to bed the evening before the first debate and imagine what it will be like.
9. Arrive at first debate (before small, non-critical audience).
10. Make introductory remarks to first audience.
11. Listen to opponent's remarks and plan my rebuttal.
12. Deliver my rebuttal.
13. Think about the second debate the night before it occurs.
14. Arrive at second debate (before larger, more important audience.)
15. Deliver my remarks and respond to opponent before second audience.
16. Think about PTA debate three days before the meeting.

17. Think about PTA debate night before the meeting.
18. Arrive at P.T.A. meeting.
19. Step up to speak.
20. Deliver introductory remarks to P.T.A.
21. Listen to opponent's remarks and plan rebuttal.
22. Deliver rebuttal to opponent's remarks.

Notice how small the space between each step is. It appears as if there's hardly any challenge at all in moving one notch higher. Of course, this is precisely the point of hierarchy building, for after moving through a series of goals that are not overly challenging, June found herself speaking to the important group with little apprehension. The principle here is rather like the painless process of saving a few cents a day for a long-wanted vacation, rather than trying to scrape up the money all at once.

After looking over June's hierarchy, you might have chosen different steps or arranged the ones she picked in a different order. Setting up these intermediate goals is a personal process, and the important thing is to arrange yours in a way that best suits you. Therefore, the fact that you were thinking about how you could overcome your own fear of speaking is a good sign, for this is exactly how you would begin to do so.

As with the shaping procedures in Chapter 4, an anxiety hierarchy can be arranged in several ways. You might, for instance, approach your ultimate target with a series of time-oriented steps, starting long before the event occurs and moving steadily closer. Another way to set up a hierarchy is by approaching various *people*, first those with whom you feel most comfortable and gradually moving on to those who are more threatening. If you become nervous while talking about certain *subjects*, then your hierarchy could start with topics you feel most comfortable discussing and escalate toward the ones you find difficult. The important thing to realize is that your hierarchy should be organized in a manner that best allows you to move in a step-by-step process toward your ultimate goal. Whatever process you use, be sure that your first step generates only a slight amount of anxiety, and keep the gaps between each succeeding step small.

Construct your anxiety hierarchy for the fearful situation you have chosen to work on in this chapter. If you have not chosen a situation, do so now, following the criteria on pages 95–96.

1. Begin by cutting up the cards on Duplicate Activities page 279 or obtain a pack of three-by-five-inch cards. On one of these cards describe the most fearful situation you would be likely to face that relates to the subject you've chosen. For instance, if your anxiety relates to expressing affection, describe the person with whom you would feel most uncomfortable sharing your feelings, and the situation in which your dreaded encounter would take place.

► ANXIETY SITUATION CARDS

1. Cut along the lines.
2. Describe one specific situation in your anxiety hierarchy on each card.
3. Rank orders cards from least to most threatening.
4. Assign a SUDS number to each in the space provided.
5. Write additional situation cards as necessary to keep SUDS level increases gradual.
6. Number each card in the space provided.

2. On the second card describe a situation that would cause you to feel only slight anxiety. <u>Be sure to make this and all your descriptions specific enough so that you will be able to picture each as a scene in your mind.</u> As an example, your least anxious card in the area of expressing affection might read, "At the end of our evening together, telling my friend C. that I've enjoyed myself."

3. Now describe in writing a third scene relating to your hierarchy, then insert it between your most and least anxious cards.

4. Continue this process with other cards. As you finish each one, place it in the spot that corresponds with the level of difficulty it presents for you. Continue this process until you have recorded and arranged enough scenes to provide a gradually increasing hierarchy of situations. Complete this step before going on.

5. The magnitude of your scenes should increase in evenly graduated steps, so that the process of mastering each one is smooth. To be sure that your hierarchy does this, you can assign each card a numerical rating, forming a SUDS (subjective units of disturbance) scale. Begin by writing the number 100 on the most fearful situation you have described. Consider a rating of 0 to represent the feeling of total relaxation and confidence. Now assign a SUDS number to each of the cards you have written. Do this before going on.

6. Look at the number of SUDS points between each card. A truly gradual hierarchy should have no more than 5 to 10 points between each item. (At the top end of your scale the space might well be closer to 5 points.) A large gap between two cards—say 20 points or more—indicates that this step is probably too big. In such cases you should now write descriptions for intervening scenes to make your transition easier. Remember, with this method it's always preferable to risk making your steps unnecessarily small rather than taking the chance of their being too great. After you have finished compiling your set of cards, put it aside while you read the next section. You will use it shortly.

Progressive Relaxation So far the hierarchy recorded on your cards isn't so different from the intermediate goals you set up in Chapter 4. The main distinction is that the difficulties you have described here should be caused by your anxiety rather than a lack of the know-how to carry them out.

Now, however, we come to relaxation training—a major feature of the desensitization process that sets this method apart from the skills-oriented procedures you've already learned. In this section you'll discover how to relax yourself progressively, so that eventually you'll be able to carry these calm feelings into the situations you've chosen to work on.

The value of relaxation training was first explored systematically by Edmund Jacobson of Harvard University. His work revealed that a person's subjective description of anxiety was accompanied by the physiological

reaction of shortened, tensed muscle fibers. When these fibers were relaxed, the feelings of anxiety dissipated. Jacobson concluded that one way
to relieve anxiety was to develop a process whereby people could consciously achieve this state of relaxation. After much work he developed
such a procedure, which involved the tensing and relaxing of various
muscle groups in the body until the subject could gain sufficient control to
eliminate the contractions at will. The major shortcoming of Jacobson's procedure was the time required to learn it—a total of 56 sessions of from one
to nine hours each.

A breakthrough occurred when Joseph Wolpe of Temple University modified the relaxation method so that it could be learned in six 20-minute
sessions, supplemented by 30 minutes of daily home practice between
each session.

This deep muscle relaxation method of Wolpe's is the one you will learn
now. It rarely takes more than 10 sessions of 30 minutes or so practiced
twice daily—about five hours of your time. This effort should be a good investment, for it will pay the dividend of your being able to achieve full
relaxation whenever you desire.

As outlined here, progressive relaxation training covers four stages, each
of which gives you increasingly greater control over your body. You might
find it possible to skip one or more of these steps and still reach the last one
without any loss of effectiveness. If this seems possible, fine. On the other
hand, be sure to move slowly enough to gain the full benefit of the procedure.

Your relaxation sessions should take place in a quiet spot where you will
not be disturbed. Find a comfortable seat that will support your arms, legs,
and head. You will probably find the process works best if you can dim the
lights and close your eyes while performing the activities in these instructions. You will learn to relax each of 16 muscle groups in your body one at a
time, first by tensing each one as much as possible for a few seconds and
then relaxing that tension all at once. Just as you would build up the mo-
mentum of a pendulum's swing in one direction by first pulling it back the
opposite way, you can achieve greater relaxation by immediately releasing
your maximally tensed muscles. In addition, tensing a particular group of
muscles will give you a way to focus your attention on that part of your
body, helping you to become more aware of what goes on there as you communicate in various situations. Finally, the vivid contrast between tension
and relaxation will let you clearly appreciate the difference between these
two states.

Basic Relaxation Procedure

1. The first step in relaxation training calls for you to tense the muscles
   of your *dominant hand and forearm* (i.e., if you are right-handed,
   start with that side of your body.) Tense these muscles by making a

tight fist, so that you can feel the tightness in your hand and up into your lower arm. Hold that position for five to seven seconds, then relax it *immediately*. Now let your hand hang limp, noting the looseness that now flows through that area. Enjoy that sensation for about 20 seconds.

Repeat this procedure as many times as necessary to get a deep feeling of relaxation. After you've finished the dominant hand and forearm, move on to each of the following steps in turn. As you progress, make sure to repeat each procedure until the muscles in question are as relaxed as the ones you just finished. In other words, as you move down the list, your body should become looser and looser. It may take you as much as 40 minutes to move through the list the first time, but after a few sessions you should achieve a state of relaxation almost immediately, without the need to tense your muscles.

Here are the remaining steps of the relaxation procedure. Be sure to move on to each after you have mastered the preceding one.

2. *Dominant biceps.* Push down on the arm of your chair until the bicep muscles become tense without affecting the relaxed hand and forearm. Hold five to seven seconds and release immediately.
3. *Nondominant hand and forearm.* Repeat the procedure described in Step 1. Hold five to seven seconds and relax.
4. *Nondominant biceps.* Repeat the procedure in Step 2. Hold five to seven seconds and relax.
5. *Upper face.* Lift eyebrows as high as possible, tensing your scalp—or frown hard. Hold five to seven seconds and relax.
6. *Central face.* Squint eyes tightly and wrinkle nose. Hold and relax.
7. *Lower face.* Grit teeth and pull back corners of mouth, forming a grimace. Hold five to seven seconds and relax.
8. *Neck and throat.* Pull chin downward toward chest while at the same time trying to avoid actually touching the chest. Feel the muscles strain. Hold five to seven seconds and relax.
9. *Chest, shoulders and back.* Take a deep breath, hold it, and pull shoulder blades together. Hold five to seven seconds and relax.
10. *Abdomen.* Make stomach hard, as if getting ready for someone to hit you. Hold five to seven seconds and relax.
11. *Right upper leg and thigh.* Tighten the big muscles on the top side and the two smaller ones on the bottom. Hold five to seven seconds and relax.
12. *Right calf.* Pull toes upward until calf muscles tighten. Hold five to seven seconds and relax.
13. *Right foot.* Point toe, arch the foot, and curl your toes. Hold five to seven seconds and relax.

14. *Left upper leg and thigh.* Repeat the procedure for step 11. Hold five to seven seconds and relax.
15. *Left calf.* Repeat the procedure for Step 12. Hold five to seven seconds and relax.
16. *Left foot.* Repeat the procedure for Step 13. Hold five to seven seconds and relax.

During this process it's important to move at your own pace, making sure you actually feel fully relaxed in one group before going on to the next. If you develop any cramps while going through one of the steps, relax and try it again without tensing quite so much. If you find any of the steps difficult to carry out, it's all right to invent another procedure that accomplishes the same purpose as long as it doesn't force you to tense any of the muscle groups you've already relaxed.

Seven Group Procedure

After you have been able to fully relax every muscle group described above for two sessions, you are ready to try the next step. It involves reducing the number of muscle groups to seven by combining several of the early ones. Try these steps until you are able to achieve full relaxation of all groups within a 15-minute period, or less.

1. *All the muscles in your dominant arm,* including hand, forearm, and biceps. Hold five to seven seconds and relax.
2. *Muscles of the nondominant arm.* Repeat the same procedure as in Step 1. Hold five to seven seconds and relax.
3. *Facial muscles.* Squint eyes, frown hard, wrinkle nose, and grit teeth. Hold five to seven seconds and relax.
4. *Neck muscles.* Repeat the same procedure you learned in your earlier sessions. Hold five to seven seconds and relax.
5. *Chest, back, shoulders, and abdomen.* Take a deep breath and hold it while pulling shoulder blades together and tensing abdomen. Hold five to seven seconds and relax.
6. *Right thigh, calf, and foot.* Lift leg slightly, point toes, and twist foot inward. Hold five to seven seconds and relax.
7. *Left thigh, calf, and foot.* Repeat same process as above. Hold five to seven seconds and relax.

Four Group Procedure

Once you can easily relax all of the muscle groups using the above procedure, you can move on to the next step. This consists of combining the previous seven groups into four larger ones as described below. Practice these four groups using the same method as before until you can relax them all within five minutes or less.

1. *Muscles of both hands, forearms, and biceps.* Tense all of these at once. Hold five to seven seconds and relax.
2. *Face and neck muscles.* Combine the procedures you already have learned for these areas. Hold five to seven seconds and relax.
3. *Chest, back, shoulders, and abdomen.* Use the same procedure as described in Step 5 of the previous phase. Hold five to seven seconds and relax.
4. *Both upper legs, calfs, and feet.* Combine the same procedures described above. Hold five to seven seconds and relax.

Recall Procedure

Upon mastering these groups, you are ready to practice relaxing the four muscle groups without first tensing them. You can accomplish this by carefully thinking about the muscles in question and then recalling how it feels to relax them totally. After the recollection of that feeling is clear in your mind, go ahead and actually try to let lose of the muscles, taking half a minute or so to let the tension flow from that part of your body. If any tension at all remains after doing this, focus your attention on it and allow yourself to relax that part. If you have any difficulty accomplishing this step, simply go back and work on the tension-release procedure in the preceding paragraph until you're ready to try this step again.

Counting Procedure

The final step in progressive relaxation training will enable you to relax your entire body at once. You'll accomplish this by recalling how it feels to be free of tension, then achieving this state by counting slowly backward from ten to one. At each number allow more tenseness to flow from your body, so that by the time you reach Step 1, you feel totally relaxed. A valuable way to manage this process is to allow the tension to leave each part of your body, slowly, rather like toothpaste is squeezed from a tube. At Step 10 start allowing the anxiety to flow from your hands and arms. Next feel your biceps, then scalp, face, neck, shoulders, and so on loosen up. By the time you reach the count of one, the last bits of tension should have flowed down your legs and out through your toes.

After you've achieved this level of skill, you should be able to relax yourself well in *most* settings. Often saying the word "relax" to yourself will be sufficient to erase most of the tension you are experiencing. Of course, like June you might still feel anxious in the situations you developed in your hierarchy, but the next procedure will take care of that.

DESENSITIZATION

The term *desensitization* is not limited to personal adjustment; it is also used in the medical world. A patient suffering from an allergic reaction to some substance—perhaps a certain food or pollen—is exposed to a gradually increasing dosage of that item. The first dose is so small that it causes no reaction, yet the body builds up a slight tolerance to the offensive material. A second exposure is slightly greater than the first, but the increase is so gradual that it does not cause any reaction. Over a period of time a number of slowly increased doses of the material are administered, so that the patient builds up an ability to tolerate the formerly irritating substance. The body no longer overreacts to something it once found toxic—hence the term desensitization. A few summers ago my family and I took advantage of this principle by slowly adding small quantities of the irritating agent in poison oak to our diets, increasing the dosage by only a drop or two per week. By the time we left for a camping vacation the formerly irritating plant had no effect on us. The treatment was successful, and for the first time we were able to spend a month in poison oak country without even the slightest itching.

You can follow this same procedure as a way of desensitizing yourself to a previously threatening situation. Starting with the lowest item on your SUDS hierarchy, you'll begin to replace the feelings of anxiety you formerly experienced with some incompatible response, usually relaxation. Since this first situation produced only slight anxiety to begin with, you should find it easy to inhibit your former fearful response. Once you're able to do this, you'll repeat the same procedure for each succeeding item, so that in a relatively short time you'll be able to face the situation that you formerly found most threatening with much increased confidence and relaxation.

There are two ways to desensitize yourself to a fearful situation. The first is termed *in vivo* (from the Latin, "in life"). Here you actually put yourself in the situations that have made you anxious, beginning of course with the least threatening. As you encounter these situations, you replace your old feelings of fear with some incompatible state. If your shaping hierarchy is well chosen and gradual enough, your early successes will make it much easier to tackle the more threatening ones with confidence and no unnecessary tension.

The second type of desensitization follows the same principles, but instead of approaching the hierarchy situations in real life, you do so in your imagination. Incredible as it might seem, coping wit a challenging encounter in a vivid fantasy carries over to similar situations in real life.

Let's take a look at these two procedures and see when and how to use each.

In Vivo Desensitization. Whenever possible, it's best to move up your anxiety ladder by confronting each threatening situation in real life. Bob, a professional photographer, had a fear of approaching subjects to request permission to photograph them. Curiously enough, Bob's fear increased with the age of the person he wanted to photograph: he had little trouble asking young children, but he felt increasingly anxious dealing with young adults, middle-aged, and elderly people. Since his job permitted him to select which subjects he would choose first, this progression formed a perfect hierarchy. Bob started by using the relaxation method you just learned to calm himself while approaching children under the age of six or so. Next, he repeated the same procedure with seven- to ten-year-olds, and so on up the age ladder. By moving in small steps and using his newfound relaxation skills to inhibit the anxiety he did feel, Bob soon gained the ability to approach even the oldest, gruffest appearing people. And while he was turned down occasionally, his new confidence helped put these occasions into perspective.

Psychologist Herbert Fensterheim describes how a patient of his used the *in vivo* methods to desensitize his fear of job interviews. He ingeniously decided to apply for jobs he didn't want or knew he wouldn't get. Since his career didn't hinge on his behavior in these situations, relaxing in them was easy, and gave him the chance to become comfortable in a nonthreatening setting. The confidence he gained in these no-risk activities made it easier for him to relax in the later interviews, which did count.

Relaxation isn't the only feeling you can use to overcome fears in real-life situations. You should consider any other response that is incompatible with anxiety. One man managed to overcome his fear of flying by choosing an aisle seat and engaging in sexual fantasies involving himself and the attractive stewardesses. In this way he both created an emotion that was incompatible with his fear and reinforced the experience of flying which had previously been so unpleasant. In a similar way you could use other states to override your fear: curiosity, anger, excitement, hunger, and so on. One student developed a hierarchy for coping with his fear of approaching strangers while traveling. Since a traveler is always looking for something—an honest car mechanic, a good restaurant, and so on—this man used his needs to provide the reason for approaching strangers. He began by asking street directions, then graduated to inquiring about a place to stay or eat, and then eventually was able to share his personal interests and seek out others who shared them. In this case his curiosity replaced the momentarily less urgent feelings of anxiety, thereby giving him the answers to his questions and increasing his confidence at the same time.

Take a look at the goal you described on page 83. Does it lend itself to in vivo desensitization? If so, what incompatible emotion will you use to counteract the fear you have experienced in the past?

Systematic Self-Desensitization. *In vivo* desensitization requires you to regulate the time and magnitude of the threatening situations you face, so that you can cope with the less trying ones before going on to the more difficult ones. While this is a desirable way of approaching your goal, it isn't always practical: sometimes you can't control exactly when a threatening situation will occur or whether a high-anxiety encounter might precede a low-anxiety one. At times like this the whole principle of shaping is distorted, leaving you no better off than you were before. In these cases the proper course is to use self-desensitization. As mentioned earlier, this process involves visualizing each hierarchy item in your imagination and, as you do so, replacing it with an incompatible emotion. You can thus control the order and frequency with which you encounter each item.

A large body of evidence suggests that systematic desensitization is a highly effective way of managing anxiety; used under the supervision of a professional, recent research suggests that it can be used successfully by individuals on their own. Of course, if you do experience difficulties, you should consult a trained professional for help. In order to work for you, it's absolutely essential that you faithfully follow the steps outlined below.

Visualization Practice. Since you will be moving through your anxiety hierarchy in your mind, it's important that you be able to picture the situations there as vividly as possible. This means that you should be able to imagine each scene as if you were actually there. The sensations you experience should be like those in a clear dream, in the first person, rather than the pictures you see as a spectator in a movie. A moment's thought will show that you already have such fantasies, for you often experience intense feelings of fear, happiness, and other emotions while imagining scenes that involve you.

Take a few minutes now and test your ability to visualize a scene.

1. Start by finding a comfortable spot where you won't be disturbed for 10 or 15 minutes. Seat yourself, relax, and close your eyes.

2. Next picture a spot that is very familiar to you—perhaps your room at home or the place where you work. Start by noticing exactly where in this fantasy you are located. Are you sitting in a chair? Which one? Are you standing? Where? What time of day or night is it? How do you know? Become aware of the temperature—is it warm or cool? Are you confortable?

Notice the other furniture present, if any. See the colors and textures. In your imagination go ahead and touch a few objects and see how it feels to move around.

Are there any other people present? Who are they? What are they doing? Where are they located? What are their expressions? If they're talking, what are they saying? In what tone of voice? How do you reply?

Do you hear any other sounds—background noise, traffic, voices, music. . . . Are you hungry or thirsty? If so, imagine yourself satisfying that need if the fantasy permits.

3. Stop the image. Erase it from you mind immediately and completely. Now relax, using the skills you learned in the previous pages.

4. Now go ahead and reconstruct the scene. You should be able to bring it all back quickly.

5. Finally, let the scene go again, relax, and open your eyes.

(continued)

Be sure to practice this activity until you can carry it out successfully. The entire process of self-desensitization depends on the ability to visualize a situation clearly, so your mastery of this step is essential to your later success.

Desensitization Proper. Desensitization to the entire hierarchy will take several sessions of about 15 to 30 minutes each. As before, each session should take place in a quiet spot where you can seat yourself comfortably. Have your stack of hierarchy cards at hand, organized with the least threatening on top and the highest at the bottom. At the beginning of the first session take a minute or so to relax yourself, then look at the first card and visualize the scene described there. Be sure your mental image is vivid—the value of this process comes from re-creating the scene as clearly as possible in your imagination. The image for the first card should be as clear to you as the scene you pictured in your visualization practice. Be sure and hold the picture on your card; don't allow yourself to drift to another scene. Now try to hold the image for about 20 seconds. As you do so, keep picturing yourself actually in the situation. Notice how you are acting, that it is as effective as the behavior of others. Let yourself actually *be there.* If you can hold the image for 20 seconds without experiencing any anxiety, stop the mental picture and relax. Enjoy this feeling for about a minute, then repeat the scene again. After relaxing for another minute, repeat the same procedure with the next card. Continue this process for each scene in your hierarchy, until you are able to imagine yourself in the highest SUDS setting and still remaining calm. Be sure that you can picture each scene calmly twice before moving on.

It is normal to sometimes experience anxiety while visualizing a scene. If this occurs, stop picturing it immediately and relax. Take a full minute to experience these calm feelings, then try picturing the scene again. If you find you cannot hold a scene for the full 20 seconds without becoming anxious, then consider the shorter period an intermediate step and fantasize for this length of time before gradually increasing your exposure to the full length. If you become anxious as soon as you start picturing an item, drop it and return to the previous card in your stack. Consider whether you need to insert another intermediate step that will serve as a transition to the one you found threatening. One way of doing this is to break a difficult scene into its parts, and then to gradually add the parts that make the situation difficult to manage. For example, if your difficult scene involves approaching strangers for directions in an unfamiliar city, first try the same scene in a town you're more familiar with. Remember, there's nothing sacred about your original hierarchy; if you can improve it by changing or adding an item, by all means do so.

At the most you should expect to cover three items in a session. This, however, is an outside number. It's perfectly fine to devote an entire 15- to

30-minute period to one item, which you could practice visualizing for gradually longer periods. Realize that there's no need to rush; any time you spend now is well worth it, considering the results you stand to gain.

Problems with Self-Desensitization. Any problems you have with your desensitization sessions are probably due to one of three reasons. First, you might suffer from vague imagery, finding it difficult to picture the items vividly in your mind. If this is the case, return to the visualization practice described earlier and imagine familiar scenes in great detail until your skill increases. In your imagination focus on the details of any personal involvement for greater realism. You might even focus on actual dialogue to bring the image closer to reality (Marquis, Morgan, and Piaget, 1974).

A second difficulty might involve your inability to hold a scene for the full 20-second period. As you just read, in this event you should simply apply the principles of shaping, starting with an image of only a few seconds, gradually building up the duration to the full time.

The third common problem some people encounter is a difficulty in relaxing. The most common reason for this is a failure to practice the relaxation exercises thoroughly. If this applies to you, be sure to follow each of the steps in this procedure before trying desensitization proper. In other cases, however, you might have more success relaxing by replacing the exercises with mental images of pleasant situations. Such images might include past experiences you recall with pleasure or fantasies that help you feel calm, joyful, or in some other state that is incompatible with anxiety.

In contrast to these problems there are a few cases in which you might need the help of a professional to guide you through the desensitization process: You might have difficulty stopping the anxiety-producing fantasies during the desensitization session; you might find these images recurring at other times and be unable to make them stop; you might be unable to master some technique for relaxation after repeated practice; or you might have trouble reaching the top of your hierarchy after carefully constructing a shaping ladder. Systematic desensitization is practiced in a wide range of settings, but the most likely place to find a person trained in its application is in a college counseling center, psychological or psychiatric clinic, or from a psychologist or psychiatrist in private practice. Most professionals who practice the method consider it a branch of behavior therapy, so it is a good idea to use this label when seeking assistance.

Is the goal you described on page 83 suitable for systematic self-desensitization? Explain below why or why not:

_____

_____

_____

Combining Procedures In this and the preceding chapter you have learned several methods for communicating more effectively—disputing irrational thoughts, behavior rehearsal, relaxation training, *in vivo* and systematic self-desensitization. Although each of these approaches can be practiced separately, it's often best to combine them to reach a communication goal.

You might, for instance, construct a hierarchy that calls for both *in vivo* and self-desensitization. Clint, a newspaper advertising salesman, took this approach as a way of approaching new customers. He first constructed a hierarchy of gradually more challenging prospects. Before each appointment he would visualize the discussion in his mind, practicing relaxation techniques until he could picture it without anxiety. Then he would actually make the call, again using his relaxation skills as a way of dealing with any residual anxiety that the fantasy had not cleared up. The combination of both imagined and real-life exposure proved to be perfect for Clint. In less than a month he was handling all his appointments with much increased confidence.

Some other goals involve a need for both increased skill and relaxation. In these cases it's a good idea to combine desensitization with behavior rehearsal. Mary Ann used this approach in her new role as a teaching assistant for undergraduates in a large university. She began by developing a hierarchy of situations, part of which follows:

1. Preparing lesson plans for the semester.
2. Discussing the plans with my supervising professor.
3. Preparing for the first day of class.
4. Walking into class the first day.
5. Making introductory remarks to the class.
6. Giving my first lecture on the subject.
7. Answering questions about the lecture.
8. Answering student questions about the way I've graded their midterm exams.

Mary Ann used self-desensitization to prepare herself for Steps 1 and 2. Once she felt comfortable talking to her supervising professor, she was able to draw up an outline for the first day of class in comfort. Next she enlisted the help of a friend to rehearse how she would present the material to her students, using her newfound relaxation skills whenever she felt uncomfortable. During her actual presentation she used the relaxation techniques again whenever necessary. Mary Ann reported that this combination worked well for her. The behavior rehearsal enabled her to develop and practice the skill necessary for handling the new situation, and the desensitization helped her approach each new step with excitement rather than fear.

Now consider which method or combination of methods you have learned about so far that would be most appropriate for the goal you listed on page 83. Read the example, then describe your plan in detail.

EXAMPLE When I talk with men I respect and who I fear might not respect me, I become nervous and avoid eye contact with them. I've already constructed a hierarchy of people and situations, using the cards on page 97. I'll approach each item by (a) practicing the relaxation exercises; (b) using a combination of self-desensitization and covert behavior rehearsal to calmly visualize dealing successfully with the person in question, and (c) using the in vivo method to stay relaxed while I keep eye contact in the actual situation.

GOAL AND PLAN _____

_____

_____

_____

_____

_____

_____

_____

SUMMARY

In many cases your fear of communicating comes from not knowing how to act in a certain situation. When this is the case you can use the information in other chapters of this book to learn and practice the needed skill. As you become better at the behavior in question, your anxiety should disappear.

At other times, however, you may be fearful to communicate in a certain situation even though you know how you ought to act. At times like these there are two ways to overcome your apprehension.

The first involves recognizing the irrational belief which leads you to interpret an event in a manner which results in nervous or anxious feelings. You can then dispute this belief, and in so doing usually feel more relaxed and confident.

When irrational beliefs are not the cause of your nervousness, an effective method for dealing with your anxiety is to first establish a hierarchy of gradually more threatening situations. Next, apply the technique of progressive relaxation to each item in turn, either by *in vivo* (real life) desensitization or systematic self-desensitization in which you visualize each situation. Often it is most effective to combine two or more of the methods in this book to reduce anxiety.

6
Self-Modification: Blueprint for Communication Change

Sometimes the path to assertive communication is an easy one. After reading the preceding chapters and examining other sections of the book, it's likely that you are already expressing yourself more effectively. Many readers comment that some of the principles described in this book are so simple that it is hard to understand why they've failed to practice them before. Often they report that the process of simply defining a problem clearly is enough to bring about change. In other cases skills such as keeping eye contact and using core statements (Chapter 4), open-ended questions (Chapter 7), and "I" language (Chapter 9) meet with success almost immediately. Even goals that at first seemed difficult to use gradually become easier when they are approached via the behavior-rehearsal and desensitization methods described previously.

On the other hand there are some communication problems that you may not be able to solve quickly or simply. There are usually two reasons for such difficulties. First, *there may be no immediate reinforcement for your new behavior.* Sometimes the rewards for a new style of self-expression don't come immediately: In fact, the first results of such a change can occasionally be punishing, as Marge unhappily discovered. When she first introduced herself, Marge gave the impression of being a shy and somewhat timid person. She told of her 15-year marriage to a verbal, strong-willed husband who believed that a woman was meant to be a homemaker, mother, and social asset to her husband's career. Having also grown up in a similar environment, Marge reported that she had accepted this arrangement for the first years of her marriage. Recently, she had realized that such a life was stifling; she stated that it deprived her of her self-esteem and kept her from exploring her own interests. After some discussion Marge translated these feelings into the behavioral goals of speaking up when she disagreed with her husband's decisions and insisting on the right to return on a part-time basis to her career as a nurse. Marge was wise enough to start asserting herself gradually since the change would be a big one for both her and her husband; but in spite of this caution, at first even her modest attempts at self-expression met with resistance.

During this trying period Marge designed a self-modification project with the help of a marriage and family counselor who advised her to further reduce the magnitude of her initial assertions to a degree that her husband could accept without too much resistance. During this phase of her project the counselor also made sure that Marge was reinforced for her attempts to speak up by receiving recognition and praise for her courage and skill from the assertiveness-building group she was attending. This support helped Marge to stand up for herself as she made these difficult first steps at self-expression. After a few months this plan paid off: her husband noticed that, contrary to his fears, Marge's new style of communication did not detract from her femininity or from his stature in the family. At last report their relationship was better than ever before, and still improving.

In addition to not receiving immediate reinforcement, a second reason why a target behavior may not be immediately attainable is because *it is too complex to learn all at once.* This is often true for the person who wants to become a better conversationalist. While reaching such a target would most certainly result in powerful rewards, observing a model who exhibits such conversational skills will show that this is an extremely complex talent. Chapter 7 lists several elements of this skill, but putting them all together is too big a task for many shy communicators to manage through simple behavior rehearsal or desensitization. Such a problem occurred for Dave, the man described in Chapter 3 whose aim was to converse skillfully and comfortably with attractive eligible women. It soon became obvious to him that reaching such a goal would call for a more sophisticated approach than merely reducing his anxiety or trying simply to practice speaking up whenever the talk died down; like Marge, he reached his target through self-modification techniques.

This chapter describes a method for learning new ways of communicating, both in cases where a target is complex and in instances when it isn't immediately reinforced. This approach doesn't differ in type from the information you have already learned; rather, it applies these and other principles of learning in a more systematic and detailed manner. This method will require a clear commitment and strong effort from you, for it requires that you constantly observe and record your own target behavior. If you follow the instructions faithfully, your efforts will be rewarded in two ways. First, the actual task of working on your project includes provisions for self-reinforcement. In other words, if you plan thoughtfully, you will gain pleasant consequences just for doing the project itself. Second, your project will ultimately result in mastery of an important communication behavior that you presently find difficult to carry out. When you consider the length of time you probably have suffered from many assertive problems, the payoff for faithfully applying the following information is indeed great.

Before going any further in this chapter, you should understand that it isn't designed to be read in one sitting. Instead, you should plan to approach the task of self-modification in steps, reading a section and applying the information to your assertive goal before going on.

ESTABLISH A BEHAVIORAL GOAL

As in the methods you have already learned, the first step in your self-modification project will be to set a behavioral goal. Be sure your goal is complete and specific. Remember, good results depend on a clear goal. Specify the people who are involved in your target situation and the circumstances in which it occurs. Describe in detail exactly how you want to behave in these circumstances. For instance, don't say "I want to become a better conversationalist," but rather, "I want to ask open-ended questions, offer self-disclosure about my opinions and feelings, give sincere compliments, and follow up on free information." If you haven't already done so, this is the time to observe models, visualize your idealized self-image, and use the Index and Contents of this book to find out exactly what behaviors will make up your target. A review of the checklist on pages 62–63 will help ensure that you have stated this goal in the clearest possible terms.

The self-modification project described in this chapter will help you reach assertive goals that you have so far found difficult. Begin your project by choosing a target from your list of Communication Goals in Appendix II. Be sure that the item you choose

—is important enough to justify your time and effort in a self-modification project.

—does not seem attainable by the methods you have already learned: observation of models, behavior rehearsal, coaching, and desensitization.

List the goal you have chosen in the appropriate space on your Self-Modification Progress Chart in Appendix III.

Remember, the information in this chapter will prove effective only if you complete each activity before going on.

ESTABLISH A BASELINE

It is impossible to know exactly how far you have come toward assertive communication without knowing where you began. For this reason your self-modification project must have a *baseline*—a record of the frequency with which you are now practicing your target behavior. A baseline can serve two functions. Assuming your assertiveness-building project is successful, it will graphically show your progress, and in so doing give you the reinforcement to keep on the same course. On the other hand, if the frequency of your assertive acts does not rise above the baseline rate, you will know that some part of your plan is ineffective and needs changing. In either case the baseline provides an invaluable standard against which you can measure your progress.

What Should You Count? In establishing a baseline you should count the frequency of the assertive behavior you want to increase, such as the goal you listed on your Self-Modification Progress Chart. There are four methods of counting. Each works best for a different kind of target. Consider them all and then decide which method is best suited for the target you have chosen.

1. Frequency. Counting the number of times you engage in your target is the most straightforward way of recording behavior. The manager of a large food market realized that a disproportionate amount of his conversations with employees involved criticism of their work, while he rarely complimented the jobs they did well. Having decided that competent work should be rewarded instead of taken for granted, he set out to offer praise whenever it was deserved. During his baseline period the supervisor simply counted each time he praised a subordinate. This method of counting the frequency of occurrences works well in most cases where opportunities to practice the target occur on a fairly regular basis and when each instance of the target behavior is clearly distinguishable:—saying hello to strangers, making requests, and admitting mistakes, for example.

2. Duration. Often the goal is to increase the length of time during which you engage in an already existing behavior. One student described her relationship with a neighbor as being cordial but superficial. Whenever the two women encountered each other they exchanged greetings but seldom carried the conversation beyond a few words. The goal in this case was

not to have more meetings with her neighbor, but rather to increase the length of time spent during each talk. In cases such as this you will need to record the amount of time you spend engaging in the target behavior during each instance, then compute the total of all such occasions to find your baseline rate.

3. All or None. Sometimes a behavior is difficult to count accurately for one of two reasons: Either it occurs with extremely high frequency or it is difficult to separate into discrete units. For instance, a teacher learned that he used the word "uh" almost constantly in his lectures. Counting the exact number of such utterances in an hour would have totally distracted him from the topic he was explaining, thus making the frequency method impractical. He therefore divided the 50-minute class period into five 10-minute segments, and established a baseline by recording the number of intervals in which he uttered even a single "uh." Now he only had to count one "uh" each five minutes. The goal then became to increase the number of "uh"-free segments. In the same way a woman who was unhappy with the constant interruptions she reported making while speaking with friends found her base rate by recording the number of five-minute intervals that were free of interruptions.

4. Percentage. Often the opportunities for engaging in a target behavior vary radically over daily or weekly periods. In such cases the three methods described above might not produce a representative base rate, for the recording period might contain an abnormally high or low number of chances to practice the target. In such instances you can gain a more accurate measure of your behavior by calculating the percentage of times in which you engage in your target behavior when presented with an opportunity to do so. This was the case for Laura, a single mother of two who attended school and worked at a part-time job in addition to caring for her children. As you can imagine, this busy schedule often left her feeling tired, and at such times she found the prospect of a quiet evening at home more attractive than going out with friends. Because she had such a difficult time declining invitations even when she was exhausted, Laura made her goal an increased ability to say no. At first the frequency method—simply counting the number of times she turned down unwanted requests—seemed most logical. But shortly after she began her baseline recording period, two problems became apparent. First, the number of invitations she received varied from week to week; second, her interest in accepting them fluctuated considerably from one time to another. Thus, a low frequency of refusals might sometimes have been caused by her unassertiveness, but it could also have been because of the social plans of others or her inner desire for companionship. With a goal like Laura's, the percentage method was the appropriate way to account for these variables. This method required her to record two sets of figures: first, the target behavior itself (number of unwanted invitations she refused), and second, the opportunities for

engaging in the target behavior (number of undesired invitations she received). The percentage of refused requests constituted her baseline:

$$\frac{5 \text{ refusals}}{14 \text{ opportunities}} = 36 \text{ percent success rate}$$

The value of the percentage method lies in its adaptability to varying situations, as the figures below illustrate. Laura's frequency of declining unwanted requests over a month was as follows:

week	1	2	3	4
refusals	5	2	1	2

By counting only the frequency of refusals it appears that Laura was actually becoming less assertive as time passed. However, the additional information provided by the percentage method shows quite the opposite.

week	1	2	3	4
refusals	5	2	1	2
undesired invitations	14	5	2	3
success rate	37%	40%	50%	67%

The percentage method shows that Laura had actually been moving closer to her goal. The apparent decline was related to the varying number of opportunities she had to assert herself.

In summary, the method you choose for establishing a baseline and recording your progress depends on the nature of your goal. Use the frequency method when you can easily count separate instances in which you engage in your target behavior and when these instances occur at a relatively constant rate. When the effectiveness of your target behavior depends on how long you engage in it, use the duration method. When the high frequency of a target behavior makes counting difficult or when it is hard to distinguish between separate instances of the behavior, use the all-or-none method. Finally, when the opportunities to practice vary widely, use the percentage system.

Now turn to page 267 and review the target behavior you listed there. Use the following checklist to decide which method is most appropriate for recording that behavior during your self-modification project.

Frequency Method

    (   ) opportunities to engage in the target occur on a regular basis

    (   ) each instance of the target is equal to the others (same length, difficulty, etc.)

Duration Method
( ) length of time engaged in the behavior is a measure of your
    success
All-or-None Method
( ) behavior occurs with such frequency that counting every in-
    stance is impractical
( ) behavior is difficult to separate into discrete units
Percentage Method
( ) opportunities to engage in target behavior occur on an irregular
    basis

DECIDE ON A METHOD FOR RECORDING YOUR TARGET BEHAVIOR BEFORE READING

FURTHER. LIST THE METHOD YOU HAVE CHOSEN HERE: _____.

Make Your Data Reliable You should be sure that the method of recording
you have just chosen is a consistent, reliable one, for an unreliable system
will give a misleading record of your progress. A recording system is said to
be reliable if the same event is recorded in the same way every time it
occurs. To use a common example, a scale can be considered reliable if it
registers the same weight each time a five-pound brick is placed upon it.[1]
There are several steps you can take to ensure the reliability of your baseline data.

1. Make Sure Your Target Behavior Is Unambiguous.   Suppose that your
goal is to increase the number of times you approach strangers at social occasions. Your tally of these occurrences will be reliable only if you always
use the same criteria to define an act of "approaching," who constitutes a
"stranger," and what you consider to be a "social occasion." For instance, if
you consider simply smiling at someone an approach in one case, then you
should always count it as such; don't decide at a later time to record only instances when you make verbal contact. It's fine to define as strangers people with whom you have previously exchanged only a few words, but after
doing so you should not decide in mid-project to count only those people
you've never met at all. Decide in advance what you mean by "social occasions" and stick to that definition. If you have carefully read and followed
the instructions for goal setting as described in Chapter 3, you should have
no problem with ambiguity. To be sure your target is clear, it might be wise
to check it against the criteria listed in the chart on pages 62–63.

2. Record Every Occurrence of the Target Behavior as It Happens.   One
of the biggest problems you will face in your assertiveness project is the
tendency to be an irregular counter. It is absolutely essential to record

[1] Reliability does not guarantee *validity*. A scale that consistently registers a five-pound
brick as weighing ten pounds is certainly reliable, but we can depend on it to be reliably
incorrect. In the same way, you must be certain that the behaviors you are observing are not
only consistently measured but are truly important indicators of assertiveness.

every instance of your target behavior when it occurs. You may be tempted to trust your memory, planning to make note of your behavior at a later time. Do not do this! Realize that the minor inconvenience of counting is only a temporary means to the end of reaching your target behavior, and that it will soon be over. Be a faithful, consistent counter.

Experience and research prove that remembered data is usually inaccurate data. There are two reasons for this. First, it is difficult to recall a large number of facts for a long time when you are constantly being bombarded with other information. If your goal is to raise the quantity of your remarks in conversations, the excitement that will come from your increased involvement will make it difficult to remember the actual number of comments you make. After all, if you devote much of your energy to counting and remembering your remarks, you will probably miss most of what other people are saying, thus defeating your original purpose. In the same way, many other assertive behaviors are difficult to recall accurately: the times you speak in a loud tone of voice, the percentage of times you ask for additional information when criticized, or the duration of a conversation.

A second problem that comes from trying to remember data is the tendency to distort what actually happened when the facts are unpleasant. Suppose that you want to increase your interruption-free five-minute segments of conversation. After the first hour of self-observation there have only been two such instances. As the day wears on, you recall only three more interruption-free segments out of a total of four hours of conversation. When the time comes to record your behavior, you have only five segments, or a total of 25 minutes free from interrupting out of five hours of listening. But in your heart you know that you aren't that bad! You rationalize that you must have forgotten a few segments, so you consult your self-image and record a total of ten segments. Presto! The "facts" now fit your self-concept, however invalid they may be. *Always record events as they occur.*

3. **Use an Independent Observer Whenever Possible.** People are not naturally accurate observers of their own behavior. For this reason you should get a friend to monitor the frequency of your target behaviors. Of course, it is not always possible to have others observe you. The behavior in which you are engaging might occur in a variety of settings, some of which will not include your confederate. In other instances you might be focusing on an activity that is not observable by others, such as imagining catastrophic fantasies in which you fail miserably or covertly making unflattering comments about yourself (e.g., "I don't have anything worth saying"). But in all cases the reliability of your data will be much greater if it is corroborated by another observer.

Methods of Recording Data The last section made clear the importance of recording each occurrence of your target behavior as soon as it happens.

The question now arises as to how to do this recording in the easiest, most accurate way. If counting becomes too much of a chore—too punishing, in other words—then you will be less likely to do a good job, as the story of Marty illustrates. Marty's wife had accused him of being inattentive in their frequent discussions about how to raise their two children. An analysis of the problem showed that the specific behavior she found annoying was Marty's tendency to look around the room and fiddle with his hands as they talked, suggesting to her that the subject was unpleasant or boring. Marty's target, then, became to maintain eye contact and keep his hands still during 10-minute segments of conversation. After the project began, Marty kept track of his progress on a small slip of paper that he carried with him. Unfortunately, this system caused problems almost immediately. As Marty's wife put it: "You do fine for a while, but it drives me crazy when you pull out that notepad every ten minutes." In other words, the very act of recording the behavior conflicted with Marty's target. As long as he used the paper and pencil method of collecting data, he would never satisfy his wife.

A second type of recording problem was encountered by Doug, an avid volleyball player who reported a desire to handle himself more aggressively on the court. He translated this desire into the target behavior of loudly calling "mine" when teammates began to charge shots he felt he could handle. "You said it was important to record each behavior as soon as it happens," he stated. "But how can I do that when I'm in the middle of a game? I can't exactly carry a clipboard around with me, you know."

Problems like these highlight the characteristics that any method of recording behavior should possess. First, it should be *unobtrusive* so you will not call undue attention to your counting. Second, it should be *easy to operate*, so you can count a behavior without interrupting your other activities. Finally, it should be *portable* enough to be always present in your target situations. In many cases simply carrying a three-by-five-inch card and a pencil with you is an effective recording method. A man who wanted to ask salespeople for assistance while shopping kept such a card in his pocket. Since he always brought his checkbook along on such journeys, the apparatus was always ready for use. A commercial photographer who found it difficult to ask potential subjects if he could photograph them recorded his progress on a piece of paper taped to his camera case. A student who wanted to ask more questions in class set aside a page in her notebook for recording purposes.

In other cases the paper-and-pencil method is not practical. Doug, the volleyball player, invested in a wrist-mounted gold stroke counter, such as can be found at most sporting goods stores. Such devices have two separate scales, making them ideal for calculating the percentages. On one side of his counter Doug recorded the number of balls that came his way (waiting until after the point had been made, of course), while on the other he counted the times he called other players away in a loud voice. Devices similar to the one Doug used are sold in variety stores, primarily to shoppers who use them to keep track of their total purchases. These small, flat plastic devices fit comfortably into a pocket or purse, where they can be unobtrusively used to record the frequency of greetings, smiles, volunteered opinions, questions asked, and other behaviors that would be interrupted by more visible methods of self-monitoring. Marty used such an instrument to record periods of attentiveness without disturbing his wife.

The range of unobtrusive, portable, easily operated ways to record behavior is only limited by one's imagination. One student reported starting the day with a precounted number of pennies in his left pocket. Each time he engaged in his target behavior, he would transfer one coin to the right pocket. At the end of the day he merely had to count the pennies to note his progress. Other readers have suggested using the date indicator on a watch, knots tied in a string, matches torn out of a fresh book, or pieces of candy or breath mints consumed from a precounted pack to record the number of target behaviors practiced in a given time period.
practiced in a given time period.

Choose a method of recording behaviors for your Self-Modification Project. Remember to choose a system that is

— portable enough to use in all situations where your target behavior will occur;
— unobtrusive enough to not call undue attention to your recording;
— easy to operate so that you can count behaviors without interrupting your normal activities.

List the system you will choose here. _____

_____

_____

DO NOT GO ON UNTIL YOU HAVE SELECTED A RECORDING SYSTEM.

Chart Your Progress   After you have developed a satisfactory method for counting the incidence of your target behavior, you will need to set up a way of analyzing your progress over the duration of your project. In most instances the best vehicle for this purpose is a graph. To see how such a device works, observe Marty's graph after six days (page 120).

This graph clearly shows the pattern of Marty's attentiveness. Considering the fact that he spent several hours per day with his wife, the graph indicates that there are no radical swings from one day to another, which suggests that both the opportunities to listen to his wife and the way he handles such chances are consistent. If the graph had shown wide swings from one day to another, the data might have suggested that different cir-

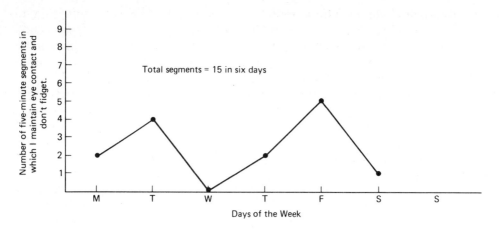

cumstances affected Marty's attention span—problems that came up at work, variations in the time he and his wife spent together, or the amount of tension or fatigue under which he was operating on given days. Wide fluctuations might have also indicated that the opportunities to listen to his wife varied, perhaps due to the time they spent together. In this case he might have used the percentage method of recording to gain a more valid measure of his behavior.

Doug used such a percentage method to graph his progress on the volleyball court. Note that instead of keeping a day-by-day chart he wisely only recorded data for the dates on which he actually played ball.

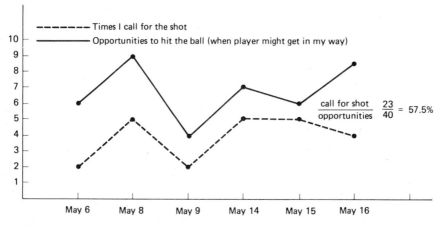

Doug calculated the percentage of shots called for simply by adding the total number of opportunities he had to yell "mine" and dividing it into the number of times he actually called out in those circumstances. Simple arithmetic gave him the answer.

Length of the Baseline Period There is no single proper length of time to record baseline data. Since the purpose of this period is to get an idea of how frequently you practice a target behavior before beginning your intervention, the general principle is to make your baseline period long enough to constitute a representative sample of your behavior. Assuming that the rate of behavior is fairly constant, a baseline of one week is usually sufficient. On the other hand, if you notice wide day-to-day variations in your data or if the behavior you are counting does not occur daily, then a longer period may be called for. If the baseline period occurs during a period that is not typical of your normal lifestyle, you should consider extending the period in order to make it more accurately reflect your starting point. A look at the data and daily variations on your graph, plus an examination of whether this was a typical period for you will usually give a good idea of how long you will need to record baseline data before being sure that it reflects your typical style of communication.

Start recording your baseline now, using the Self-Modification Progress Chart in Appendix III. Sample charts are provided as models in Appendix IV. Remember that in order to make your project successful you must faithfully count each instance of your target behavior from now until you reach your goal. In order to remind yourself about the need for faithful record-keeping, post the Self-Modification Progress Chart in a place where you will see and use it every day—on your bathroom mirror, closet door, refrigerator, or some other conspicuous spot.

POST YOUR CHART NOW IF POSSIBLE, AND CERTAINLY BEFORE YOU GO TO BED TONIGHT.

Premature Improvement during the Baseline Period At some point during the baseline period you may find that the figures recording your preintervention behavior are invalid, since the very act of observing yourself will have led you to start acting more assertively. This phenomenon has been labeled "reactivity," since the target behavior seems to react to the process of measuring.

Do not be upset if your behavior improves reflecting your process of self-monitoring. The only negative consequence will be that your baseline measure will be inaccurately high, making your ultimate progress greater than your figures will show. Of course, you will be aware of this fact, and it seems like a small price to pay for the results you are already achieving for your time and effort.

Another word needs to be said about the immediate improvement that often comes from simply observing your behavior. It appears that the increases in desired behaviors that come from reactivity are often temporary.

For this reason you should not suppose that the immediate changes in your style of communication will necessarily be lasting ones. In most cases you will need to use the methods discussed in the rest of this chapter to make them permanent.

Quantify Your Goal At the end of the baseline period you will have a fairly accurate picture of the frequency with which you presently engage in your target behavior. With this figure in mind you can specify exactly how often you want to act in that new, desirable way. In other words, you can now complete the setting of your target by specifying how many times you would like to act assertively in a given period.

Recall Doug, the volleyball player. As the graph on page 120 shows, his baseline figures of calling "mine" for shots he felt he could handle was approximately 58 percent. With this figure in mind Doug decided that a target of 90 percent would be satisfying. Marty, the husband who wanted to increase his figet-free conversations with his wife, decided to double his baseline rate of 15 segments per week to 30.

How can you decide on the optimum frequency for your target? Your first decision might be to strive for perfection: Never to fidget, always to call for volleyball shots, to speak with complete confidence before a group, never to allow unwanted silences to intrude into conversations, and so on. While you might indeed want to aim at the ultimate goal, there are two reasons why you might decide to set a more modest target. First, even if it were realistic to expect you to behave "perfectly," you might not want to do so. The perfect conversationalist or public speaker, the person who always gives and receives compliments gracefully, or the totally confident communicator often appears slightly inhuman. In many cases people's imperfections are as attractive as their strengths. One of the features I most appreciate about my wife is her even temper and general good humor. On the other hand, our life together would be much less satisfying and exciting without an occasional lapse in her mild disposition. These bursts of anger allow me to feel more human when I lose my temper or behave foolishly. In addition, our occasional fights are effective ways of clearing up some of the small gripes that we harbor against each other from time to time. Also, like most people, my wife needs some way to ventilate the frustrations that build up from living in an imperfect world, and an outburst of anger can be an excellent cathartic. Finally, while her flashes of temper (as well as mine) are often unpleasant as they occur, they provide the opportunity for us to make up later, which is usually enjoyable enough to make the previous unhappiness worthwhile. All this is to say that the life of a totally assertive communicator might not be as desirable as it first seems.

Besides the desire to retain some of your endearing "flaws," there is a second reason you might want to set your assertive target short of perfection. Often the optimal level for practicing a behavior is less than 100 percent. Consider, for example, the goal of reducing the frequency with which you interrupt others in mid-sentence. When carried to excess, this interrupting is clearly an irritating habit. On the other hand, there might be times when such intrusions are desirable or even necessary. For instance, you might want to speak up when someone is repeating a message you have already heard or when you need to share an urgent message. At times such as these the goal of never interrupting becomes just as undesirable as does that of frequently intruding. As you review your baseline data with the idea of quantifying your target, consider what the optimal level of behavior would be for you.

When you are satisfied that you have enough data to reflect accurately your present level of assertive behavior, terminate your baseline period and quantify your target. On your Self-Modification Progress Chart draw a vertical line at the end of your baseline (see the sample charts in Appendix IV for examples). Next, record your present level of performance by figuring whichever is appropriate: a daily average, weekly total, or percentage of success. You now have a standard against which to measure your progress. Finally, set an ultimate frequency with which you want to perform your target behavior.

SHAPING: ONE STEP AT A TIME

At this point your baseline provides a clear measure of your present level of assertiveness and your target gives you a clear goal. The obvious question now is, "How do I get from here to there?"

One of the keys to a systematic learning of assertiveness is the process of shaping, or successive approximation, which was briefly discussed in Chapters 4 and 5. Recall that shaping consists of teaching a new behavior through a series of intermediate steps; first rewarding a crude approximation of the target and then, as it is mastered, gradually reinforcing behaviors that are closer and closer to the ultimate goal. Thus, rather than mastering a skill all at once, the learner moves steadily closer to the desired way of communicating.

The next step in your self-modification project will be to set up a series of intermediate goals by which you will move toward your final target. As you establish these steps, remember the two most important rules of shaping: (1) *No intermediate step is too small.* (2) *You can never start at too basic a level.* The value of the shaping process comes from steady progress rather than drastic changes, so you should be content to move at a modest but constant rate. Actually, what might first seem like a slow rate of change is in truth relatively quick. Seldom will a series of intermediate steps take more than a few months to complete, and considering how long most people have been saddled with their communication problems, such a schedule seems rapid indeed.

Types of Intermediate Steps There are a number of methods for dividing a target into intermediate steps. The one you choose will depend on the nature of your goal.

  1. Frequency.   As this is the easiest method for establishing steps, use it whenever there is no special advantage in any of the alternate methods listed below. To establish intermediate goals involving frequencies, simply divide the difference between your baseline rate and your ultimate goal into manageable segments.

  Sarah, a sales clerk at a department store, wanted to offer assistance to a greater number of customers during her work. She recorded a week-long baseline average of 19 approaches per day for her four-hour shift. Then, after observing the amount of traffic in her area, she set a goal of 35 contacts per shift. Thus she needed to approach an average of 16 additional customers per day. Taking the advice that no step is too small, she set an increase of one customer per day as her first intermediate goal. Sarah found that this target was extremely easy, and she reached it in one week. She made her next week's goal an increase of two additional daily contacts, which she also achieved in a week. Thereafter she maintained this rate of two additional contacts per week, and arrived at her ultimate target in just over two months. (Shortly after completing her project, Sarah received compliments and a raise from her approving manager.)

FREQUENCY APROACH: SARAH

Target Behavior

<u>Who</u>: Customers at work
<u>Circumstances</u>: When they first enter my department
<u>Desired Behavior</u>: Approach them and offer my assistance

Baseline

19 approaches per day

Target Frequency

35 approaches per day

Intermediate Steps

  1. 20 approaches per day
  2. 22 approaches per day
  3. 24 approaches per day
  4. 26 approaches per day

5. 28 approaches per day
6. 30 approaches per day
7. 32 approaches per day
8. 34 approaches per day

---

2. **Person.** This method is appropriate when your target behavior is more difficult to practice with some people than with others. In these situations the best approach is to express yourself with the less troubling people at first, gradually moving on to the more difficult ones. By progressing in this manner you can apply the actions that proved successful in your earlier attempts to the later, more difficult settings.

PERSON APPROACH: GUS

Target Behavior

<u>Who</u>: Friends, parents, and boss
<u>Circumstances</u>: When I'm offered an invitation I don't want to accept
<u>Desired Behavior</u>: Decline with thanks, explaining that it's important to spend my rare free time with my family.

Baseline

40 percent effective average over all situations described below

Target Frequency

90 percent effectiveness average over all situations described below

Intermediate Steps

1. Concentrate on declining offers of friends for parties, bridge, golf, etc.
2. Concentrate on declining unwanted invitations from parents, plus step 1
3. Concentrate on declining offers of boss to "have a few drinks" after work, plus steps 1 and 2

Gus used a person hierarchy with his target of declining invitations to events that interfered with the time he preferred to spend with his family. After reviewing all the instances in which he was faced with such invitations, he decided that the easiest offers to decline would be those extended by friends for dinner parties, bridge, or golf. The next step in Gus's hierarchy involved his parents. Whenever Gus declined their biweekly invitation to make the four-hour round trip drive to their home, he was met with deep sighs, assurances that the parents were "used to being alone," and other guilt-inducing strategies. After his initial success with his friends, Gus was able to explain to his parents that he did enjoy visiting them every month or six weeks, but that he also needed time with his own family. Although this message didn't decrease his parents' attempts at manipulation, by asserting himself Gus realized that he wasn't responsible for the way they responded to his legitimate requests. Bolstered by this knowledge, Gus was ready to move on. The final step in his project involved his boss, who often suggested that they drop by the local saloon for a few drinks after work. Armed with the confidence of his previous assertions, Gus calmly and honestly explained that while the socializing was truly fun, his time with his family was precious to him, and thus regular sessions would be impossible. He did, however, assure his boss that an occasional Friday afternoon celebration of the week's end definitely sounded attractive.

3. Situation. In some cases your ultimate target may center on only one person, but expressing yourself with that person is more difficult in some situations than in others. At such times you should organize your intermediate goals to reflect these different contexts.

SITUATION APPROACH: ROY

Target Behavior

Who: Marcia

Circumstances: When she acts as if she's positive about a fact or opinion and I'm not sure of my position.

Desired Behavior: I want to express my uncertainty instead of falsely acting positive.

Baseline

15 percent of total opportunities

Target Frequency

100 percent of opportunities

Intermediate Steps

1. Increase expressions of uncertainty to 25 percent of opportunities
2. Increase expressions of uncertainty to 35 percent of opportunities
3. Increase expressions of uncertainty to 45 percent of opportunities
4. Increase expressions of uncertainty to 55 percent of opportunities
5. Increase expressions of uncertainty to 65 percent of opportunities
6. Increase expressions of uncertainty to 75 percent of opportunities
7. Increase expressions of uncertainty to 85 percent of opportunities

8. Increase expressions of uncertainty to 95 percent of opportunities
9. Increase expressions of uncertainty to 100 percent of opportunities

Roy's goal was to admit when he was unsure about a subject, rather than pretending to know the answer. He found this difficult only in the presence of Marcia, a close friend and co-owner of their interior decorating service. Roy claimed that his partner's dogmatism caused him to act equally certain about the subject at hand, inevitably leading to an argument. This escalating stubbornness was threatening to destroy both the friendship and the business.

Rather than trying to change his behavior all at once, Roy decided to approach his target of expressing his uncertainty in small steps. After reviewing all the circumstances in which he acted dogmatically, he decided that the easiest situations to change were social discussions with Marcia in which the subject of politics came up. Since Roy had no strong feelings on the subject, he felt that he wouldn't be sacrificing too much of his dignity by admitting his lack of a strong position about a candidate or an issue. The next most challenging opportunity involved disagreements about environmental issues, followed by discussions about the work of their competitors, and their ways of redesigning a client's home or office. The ultimate test of Roy's willingness to admit his uncertainty called for his candid response while talking about whether to expand their business into a second city by inviting another designer to join their partnership.

4. Elements. Sometimes the most appropriate way to master a complex communication skill is to break it into its separate components, which you can then work on one at a time. Dave, the man described in Chapter 3 who wanted to become better at conversing with attractive, eligible women, used an elements approach to reach his goal. Observation of models plus a review of Chapter 7 showed that he could best reach his target by mastering several skills—asking open-ended questions, volunteering feelings and facts about himself through self-disclosure, following up on free information offered by the female, and expressing sincere compliments. Dave wisely chose to work on these elements one at a time, in effect carrying out several small projects in order to reach his final goal.

ELEMENTS APPROACH: DAVE

Target Behavior

<u>Who</u>: Attractive, eligible women

<u>Circumstances</u>: At parties, while standing in lines, and occasional other situations

<u>Desired Behavior:</u> Carry on conversations without silences longer than 20 seconds, finish all sentences I start. Make eye contact while speaking and listening.

Baseline

No successful conversations longer than three minutes

Target Frequency

Be able to meet above criteria in 80 percent of my conversations, allowing them to go on for as long as I feel is appropriate.

Intermediate Steps

1. Ask open-ended questions
   a. ask at least one per conversation
   b. ask at least two per conversation
   c. ask at least three per conversation
2. Volunteer ideas and feelings through self-disclosure
   a. volunteer at least one piece of self-disclosure per conversation
   b. volunteer at least two pieces of self-disclosure per conversation
   c. volunteer at least three pieces of self-disclosure per conversation
   d. volunteer at least four pieces of self-disclosure per conversation
3. Follow up on free information
   a. ask at least one question based on free information
   b. ask at least two questions based on free information
   c. ask at least three questions based on free information
   d. ask at least four questions based on free information
4. Volunteer sincere compliments
   a. express a sincere compliment in a quarter of my conversations
   b. express a sincere compliment in one half of my conversations
   c. express a sincere compliment in three quarters of my conversations

---

Use of the elements approach calls for a slightly different method of recording your progress (see sample Progress Chart II, Appendix IV). In addition to graphing the (hopefully increasing) frequency of times you engage in your target behavior, you will need to keep a separate record of your intermediate steps. This is necessary since these steps call for different units of measurement than the ultimate target does. If you decide to use the elements approach, use the supplementary chart in Appendix III to record your intermediate steps. At the same time you are working on your intermediate steps, keep an eye on the graph measuring your ultimate target. It will show you whether the intermediate steps you have chosen are in fact good stepping-stones; for as you gradually become more proficient at each element, you should begin to see an increase in the frequency of your final target.

5. Combination.   In some cases you may find it desirable to combine two or more of the above approaches to establish the most workable series of intermediate steps. Recall Marge, the woman described on page 111 who wanted to express her opinions and needs more forcefully to her husband. Marge was determined to stand up for herself, but in the face of her husband's strong resistance to her comments she was wise enough to change her behavior gradually. The step-by-step approach described in this chapter made it easier for her husband to adjust to the new style of communicating and at the same time allowed Marge to become skillful at the easier kinds of self-expression before going on to more challenging assertions.

COMBINATION APPROACH: MARGE

Target Behavior

<u>Who</u>: My husband

<u>Circumstances</u>: When we disagree, and when the subject of my returning to nursing arises

<u>Desired Behavior</u>: I want to express my position until I am satisfied that my husband has understood me (while at the same time listening to his side)

Baseline

I speak up in only 15 percent of our disagreements, and never any more about the subject of nursing.

Target Frequency

I want to speak up in about 80 percent of our disagreements and whenever I feel the subject of my nursing is important enough to mention.

Intermediate Steps

1. Express myself 25 percent of the time during trivial disagreements (ways to spend a free evening, discussions on current events, etc.)
2. Express myself 40 percent of the time during trivial disagreements
3. Express myself 60 percent of the time during trivial disagreements
4. Express myself 80 percent of the time during trivial disagreements
5. Express myself in 25 percent of our major disagreements (child raising issues, major financial purchases, the future of our relationship)
6. Express myself in 35 percent of our major disagreements
7. Express myself in 45 percent of our major disagreements
8. Express myself in 55 percent of our major disagreements
9. Express myself in 65 percent of our major disagreements
10. Express myself in 75 percent of our major disagreements

11. Express myself in 80 percent of our major disagreements
12. Express my feelings about returning to my nursing career whenever I feel it's appropriate

---

At first Marge considered approaching her goal through a simple frequency method, in which she would gradually state her opinions or needs more and more often. However, this method failed to take advantage of the fact that her husband would probably be more receptive to assertive responses on some subjects than on others. By combining the situation and frequency strategies she developed the hierarchy shown below. In the same way you should be sure to consider all of the above methods before mapping out your intermediate steps. Be sure to use the most useful features of each in order to arrive at a series of stepping-stones that will give you the greatest chance of reaching your ultimate target.

A Few Words of Advice In a short time you will set intermediate steps for your self-modification project. *These goals are not sacred: Once you have established them, feel free to change any part of your project if events prove this to be necessary.*

If you have trouble moving from one step to another, you may want to decrease the interval between each one to make the transition easier. On the other hand, your progress may be so rapid that you can eliminate some of your subgoals and still progress easily.

You might want to rearrange the steps in a more workable order. Dave, for instance, discovered that it was relatively easy for him to get a conversation going by offering a sincere compliment, and so he placed this subgoal ahead of the more challenging one of following up free information.

Finally, you might even decide to redefine your ultimate target after beginning your project. Many readers who start out desiring to approach strangers more often discover later that such overtures of friendship often aren't worth the effort, and so they decide to approach a more limited number of people.

Now it is time to set up intermediate goals through which you will gradually move toward your target behavior. Review the various methods of establishing such goals and choose the one that is most appropriate for you. Space your goals closely enough to virtually guarantee your success in reaching each one: Start just slightly above your baseline rate, and remember that no step is too small. Enter the steps you choose on your Self-Modification Progress Chart in pencil now (you may decide to revise them later).

COMPLETE THIS STEP BEFORE GOING FURTHER

THE INTERVENTION PLAN:
REINFORCE DESIRED BEHAVIORS

The Need for Reinforcers As you read in Chapter 3, a behavior is likely to occur more often when it is reinforced. This principle explains why people behave assertively in the first place: they receive a payoff for doing so. Sometimes this payoff comes in social benefits—for instance, meeting new people or growing closer to old friends. At other times the rewards[2] are material, such as a higher salary based on better ability to manage employees or sell a product. In still other cases the rewards are strictly personal—the feeling of satisfaction that comes from expressing yourself well or standing up for your beliefs. In all these cases the point is the same: We already act assertively because desirable consequences follow such behaviors.

Why then don't you behave more assertively? By now your list of communication goals in Appendix II gives you a clear picture of how you want to act, and you can probably imagine the rewards that would come from such behavior.

One reason you might find it difficult to change is that you are being reinforced for behaving as you do now. Carla, for instance, claimed she wanted to share complaints she had with her boyfriend when they occurred instead of giving him the "silent treatment." Upon closer examination she learned that withholding her complaints and her affection did have several benefits: Her boyfriend treated her with much more consideration than usual, he often was willing to volunteer his shortcomings in order to have her warm up again, and she received the satisfaction of punishing him for failing to please her. When she looked at the consequences of her behavior, it became apparent that while on the whole her silences might have been undesirable, they did have reinforcing consequences.[3]

There is a second reason why change is sometimes difficult. Although your ultimate target might clearly be reinforcing, often the events you have to go through to reach it can be punishing. Recall what we said at the beginning of this chapter about Marge, who wanted to express her opinions and needs to her husband. While her ultimate goal of self-expression was cer-

---

[2] Although there are types of reinforcers that are not rewards (Watson and Tharp, 1972), our discussion here will not focus on them and thus will use the two terms interchangeably.

[3] A behavior doesn't have to be reinforced every time it occurs in order to be maintained. In fact, a behavior that is only intermittently rewarded will be harder to extinguish than one that does result in a payoff each time it occurs. To use a common example, gamblers will spend large amounts of time and money feeding coins into slot machines that rarely pay off.

tainly attractive, she correctly expected to meet a great deal of resistance from her husband along the way. Similarly, while your intermediate steps might not always be punishing, sometimes they call for a considerable amount of time and energy—counting behaviors, keeping graphs, and so on—that might not seem worth the effort.

The purpose of this project is to deal with problems like these; to make the transition from your baseline rate to your target reinforcing enough so that you will enthusiastically follow all the steps necessary for change. The method you will use is based on a simple idea: *Manage your environment to make sure that you are reinforced for each of your intermediate steps.* By reinforcing these successive approximations of your target you will deliberately make it worth your while to complete each step, heading toward the time when your new behavior will be reinforcing enough to maintain itself without any attention from you. This part of Chapter 6 will show you how to select and manage reinforcers to keep you moving toward this goal.

Types of Reinforcers What things can you use to reinforce your progress? To make the best choice, it is helpful to organize reinforcers into four categories: tangible, social, activity, and intrinsic.

1. Tangible. These are material items. Food, for example, is a powerful reward for many people. You undoubtedly have certain special treats that would be excellent rewards for engaging in a target behavior. Another category of tangible reinforcers are items that improve your personal appearance—new clothes, hair styling, and so on. Articles that you can use in pleasurable activities can also be reinforcing: The prospect of new books, records, sheet music, sports equipment, and so on will most likely encourage you to increase a desired activity. You probably can think of other tangible items that are reinforcing for you. The Reinforcement Checklist on pages 135–144 will help you consider the possibilities.

2. Social. As the name implies, social reinforcers consist of the ways other people act that you find desirable. Approval, physical affection, conversation, and smiles are all examples of social reinforcement. It is social reinforcers that will most often provide the major payoff for learning new communication skills, and once you are expressing yourself more assertively, they will probably come automatically from people not involved in your project. For now, however, enlist the cooperation of others to reinforce your desirable behaviors. In most cases people will be happy to help you improve your communication skills—praising you, doing favors, and so on—especially since your improvement will often help them as well. Carla's boyfriend was happy to give her a backrub each time she shared a problem she was experiencing in their relationship. Not only did this reward encourage Carla to speak her mind, but the pleasant prospect of finishing the discussion with the backrub tended to make their talks last a shorter time and end more happily.

3. **Activity.** While some desirable activities overlap with items in the social category, you can often think of new reinforcers by reviewing the things you like to do. Attendance at such events as concerts, movies, plays, and so on is often effective. Participating in sports or musical activities can be useful. Indulging yourself by reading a book, watching television, or doing a crossword puzzle is also pleasant. Simply pay attention to the kind of activities you daydream about, and you will probably soon have a long list of reinforcers.

A list of enjoyable activities can offer a variety of low-cost reinforcers, a fact appreciated by many who can't afford tangible rewards. Taking walks, for instance, costs nothing but can be very rewarding. The same holds true for working in the garden, taking naps, sunbathing, or jogging. Many busy people find an extremely attractive reinforcer to be half an hour of free time that can be wasted with no guilty feelings.

Even when no low-cost rewards seem to be available, you can still find reinforcers by using the Premack principle, named after the researcher who first described it. The idea here is to earn a behavior you previously took for granted by making it contingent on practicing your target. Alex, for example, allowed himself to read the newspaper with his breakfast only if he greeted his wife with a pleasant "good morning." Kristin earned the right to enjoy her evening jogging session only after asking her daily quota of questions in class.

4. **Intrinsic.** These reinforcers are the feelings of satisfaction, pride, accomplishment, or relief that you gain by communicating more effectively. It is possible to give yourself intrinsic reinforcers by making a point of recognizing your accomplishments. While intrinsic reinforcers can be powerful influences in maintaining a behavior, they are generally more difficult to give yourself as part of a self-modification program. You probably would be wise to choose a reinforcer from one of the other three categories and trust that the intrinsic feelings of accomplishment will almost surely follow and add to the effectiveness of your program.

Criteria for Choosing Your Reinforcer There are several guidelines you can follow to make sure that the reinforcers you pick will be most effective in moving you toward your assertive goal.

First, any reinforcer you choose should be important to you. In other words, you should want to engage in your target behavior in order to earn the reinforcer. Since a consequence that might be reinforcing for another person might be totally unattractive to you, be sure to only pick items with personal appeal.

Next, the reinforcer you choose to strengthen your desired behavior should be more powerful than any benefits that come from acting in your old, unsatisfying ways. Carla, for instance, first decided to reward her straightforwardness toward her boyfriend with a new record album, but found that the enjoyment of making him squirm with her silence was far sweeter than any music. Upon realizing this fact, she began searching for a new reward that she valued more than the sight of her boyfriend's discomfort.

The third guideline is that your reinforcer should not be so important that you would suffer greatly by failing to earn it. Dottie, for instance, originally decided to earn her lunch by calmly responding to her children's frequent whining in the morning. This strategy had two shortcomings: First, if the children failed to whine, Dottie went hungry. Second, when Dottie failed to respond calmly, she found it impossible to function effectively in her afternoon job as a teacher's aide if she skipped lunch. If the consequences of failing to earn a reward are too unpleasant, the prospect of carrying out your project will be so punishing that you might drop it entirely. In other words, seek the happy medium of a reinforcer that is important enough to work toward but dispensable enough to live without.

Fourth, your reinforcer should not be one that will lose its effectiveness through use. Actually, there is no reason for having only one reinforcer on your project. One way to keep from becoming tired of a reinforcer is to create a list of rewards that offer plenty of variety. One student who wanted to ensure his participation in class developed a list of reinforcers from which to choose—buy a new science fiction novel, treat himself to an afternoon nap, or enjoy a game of pool with his friends.

Fifth, your reinforcer should be accessible. While it might be desirable to reward each act of assertiveness with a 50-dollar bill or a week's vacation from work, such consequences are beyond most peoples' resources. This limitation might first seem to eliminate a large number of tangible and activity reinforcers that you could not expect to give yourself each time you practice a target behavior. Fortunately, however, a system of *token* reinforcers makes more significant items accessible. The idea is to earn a certain number of tokens or points each time you perform a desired behavior. You can then trade in a predetermined number of these points for the eventual reinforcer. Will's greatest wish was to take a skiing trip to a distant resort during his winter vacation. He knew that the only way he would be able to manage such a trip was to begin putting money aside several months in advance. Since he found saving difficult, he decided to combine a thrift program with his communication goal of smiling more at customers where he worked. Each smile earned him 25 cents, and within eight weeks he not only had earned enough for the trip, but also had money to buy a new set of ski poles.

To add a bit of variety to your project it is possible to set up a redemption schedule for the points you earn for each desired behavior. Nellie, a teacher, earned points for complimenting the good work of her students. She set up a schedule for cashing in her token points as follows:

1 point = 30 minutes of sunbathing or swimming
5 points = lunch at a favorite restaurant

> 10 points = new swim suit for summer
> 20 points = withdraw money from savings account and buy telephoto lens for camera

A final guideline for choosing effective reinforcers: They should be available as soon after the desired behavior as possible. Research suggests that the power of a reinforcer decreases as it is separated from the event itself. This explains why I find working on this book so difficult in spite of the fact that I hope it will some day pay a financial dividend. The gap between the time these words are written and my first royalty check will probably be upwards of two years. Some reinforcers are easy to give yourself immediately—cigarettes, candy, and so on—but it isn't always practical to follow a desired behavior with a meal, nap, or sexual intercourse.

One way to ensure rapid reinforcement is to take advantage of the point or token system just described. The idea of having immediately earned a point that is eventually redeemable usually is effective. (After all, the redeemable tokens we call "dollars" are quite powerful, although we do not always trade them in right away.) A second way to reinforce quickly is to reward your behavior immediately with a small but pleasant consequence, while reinforcing the attainment of a week's intermediate goal with a more substantial treat. The teacher mentioned earlier who wanted to reduce his "uhs" during lectures shared this goal with his students, who acknowledged his success at the end of each class. At the end of a week in which his total number of "uhs" was low enough to meet or surpass his intermediate goal, he reinforced himself with a steak dinner.

▶ ## REINFORCEMENT CHECKLIST

There are many ways you can reinforce yourself for practicing a new communication behavior. The list obviously isn't complete: But by suggesting a large number of common reinforcers it will cause you to think of other items that are especially pleasant for you. Use the list as follows:

1. As you move through each category, check any item that might serve as a reinforcer for you. In the space provided fill in any specific details that describe your potential reinforcer more fully. For instance, under the category of "visiting friends" you might list one or two special names; under "reading" you could describe a particular book or a type of reading you enjoy.
2. When you think of a possible reinforcer that is not included on this list, immediately describe it in one of the spaces provided at the end of each section.

When you have finished this page, you should have a catalog of possible reinforcers you can use for your self-modification project.

A. Material Reinforcers
    1. Foods

   a. Snacks _____

   b. Favorite meals or dishes _____

   c. Beverages _____

   d. Dining out _____

   e. _____

   f. _____

2. Clothing

   a. _____

   b. _____

   c. _____

   d. _____

3. Hobby Items

   a. Sports equpment _____

   b. Puzzles _____

   c. Photographic equipment _____

   d. Tools _____

   e. Camping gear _____

   f. Musical (instruments, music, etc.) _____

   g. _____

   h. _____

4. Personal Appearance

   a. Hair styling _____

   b. Cosmetics _____

   c. Jewelry _____

   d. _____

   e. _____

5. Home Decoration and Improvement

   a. Furniture _____

   b. Photographs of paintings _____

   c. Plants and flowers _____

    d. Appliances _____

    e. Music equipment (speaker, records, etc.) _____

    f. _____

    g. _____

6. Books and Magazines

    a. Fiction _____

    b. Current events _____

    c. Art _____

    d. Humor _____

    e. School _____

    f. _____

    g. _____

7. Transportation (car, bicycle, motorcycle, etc.)

    a. Repairs _____

    b. Accessories _____

    c. _____

    d. _____

8. Savings (set aside a specified amount for each assertive act or goal reached)

    a. For specific object _____

    b. For general savings _____

9. Other Material Reinforcers

    a. _____

    b. _____

    c. _____

    d. _____

    e. _____

    f. _____

    g. _____

B. Social Reinforcers

  10. Receiving Compliments from Others

a. _____

b. _____

c. _____

d. _____

11. Receiving Affection

    a. _____

    b. _____

    c. _____

    d. _____

12. Hearing Jokes

    a. _____

    b. _____

13. Visiting with Friends

    a. _____

    b. _____

    c. _____

    d. _____

14. Visiting with Relatives

    a. _____

    b. _____

    c. _____

    d. _____

15. Talking on the Telephone

    a. _____

    b. _____

    c. _____

16. Meeting New People

    a. _____

    b. _____

    c. _____

17. Receiving Surprise Gifts

    a. _____

    b. _____

    c. _____

18. Saying "I told you so"

    a. _____

    b. _____

    c. _____

19. Giving Parties

    a. _____

    b. _____

20. Attending Parties

    a. _____

    b. _____

21. Going on Dates

    a. _____

    b. _____

    c. _____

22. Flirting

    a. _____

    b. _____

    c. _____

23. Sex

    a. _____

    b. _____

    c. _____

    d. _____

24. Other Social Reinforcers

    a. _____

    b. _____

    c. _____

    d. _____

    e. _____

    f. _____

    g. _____

C. Activity Reinforcers

25. Traveling

    a. Driving _____

    b. Vacationing _____

    c. Visiting new place near your home _____

    d. Sightseeing _____

    e. _____

    f. _____

    g. _____

26. Exercise

    a. Cycling _____

    b. Tennis _____

    c. Golf _____

    d. Swimming _____

    e. Football _____

    f. Baseball _____

    g. Basketball _____

    h. Bowling _____

    i. Skiing _____

    j. Running _____

    k. Hiking or taking walks _____

    l. Horseback riding _____

    m. _____

    n. _____

    o. _____

p. _____

q. _____

27. Television or Radio

    a. _____

    b. _____

    c. _____

28. Reading

    a. Fiction _____

    b. Current events _____

    c. History _____

    d. Humor _____

    e. School _____

    f. Biography _____

    g. _____

    h. _____

    i. _____

29. Going to Movies, Plays or Concerts

    a. _____

    b. _____

    c. _____

30. Looking at Attractive Men or Women

    a. _____

    b. _____

    c. _____

31. Hobbies

    a. Sewing _____

    b. Crafts _____

    c. Collecting _____

    d. Art _____

    e. Puzzles _____

f. _____

g. _____

h. _____

32. Dancing

    a. _____

    b. _____

    c. _____

33. Picnicking and Camping

    a. _____

    b. _____

    c. _____

34. Gardening

    a. _____

    b. _____

    c. _____

35. Playing Cards or Gambling

    a. _____

    b. _____

36. Listening to Music

    a. Live _____

    b. Recorded, at home _____

    c. In the car _____

    d. _____

37. Cooking

    a. Your own favorite foods _____

    b. For others _____

    c. _____

    d. _____

38. Smoking

    a. _____

b. _____

39. Free time

    a. Time to "waste" without guilt _____

    b. _____

    c. _____

40. Bathing

    a. Bubble bath _____

    b. Showering _____

    c. Sauna _____

41. Sleeping

    a. Oversleep in morning _____

    b. Naps _____

    c. _____

    d. _____

42. Other Activity Reinforcers

    a. _____

    b. _____

    c. _____

    d. _____

    e. _____

    f. _____

    g. _____

3. List the reinforcers here that have met the above criteria and that you are satisfied would be most effective in your self-modification project.

_____

_____

_____

_____

_____

_____

_____

4. Now transfer some or all of these items to your Self-Modification Progress Chart. Indicate which ones you will use to reinforce single instances of desired behaviors and which you will earn for reaching intermediate goals. For examples, see the sample Progress Charts in Appendix IV.

COMPLETE THIS ACTIVITY BEFORE READING ON.

Once you have completed all the steps in this chapter, you are ready to begin the intervention period of your self-modification project: This is the time you actually start moving steadily closer to reaching your target behavior. As you do so, remember to follow the essential steps as described so far:

—Faithfully and accurately record every incidence of your target behavior *as it occurs*, and transfer your records to the Self-Modification Progress Chart each day. Don't trust your memory, and don't "wait until tomorrow" to graph the results of your efforts.

—Reinforce yourself for each instance of the target behavior as *soon as possible* after it occurs. While you might find yourself improving because of the favorable reactions your assertiveness produces in others or from the intrinsic feelings of personal growth, don't depend on these forces to change you. Deliberate and faithful self-reinforcement will give you the necessary added incentive for change during the time it takes to establish new communication habits. Make sure your reinforcers for behaving in new ways are greater than the benefits that come from your present style of self-expression.

—Keep the space between intermediate steps small. Remember that steady, lasting progress is better than dramatic but failing attempts at change. If you note that your progress is leveling off, reduce the distance between intermediate goals so that you can be sure of reaching them. Don't go on to a new intermediate goal until you have reached the one you are currently working on.

Continue now on your self-modification project until you reach your ultimate goal. If at any time you encounter difficulty, immediately review the information in this chapter and remedy the problem immediately.

PUNISHMENT AND SELF-MODIFICATION

So far there has been no mention of punishment in all the chapters devoted to helping you communicate more assertively. There are at least two reasons why punishment is not a desirable tool for change.

First, while punishment can discourage an undesirable behavior, by itself it does not teach preferable alternatives. Remember from Chapter 3 that in the face of punishment a person will engage in escape or avoidance behaviors—actions that result in elimination of the unpleasant situation. Such escape or avoidance behaviors don't necessarily teach more desirable alternatives. For example, punishing yourself severely for expressing anger in an overly aggressive manner is likely to reduce such outbursts, and in their place you *might* even express yourself more assertively. On the other hand, you could also escape the unpleasant consequences of your aggression by engaging in other, equally undesirable behaviors—sulking, being sarcastic, or avoiding people altogether. Clearly in these cases the punishment would not have produced the desired results.

What about punishing these new, undesirable behaviors so that eventually you would act in the only way that didn't result in punishing consequences? This strategy might eventually work, but it is certainly less efficient and more time-consuming that simply rewarding the originally desired outcome.

Another reason for steering clear of punishment is a common-sense one: A punishment strong enough to discourage you from communicating in an ingrained, habitual behavior might also be strong enough to discourage you from carrying out your plan at all. A project that frequently results in self-denial, discomfort, or embarrassment might lead you to ask the question, "If this is self-improvement, who needs it?" Why not reward yourself for communicating better, thus making the prospect of continuing your project one you'll anticipate with pleasure.

DOUBTS ABOUT SELF-MODIFICATION

After learning the methods in this chapter, some readers object to one or more points. They do not doubt the effectiveness of self-modification techniques, but they have reservations about the philosophy behind such methods. Because such questions occur from time to time, they need to be answered.

Q. *Isn't self-modification manipulative?*

A. Self-modification definitely operates by controlling the environment, but because you only work on improving your *own* communication and not on changing others, there is no question of deception or controlling people without their knowledge or against their will. The very deliberation with which you set goals in your project ensures that you are going into the process with your eyes wide open, fully aware of the likely results. If manipulation means deception, there is none here.

Q. *Why go through all these involved steps? Someone who truly wanted to change could probably do so without all this fuss.*

A. Some people behave in unsatisfying ways because their environment supports such actions; others do it simply out of habit. Sometimes just recognizing a more desirable alternative is enough to bring about change, but in other cases you need a boost to get into a new routine. The methods in this chapter provide this boost by ensuring that your early efforts at changing meet with success. It would be foolish to say that self-modification is the *only* way to change; on the other hand, if the method works in some cases where simply wanting to communicate better isn't enough, why not use it?

Q. *Isn't there a danger of becoming dependent on the reinforcers I give myself? I'd hate to go through life having to reward every act of assertive communication.*

A. There's little danger that you'll need to use deliberate self-modification after reaching your target, for as you become a more effective communicator, the intrinsic reinforcement that comes from your increased self-respect and confidence will take over. These feelings, accompanied by the social benefits that come from behaving more assertively, will give you plenty of incentive for maintaining the assertive behavior.

Q. *The whole process of self modification seems so mechanical. There's no mention of* FEELING *more assertive, only* ACTING *that way. Without a change in your attitude, any new behaviors are only a mask.*

A. What often begins as a self-conscious charade of assertiveness later turns into the real thing. As author Sharon A. Bower puts it, "It's often easier to act yourself into new ways of feeling than to feel yourself into new ways of acting."

Think of the first time you learned a new physical skill, such as riding a bicycle or skiing. Your first few attempts probably felt totally unnatural, yet if you persisted, the skill later became spontaneous and second nature to you. In the same way the feelings of awkwardness that sometimes accompany the initial attempts at assertiveness soon go away, leaving you feeling genuinely confident and skillful. Don't be bothered by feeling stiff at first. Be persistent and patient, and you will soon know what it feels like to express yourself effectively.

SUMMARY

This chapter has introduced you to a systematic method to teach yourself new communication skills. While it will be effective in helping you to reach most communication goals, it is most appropriately used (a) when there is little likelihood of your being reinforced for your initial attempts at self-improvement, or (b) when a skill is too complex to learn by simple observation of models, behavior rehearsal, coaching, or desensitization.

The self-modification method consists of four basic steps: First, define a behavioral goal. Second, measure a baseline rate, consisting of the frequency with which you practice the target behavior before attempting to change. This will require you to develop a system of counting and recording behaviors that is portable, unobtrusive, and easy to use. Third, divide the distance between your baseline rate and your target into intermediate steps that are modest enough to virtually guarantee you success. Fourth, devise a system of rewards to reinforce each successive approximation of your goal. These reinforcers are preferable to punishment as a device for changing behavior, as they can teach you a new skill instead of merely decreasing your old, undesired actions.

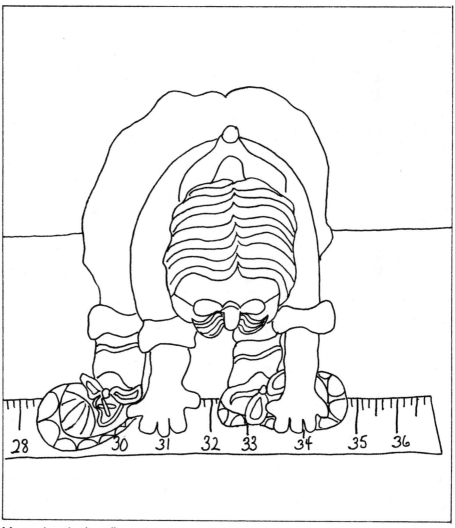

Measuring the baseline rate.

Part Three

SPECIFIC APPLICATIONS

The next three chapters focus on some of the most common assertive problems—establishing relationships and carrying on a conversation, expressing feelings, coping with criticism, managing conflicts, making requests, and when appropriate saying no to the requests of others.

Combining the specific advice from Part Three with the methods for changing behavior from Part Two gives you a good chance to improve your communication skills. The only other ingredients necessary to ensure progress are your energy and diligence.

7

Establishing Relationships through Conversation Skills

The goal stated most often in assertiveness-building groups I've led is the desire to become a better conversationalist. Men and women seem to be equally anxious to learn this skill. Age makes no difference. Physical attractiveness, education, and income also don't seem to matter. It appears that almost everyone would like to be a better conversationalist. This desire makes sense, for nearly all of the initial contacts we make, and most of the subsequent ones as well, come about through language. Since this is true, it's easy to see why the ability to start and carry on a conversation is an essential ingredient in building and maintaining comfortable, rewarding relationships.

One word of caution: While the information here will almost certainly be helpful, you ought to realize that it won't transform you into a faultless conversationalist in every situation you encounter. Even the most confident and skilled speaker isn't always successful. There can be several reasons why a particular encounter doesn't go smoothly. Sometimes you simply don't have much in common with the other people and thereby have no interest in getting to know them. In different circumstances you might find that a person doesn't want to talk with you, perhaps because of preoccupation with some other concern or just a disinclination to be social. And finally there will be times when you simply could have handled the situation better. Don't let instances like these bother you too much. Remember that the skills here will increase your *overall* rate of effectiveness in conversations; they won't guarantee you perfection in every instance. Total success isn't realistic or necessary in communication any more than it is in other endeavors. A baseball player can become an all-star by batting .330—hitting successfully only a third of the time—and a successful financier can become wealthy by investing in more moneymaking ventures than losing ones. These people don't expect or need to be perfect, and neither should you.

LEVELS OF COMMUNICATION

The term "conversation" actually covers several very different types of interaction. Failing to recognize these levels can lead to a kind of conversational crossing of wires, in which two partners appear to be discussing the same subject yet are obviously not on the same wavelength. Because the ability to distinguish between these types is critical to much of what follows, it is important to consider them here.

Picture a series of four concentric circles surrounding a core. Imagine that this core represents the essential you—your beliefs, moods, strengths, weaknesses, likes, and dislikes—every important fact and trait that makes you who you are, all rolled into one. If it were possible to share yourself to the fullest all at once, the result would be that the other person would know everything contained in that core. Since in most cases this kind of intense, immediate sharing only comes with the passage of time and growth of trust, the way we come to let others know about us is by offering information from the various levels that surround our core. Let's take a look at each of these levels and turn and see what they contain.

Clichés The layer farthest from the core consists of clichés: "How are you doing?" "Fine!" . . . 'We'll have to get together some time."

Remarks such as these usually aren't meant to be taken literally; in fact, the other person would be surprised if you responded to a casual "How are you?" with a lengthy speech on your health, state of mind, love life, and finances. Yet it's a mistake to consider clichés as meaningless, for they serve several useful functions. For instance, they can give two speakers time to size each other up and decide whether it's desirable to carry their conversation any further. Our first impressions are generally based more on the nonverbal characteristics of the other person than the words we hear spoken. Things like eye contact, vocal tone, facial expression, posture, and so on can often tell us more about another person than can the initial sentences in a conversation. Given the value of these nonverbal cues and the awkwardness of actually saying, "I want to take a few minutes to look you over before I commit myself to getting acquainted," the exchange of a few stock phrases can be just the thing to get you through this initial period comfortably.

Clichés can also serve as codes for other messages we don't usually express directly, such as "I want to acknowledge your presence" (for instance, when two acquaintances walk past each other.) Additional unstated messages often contained in clichés are "I'm interested in talking if you feel like it," or "Let's keep the conversation light and impersonal; I don't feel like sharing much about myself right now." Accompanied by a different set of nonverbal cues, a cliché can say, "I don't want to be impolite, but you'd better stay away from me for now. In all these cases clichés serve as a valuable kind of shorthand that makes it easy to keep the social wheels greased and indicates the potential for further, possibly more profound conversation.

You already know that in the first few minutes of a conversation the subject isn't as important as the opportunity to size each other up. Because this is true, you needn't be bothered by the thought of discussing a trivial topic for a few minutes. In fact, such a skill can be a useful one, for it allows you to avoid the pressure of having to say something profound or personal during a period of time when your actions are more important than words.

Either independently or in an assertiveness-building group you can learn to become more comfortable during the opening stages of a conversation by trying the following exercise. You'll need to join with two other people to accomplish it.

1. Choose one member of the trio to be the speaker; the other two participants take the role of listeners.
2. The speaker chooses a subject from a stack of inane topics written on cards.
3. The speaker then talks for a period of one to three minutes on this subject (depending on the level of anxiety present).
4. After all three participants have taken the role as speaker, they offer each other feedback on the nonverbal effect of their behavior. (A useful method to use in this step is simply to look over the checklist of nonverbal and vocal elements of assertion on pages 53–54). As with any type of behavior rehearsal, it's important to focus on the positive aspects of each person's behavior before going on to suggest areas for potential improvement.

This exercise can be enjoyable and at the same time give you a great deal of confidence during the first few minutes of conversation.

Facts   Moving inward from clichés to the next circle on the communication model brings us to the level of exchanging *facts*, such as:

—"You probably can get your car fixed at a garage in town. It looks like you need a rebuilt generator."
—"I'm a professor at a small college in California."
—"If you go camping in the mountains this weekend, you'll probably get rain."

While they may at first seem impersonal, facts can tell you a great deal about the other person, and in so doing form the basis for a future conversation. For instance, consider the three preceding pieces of information:

—You've learned that the speaker is familiar with the town and knows at least a little about how cars work. If you're interested in either of these subjects, you've found a starting point for a conversation.
—The speaker is involved in higher education. Are you? Would you like to share more about colleges or find out what subject the person teaches or learn something about California? Here's your chance.
—How does the speaker know that it might rain in the mountains? Perhaps the information came from a weather forecast, which doesn't give you much to talk about. On the other hand, your partner here might be familiar with the area you've headed for, in which case you have something in common.

Facts can be interesting in themselves, and they can be a good clue as to whether a relationship with your conversational partner is worth pursuing.

Opinions   Still closer to the core of a speaker's personality is the level of *opinions*.

—"I used to be a political volunteer for some cause in every election, but I think politics is so corrupt now that I don't even bother to vote."
—"If you like Mexican food, you've got to try Lupita's. It's great!"
—"I think Jack is a phony."

It's clear that opinions like these tell you a great deal about the other person—much more than do facts and clichés. If you know where the speaker stands on a subject, you can get a clearer picture of whether your conversation has any potential. In the same way every time you offer a personal opinion you're giving people valuable information about yourself, as well as providing some material that they can respond to in order to keep the conversation flowing.

Feelings   The fourth level of communication—and the one that's closest to one's personal core—is the realm of *feelings*. At first glance feelings might appear to be the same as opinions, but there is a big difference. As we saw above, "I think Jack is a phony" is an opinion. Now notice how much more we learn about the speaker by looking at three different feelings upon which this judgment could be based:

—"I think Jack is a phony and *I'm sad that he won't act naturally around me.*"
—"I think Jack is a phony and *I get angry when he doesn't say what's on his mind.*"
—"I think Jack is a phony and *I'm uncomfortable when I see him put on a front when everybody knows what he's doing.*"

Once you can recognize the difference between these four levels of communication, it's easy to see several reasons why it's hard to keep a conversation going. Sometimes the speakers might remain exclusively on the level of facts. This might be suitable for a business relationship but wouldn't be very likely in most other circumstances. Even worse, other communicators never get off the level of clichés. And just as a diet of rich foods can become unappealing if carried to excess, the overuse of feelings and opinions can also become disagreeable. In most cases the successful conversation is one in which the participants move from one level to another as the circumstances call for.

Another common problem occurs when two communicators want to relate to each other on different levels. If one is willing to deal only with facts and perhaps an occasional opinion, while the other insists on revealing personal feelings, the results are likely to be uncomfortable for both. Consider the following meeting between Jack and Roger at a party.

J: Hi. My name's Jack. I don't think we've met before. (*cliché*)
R: I'm Roger. Nice to meet you. (*cliché*)
J: Do you know anybody here? I've just moved in next door and don't know a soul except for the host. What's his name . . . Lou? (*fact*)
R: Lou's right. Well, I'm here with my wife—that's her over there—and we know a few other people. (*fact; Both speakers are comfortable so far.*)
J: Well, I used to have a wife, but she split. She really did me in. (*fact and opinion*)
R: Oh? (*cliché*) (He doesn't know how to reply to this comment)
J: Yeah. Everything was going along great—I thought. Then one day she told me she was in love with her gynecologist and that she wanted a divorce. I still haven't gotten over it. (*feeling and fact*)
R: Well, uh, that's too bad. (*cliché; Roger is now very uncomfortable.*)
J: I don't think I'll ever trust another woman. I'm still in love with my wife, and it's killing me. She really broke my heart. (*feeling and fact*)
R: I'm sorry. Listen, I've got to go. (*cliché*)

Clearly Jack moved to the level of sharing feelings long before Roger was prepared to accept this kind of communication. While this kind of discussion might have helped a friendship if it had come at a later time, Jack only succeeded in driving Roger away by coming on too fast. Remember the hazards of moving too quickly to a level your partner is likely to find uncomfortable.

▶ Test your ability to distinguish between the various levels of communication about which you've just read. In the spaces following the example list three genuine personal responses for each category.

SAMPLE TOPIC: The author and his writing.
   a. Facts
      1. This is the second book I've written.
      2. The first one was a text on interpersonal communication.
      3. Thanks to my efforts I was able to take a trip to Canada this past summer. I may even have enough money left over to repair my leaky roof before the rains come.
   b. Opinions
      1. I think it's been worth the effort to write the books.
      2. I think I've become a better instructor as a result of the research involved in my writing.
      3. I'm not very efficient when it comes to dividing my time between writing and fooling around.
   c. Feelings
      1. I'm flattered and proud that a first-rate company thought enough of my work to publish it.
      2. I'm getting nervous about whether I'll finish this manuscript before the publisher's deadline.
      3. Right now I'm tired of writing and think I'll spend the rest of this sunny day at the beach.

1. TOPIC: Assertiveness training
   a. Facts

      1. _____

         _____

         _____

      2. _____

         _____

         _____

      3. _____

         _____

         _____

   b. Opinions

      1. _____

2. _____

3. _____

c. Feelings

   1. _____

   2. _____

   3. _____

2. TOPIC: The next five years of your life

   a. Facts

     1. _____

     2. _____

     3. _____

   b. Opinions

     1. _____

    2. _____

    3. _____

 c. Feelings

    1. _____

    2. _____

    3. _____

3. TOPIC: The present state of this country's government
  a. Facts

    1. _____

    2. _____

    3. _____

  b. Opinions

    1. _____

2. _____

3. _____

c. Feelings

  1. _____

  2. _____

  3. _____

CONVERSATION SKILLS

Now that you're able to distinguish between the four levels of communication, it's time to see how you can use a variety of specific techniques to fit each one into your conversations. As you read on, don't get the idea that this list means there is a single style of communication that everyone ought to follow. Nothing could be further from the truth: The most effective style of relating for you has to be one that uniquely fits your own behavior won't be exactly like anyone else's—in fact, it will vary from one conversation to another depending on who you're with, what's going on, and how you're feeling. As you look over the suggestions this chapter contains, realize that they can provide the *raw material* from which you can build your own personal conversation style. Just as several builders can create totally different and beautiful homes using identical bricks, concrete, wood, and glass, you'll be able to use the ideas that follow to develop a way of approaching others that is consistent with your own personality.

Another thought: It's likely that you'll feel awkward as you practice the skills that follow. This doesn't mean that there's anything wrong with them or with you. If you have ever learned to ice skate or ride a bicycle, you'll remember that practice and perseverance changed your clumsy early attempts into a natural and more graceful style. You can expect the same thing to hold of your conversational ability. Don't expect perfection overnight.

Remember the principles of shaping from Chapters 4 and 6: Don't make unrealistic demands on yourself. It's probably wise to pick just one of the following skills to start with. If you decide to begin by practicing open-ended questions, try to use just one per day or one in a conversation. Remember that even a single step like this is an improvement over your old way of communicating. Then, as you gradually become more comfortable with the skill, you'll find yourself using it more often, until it becomes a part of your natural style.

Finally, to put this chapter into perspective, let us remember that conversation—all communication, in fact—is as much an art as a science. To continue with the earlier example, it's certainly possible for almost anybody to become a competent ice skater with practice and instruction, but few people could ever become Olympic contenders. The question isn't whether you're a perfect conversationalist (whatever that may be), but whether you're as comfortable and skillful as your potential allows.

Conversation Starters   One way to look at a conversation—or a relationship, for that matter—is as a search for common interests. This doesn't mean that you only want to meet people who agree with you, for this would become boring. But in order for a conversation to work, the participants have to be interested in at least discussing the same topics.

Some of the following suggestions for starting conversations are clearly stratagems—that is, even though they have some other ostensible purpose, their real aim is to strike up a conversation. Is this manipulative? Maybe so. Is it in any way harmful? I doubt it. Many conversations never get started and others suffer early deaths because neither partner knows how to keep them going. Any device that can help you over the initial discomfort that often comes with getting acquainted can't be harmful. Since all of the following approaches are pretty well known, people will usually recognize them for what they are. If the other person responds to your overture, it's a signal to go on; if not, they'll probably make this clear.

Basic Data.   Since you have to start this search for mutually interesting topics somewhere, exchanging what Zunin calls "name, rank and serial number" is often a good idea. What's your name? Where do you work? Where are you from? Questions such as these may be basic, but the facts they convey make up much of the reality of our lives. And in addition to being informative, this exchange of information can often lead to a number of common interests that you can pursue.

A: Hi! My name is Alyx.
B: Hello. I'm Brian.
A: Is this your first semester at the college?
B: Yes it is. How about you?
A: Me too. Do you come from around here?
B: No. I'm from a small town in Oregon named Lorane.
A: I've been there! I know a family who has a farm outside of town, off Gowdyville Road. Maybe you know them . . .

Small Talk.   Like the practice of sharing basic facts, small talk can also serve as a springboard to sharing common interests. Remember that these common phrases are simply a sociable way of saying, "I'm interested in talking. Let's see if we hit it off." Consider the following example.

R: Hot enough for you?
L: I like it. It reminds me of home—I'm from the desert.
R: Where?
L: Near Borrego Springs. I really miss it.
R: Really? I always thought of the desert as being kind of nowhere. What do you like about it? By the way, my name's Rob.
L: I'm Lee. Well, for one thing, the desert is really peaceful . . .

Compliments.   No matter what we say, most of us appreciate nothing more than a compliment. I'm not talking about insincere flattery, which usually has the effect of discouraging further conversation. When the opportunity seems right, expressing your genuine admiration or appreciation can be a good way to start a conversation.

—"That's a beautiful ring. Did you have it specially made?"
—"I hope this won't embarrass you, but you really have a nice voice. Do you sing very much?"
—"You really take good care of your car. Some day I want to have a new BMW."

Although compliments like these might come as a surprise, the recipient usually will appreciate them. Sometimes people are unsure about how to respond in such circumstances, however (see Chapter 8 for some suggestions), so it's a good idea to follow your original remark with a question or other comment that allows a graceful reply.

Requests and Offers of Assistance.   While some situations in which you need assistance are obviously a nuisance, at other times they can prove to be socially advantageous. Your request for help can be an easy way to start a conversation.

—"Excuse me. I'm lost. Can you help me find the library?"
—"I wonder if you could help me. I want to barbecue some steaks, but I don't know which cut would be best."
—"I notice that we have the same brand of bike. I can't seem to get mine to shift gears very well. Could you help me?"

In the same way an offer of help can provide a good conversational lead-in.

—"Can I give you a hand unloading that car?"
—"You look confused. Can I help you find something?"
—"That wheel looks stuck. Want me to see if I can get it loose?"

Don't think that these devices are so overworn that you'll put the other person off by using them. Remember that in the first few minutes of a conversation the nonverbal messages you send are usually more important than your words. (For a review of these elements see pages 53–54). If you're genuinely friendly and interested in learning more about the other person, these feelings will be apparent no matter what you say. When a natural subject of conversation isn't at hand, it's probably wiser to use a standard approach than to try and be especially witty or creative and risk looking awkward. Remember, the main goal in the first few minutes of a conversation is to establish contact: If you can accomplish this, you'll have plenty of time to get better acquainted.

Utilizing Free Information Sometimes an initial exchange of facts or a few clichés leads naturally into a satisfying conversation. In other cases, however, things don't progress so smoothly. Here's a familiar scene: You've just met another person. You've introduced yourselves to each other and told where you live, what you do for a living, and where you're from. You've commented on the weather. Then comes an awkward silence. After a few moments of averted glances and shifting about, either you or your partner can't stand the tension any more. One of you blurts out "Nice talking to you" or "I've got to get going," and the conversation is over before it really ever started.

It usually isn't necessary to feel at a loss for words in these situations. Most people will give you plenty of opportunities to develop a conversation by offering free *information*—data that goes beyond what you've requested or commented on. Your skill in using free information is an important part of the conversational process. Whether consciously or not, people share whatever partd of themselves they are willing to discuss. In this sense free information is often a sort of invitation to talk about whatever the person who offers it feels is appropriate.

Most conversations contain more free information than you could possibly use. For instance, look at this scene. Two strangers, Ward and Bert, are seated next to each other on an airplane flight:

W: Excuse me, do you have the time?
B: Sure. Let me see . . . My gosh, it's already one-thirty.
B: Looks like the flight will be late today. It's usually on time. (*free information— Bert must be familiar with the performance of this flight.*)
W: (*picking up on this*) Do you take this trip often?
B: At least a couple of times a month. I work for the airline, and so it's part of my job to

move around a lot. Right now, though, I'm headed up this way to see my daughter. *(Two pieces of free information here: Bert works for the airline and he has a daughter.)*

W: What do you do for the airline?

B: I'm the regional sales manager for New England, New York, and New Jersey. *(Free information about the extent of his job.)*

W: Gee, that sounds interesting. What does a job like that involve? . . .

Notice how easy it was for Ward to keep the conversation going. All he needed to do was follow up the leads offered by Bert, who seemed willing to talk about his job. Even if Ward hadn't been interested in the airline business, he could have followed up the free information Bert offered about his daughter. Where did she live. What was she doing there? What did Bert think about the way kids behave these days? Another possibility would have been to ask Bert for more information about the various states where he worked—living conditions, climate, job opportunities, and so on. In other words, the free information you choose to pursue will depend on your own interests. If you're genuinely interested in getting to know the other person, there's likely to be some data offered that you'd like to know more about.

Free information includes nonverbal clues as well as the words another person speaks. Articles of clothing, physical features, smiles, frowns, and so on often can form the basis for a conversation, as they did for Lynne and Maria:

L: I couldn't help noticing how well your dog behaves. Have you trained her a lot?

M: Thanks. When she was a pup I took her to obedience school for a few weeks, but actually most of her manners came from my brother's training. He's a graduate student in psychology. *(Free information about obedience school and her brother)*

L: What did he do—psychoanalyze the dog?

B: No, nothing that dramatic. He's doing his thesis on learning theory, and he managed to get Fido to mind so well just by using praise as a reward. Look, I'll show you . . .

Either independently or in your assertiveness-building group you can practice following up on free information with the following exercises, adapted from the work of psychologist Manuel Smith.

1. Join with two partners to form a trio. Decide who will play the roles of instigator, responder, and observer.
2. The instigator begins a conversation with the responder by making a comment or asking a question. Pick any topic that seems appropriate.
3. For a period of three or four minutes the instigator's role is to follow up on whatever free information the responder offers. The instigator isn't to offer any information, but should only reply by asking a question based on the responder's previous comment. Don't worry if this

exchange sounds a little artificial: It's an exercise and not a real conversation.

4. At the end of the three- or four-minute period the observer and questioner offer feedback to the instigator, pointing out both ways in which she handled the exercise well and bits of free information she could have followed up. The observer and instigator then suggest to the responder how he might have shared more free information items in order to help the conversation along.

5. The same procedure is repeated two more times, allowing each person to take all three roles.

Asking Open-ended Questions   Sometimes the person you're talking to will offer plenty of free information, making your conversation flow along effortlessly. But what about the partner who, out of nervousness or lack of skill, doesn't share anything to which you can respond? Consider the following scene between Andy and a stranger seated next to him at a football game.

A: This ought to be a pretty exciting second half, don't you think?
S: Yeah, it should.
A: There sure have been a lot of fumbles so far. Do you figure it'll get any better for the rest of the game?
S: I doubt it.
A: Who do you think they'll start at quarterback, the old guy or that new kid?
S: Probably the old guy.
A: Well, I sure hope he doesn't throw any more interceptions. Do you think he will?
S: I don't know. I hope not.

By this time Andy is probably so discouraged that he probably won't try to pursue the conversation any further. Perhaps that's what the tight-lipped stranger wanted, but on the other hand the dialogue might have gone more smoothly if Andy had made it easier for the stranger to respond. For instance:

A: How do you think the second half will go?
S: Probably same as the first. Lots of fumbles.
A: Yeah. I guess the muddy field accounts for that. But I've seen both teams play better when it's snowing, for God's sake. What do you think has got into them today?
S: I don't know. For the Raiders, at least, I think it's the quarterbacking. They probably ought to stick with one guy instead of switching around so much.
A: Which one do you think they should use?
S: If you-ask me, I think the old guy is over the hill. I'd bench him and let the younger one play. He'll only get better with practice. . . .

What accounted for the difference between these two conversations? The answer lies in the kind of questions Andy asked in each case. In the first instance he used *closed-ended questions*—ones that can be answered in one or at most a few words. These brief, uninformative replies contained no free information and thus left Andy no closer to knowing his partner than before he had asked them. In contrast, the questions in the second dialogue were open-ended; that is, they were worded in such a way that they called for a more detailed response.

> Instead of "Is there a lot to do in Fargo, North Dakota?" try "What kinds of things are there to do in Fargo, North Dakota?"

> Instead of "Are you happy with your job as a nurse?" try "What are some good (or bad) things about being a nurse?"

> Instead of "Are you still practicing Transcendental Meditation?" try "I'd like to hear what your experiences have been with Transcendental Meditation."

One big advantage of open-ended questions is that they allow you to direct the conversation toward whatever communication level seems appropriate at the time.

Factual level:
"Where can I find a quiet place to camp around here?"
"What kind of training do you need to become an architect?"
"What kind of luck have you had with that brand of car?"

Opinion level:
"Who do you think we should choose as a family physician? Why?"
"What do you think should be done about the welfare problem?"
"Can you suggest a few movies we might see tonight?"

Feeling level:
"How did you feel when you found out that you never really had a chance to get the job?"
"What made you finally decide to have children?"
"Why are you angry at me?"

▶ Sharpen your skill at asking open-ended question by trying the following activities, either independently or in your assertiveness-building group.

1. Write a list of five open-ended questions that you could comfortably ask in each of the following settings:

   a. Meeting a stranger at a party

   (1) _____

   _____

   (2) _____

   _____

   (3) _____

(4) _____

(5) _____

b. Talking with a traveler from another part of the country

(1) _____

(2) _____

(3) _____

(4) _____

(5) _____

c. Being introduced to a new worker at your job

(1) _____

(2) _____

(3) _____

(4) _____

(5) _____

d. Sitting next to a stranger on the first day of class or at a lecture series

(1) _____

(2) _____

(3) _____

_____

(4) _____

_____

(5) _____

_____

e. One other situation you recently experienced in which you were at a loss for conversation

(1) _____

_____

(2) _____

_____

(3) _____

_____

(4) _____

_____

(5) _____

_____

2. With two companions form a trio consisting of a questioner, responder, and observer. The questioner's role is to begin and carry on a conversation by asking only open-ended questions. The responder should only reply to these questions, not ask any questions in return. As in preceding exercises, the critic should point out both the strengths and areas of potential improvement in the questioner's behavior. Rotate the roles until each participant has filled all three parts.

3. Tune in one of the many "talk shows" or public affairs programs on television every week. Notice how the interviewer almost exclusively asks open-ended questions to encourage the guest to offer free information. Do you "interview" people—solicit their opinions, feelings, or seek information? Ask yourself how you could apply some of the skills you observed on television to these situations.

Self-Disclosure If you've been reading the dialogue in the preceding pages carefully, you might have noticed that in each case the initiator's comments consisted almost entirely of questions. They hardly ever shared facts, opinions, or feelings with their partners. A conversation like this that went on for very long would sound strange, for the initiator would appear to be cross-examining the responder without offering anything in return. In any conversation it's important that both participants practice at least some *self-disclosure*, for a relationship can grow only when the people involved share something about themselves.

Suppose that you've met someone whom you think has the qualities of a potential good friend. Using your newfound skills of asking open-ended questions and following up on the resulting free information, you become even more certain that you'd like to get to know your partner better. Now look at this exchange from the other person's perspective: What might his feelings be toward you? The answer to this question depends to a great extent on how much of yourself you've shared. It's unrealistic to expect that others will become interested in you unless you give them some data on which to form a personal opinion. Many of the people who wonder why their relationships never seem to get off the ground don't realize the importance of being willing to let others know who they are—their likes and dislikes, their talents, opinions, and feelings. Whatever attractiveness comes from mystery can only last so long—sooner or later we need to know what makes the other person tick if there is to be any kind of relationship.

Don't become intimidated by the concept of selfdisclosure, thinking that it consists exclusively of sharing your deepest thoughts and feelings. While this type of personal sharing certainly is important under the right circumstances, simply sharing some of the many facts you know and opinions you hold is equally important and valuable.

In the following dialogue see how much self-disclosure adds to a conversation. Notice how well it compliments the open-ended questions and the following up of free information. The scene occurs in the hallway of an apartment house, where Gene encounters Mandy.

G: Hi. I guess we must be neighbors. I just moved in next door. My name's Gene. (*Self-disclosure.*)

M: Hi. I'm Mandy.

G: I'm still trying to recover from this move, but this looks like a nice place. What do you think of it? (*Self-disclosure and open-ended question, soliciting Mandy's opinion.*)

M: It's a little noisy sometimes, but the people are all really nice. I keep threatening to move closer to my job, but I don't think I'd ever find a place that's as good as this. (*Free information about the apartment and her job.*)

G: (At this point Gene has the choice of talking about Mandy's job or the apartment) What kind of people live here? (*Open-ended question.*)

M: Oh, all sorts. Mr. Toscant downstairs is a retired concert violinist. He acts very gruff, but once you get past his bluster he's really a kind man. The lady next to him—I can't remember her name—has some kind of job in the government office building downtown. I don't know her very well. The family on this floor is named Smythe. He builds sailboats and Sheila is a dance student. They have the cutest little boy named Tim. They're great. (*Plenty of free information, both facts and opinions.*)

G: That's quite an assortment of people. From the way you describe them, I think I'm going to like it here. The last place I lived was a huge apartment building and nobody knew anyone else. It was pretty depressing. I'm glad to be in a more human place. (*Self-disclosure, both facts and feelings.*)

M: What brings you here? I didn't understand whether you just moved into town . . . (*Mandy asks her first question here.*)

G: Yeah. I just moved here from Chicago. I was going to school there, but I finally finished. Now I'm a full-fledged electrical engineer. (*Self-disclosure.*)

M: Wow. I'm a writer, and mechanical things are out of my league. To show you what I mean, one of my lamps has been broken for three weeks and I haven't even tried to fix it. (*Self-disclosure.*)

G: I'd be happy to take a look at it if you'd like. I kind of enjoy fixing things. (*Self-disclosure.*)

M: Well, that would be great. I really wasn't hinting around for a free repair job.

G: That's fine. It's nice to talk with a friendly person in a strange town. I'm really glad we met. (*Self-disclosure of feelings.*)

What a nice talk! Even though they're just fictional characters, I can't help hoping that Mandy and Gene grow more fond of each other. I'd like to think that the conversational skills we've discussed here have helped start a friendship.

Practice your newfound talents by again joining with two partners so that you and one other become conversationalists and the third person becomes the observer. While the observer gives coaching and feedback, one partner should begin a conversation by offering a bit of free information, to which the other responds with one item of self-disclosure. Continue the conversation in this manner for three to four minutes, then rotate the positions until everyone has experienced all three roles.

Listening In conversation silence is sometimes golden. You have probably had the pleasant experience of talking with people who gave you their total attention, who were genuinely interested in what you had to say. It's likely that you left such conversations remarking to yourself about what a fabulous communicator these persons were, only to realize later that you did practically all the talking. Your partner's behavior here illustrated an important point: Sometimes the best communicator is one who mostly listens.

There are two reasons why listening can be valuable. First, it's often true that people like to hear themselves talk. This isn't always just an act of egotism. There's nothing wrong with sharing an accomplishment you're proud of or discussing a subject with which you're intensely involved. If you're genuinely interested in what a speaker has to say at times like these, it may not be necessary to add your thoughts to the conversation. Simply let the other person share, and enjoy it.

A second situation in which listening is valuable occurs when your partner is confused or has a problem. In these cases it's often helpful for the other person to talk the dilemma out, while you remain for the most part empathetically silent.

There are really two styles of listening, each of which you can use in conversations.

Passive Listening. Often the only contribution you need to make to a conversation is what psychologist Thomas Gordon (1970) calls "door openers"—occasional short verbal messages to let your partner know that you're paying attention. Exclamations like "uh-huh," "oh," and so on might not be very original, but they suit the purpose well. Of course, it's possible to use door openers like these as a way of *pretending* to listen when your mind is really elsewhere, but that is not the intention here. On the contrary, you can often learn the most about someone else simply by giving them space to share. People are often reluctant to talk about themselves, and your utterances can serve as a signal that you want to know about them.

Active Listening. Consider the following conversation between Walter and Aaron.

W: Gretchen and I are thinking about taking the kids to Disneyland pretty soon.
A: Sounds like fun.
W: Yeah, it will be if we don't go bankrupt in the process.
A: I guess it'll be pretty expensive, huh?
W: You're damn right it will be. First there's the expense of getting there, then the admissions, then all the hot dogs and candy and soda and other food, and of course the kids will have to get shirts and hats.
A: That's a lot more than you'd like to spend, I guess.
W: Oh, it's not just Disneyland. That will be worth it. It's just everything is getting so expensive these days. We never have enough money to take care of all the things we need, let alone having any left over for fun.
A: I guess you're really having a hard time making ends meet.
W: We sure are. I don't see how we're going to make it after Gretchen has the baby.
A: So you're mostly worried about the future, huh?
W: Yeah. We'll never make it on my present wages.
A: You need a way to get more income then . . . is that what you're saying?
W: That's right. Gretchen and I both agree that it would be best for her to stay with the baby for a year or so, and I don't see how my job alone is going to get us through.
A: It seems like a dead end for you.
W: Right. It looks like I'll have to either get a new job or make some cash on the side. . . .

Take another look at Aaron's replies in this dialogue. All he did was to reflect back Walter's thoughts and feelings, without adding any judgments or advice of his own. This kind of response has been termed *active listening* (Gordon, 1970), and it consists of simply summarizing the speaker's comments in your own words. It's a highly effective tool.

Active listening works well in two kinds of situations. First, like passive listening, it's an invitation for the other person to go on talking. By paraphrasing your partner's comments you're in effect saying, "Yes, I understand that . . . what happened next?" A second use of active listening is illustrated in the scene you just read. Paraphrasing can be a tremendously helpful device for helping people clear up their own confusion. People often are capable of finding answers for their own problems, and active listening gives them a way of sorting out the ideas that, unvocalized, can be confusing.

Here's a well-known exercise to sharpen your listening skill. Choose a partner and pick a topic in which both of you are genuinely interested—a local political issue, the problems of being assertive, or some schemes that can make you rich and famous. Carry on a conversation on your chosen subject with the following rule: Neither of you can respond to the other's comment until you have made sure that you understand it fully. You can check your understanding by using the active listening technique of paraphrasing back the comment in your own words. In addition to increasing your ability to understand others better, this exercise will help you discover how useful listening can be in helping to promote a conversation.

As a way of summarizing your newfound conversation skills, try this activity.[1]

1. Join with a group of two or three other people.
2. By yourself take a moment to figure out how you could make contact with each of the other people in your group. What might you say or do? In what setting?
3. Take turns sharing your ideas with each other. Say to each participant, "I can make contact with you by . . ."
4. After you have spoken to each member, they should take turns sharing how they might modify your approach for greater success.
5. After each person has spoken and received feedback, take a few minutes on your own to imagine one other person outside the group whom you would like to contact.
6. Members then take turns sharing how they might make contact with their chosen person. Group members again offer feedback in order to help refine these approaches.
7. Now the group as a whole decides on one "super contact"—a guaranteed, surefire way to contact another person.
8. If there is more than one group, each one in turn demonstrates its super contact to the others.

[1] Based on an exercise in Kenneth G. Johnson, John J. Senatore, Mark C. Leibig, and Gene Minor, *Nothing Never Happens*. Beverly Hills, Calif.: Glencoe Press, 1974.

SUMMARY

You've almost reached the end of this chapter on establishing relationships through conversation. If you think of each person as an island, then the ability to converse comfortably and well becomes a kind of bridge, allowing us to join our island to others and share something of ourselves with different people and in turn learn more about them. A good series of interpersonal bridges is clearly important, for it's only through contact with others that we can establish relationships. On the other hand, don't hold onto the unrealistic expectation that you'll find a lasting relationship—or even a pleasant interlude—at the end of every bridge you build. It's simply not realistic to expect that you'll be interested in everyone you meet or that they'll all respond to your overtures. As before, think of your ability to communicate successfully as a "batting average"—a percentage of successfully completed attempts to reach others. The skills you've learned here should help you increase that average, so that you find yourself involved in more and more satisfying relationships.

Remember that interaction can take place on several equally valuable levels—clichés, facts, ideas, opinions, and feelings. The level you choose to explore in any conversation will depend on yourself, your partner, and the situation in which you meet. Recall the various conversation starters listed in this chapter—exchanging basic data, making small talk, offering sincere compliments, and making requests for or offers of assistance. Try to use the techniques listed here for building and maintaining a conversation—free information, open-ended questions, self-disclosure, and both active and passive listening.

Developing conversation skills.

8

Expressing Feelings and Coping with Criticism

EXPRESSING FEELINGS

Ours is a society that discourages the expression of most feelings. From the time many children are old enough to understand language, they learn that the range of acceptable emotions is limited. How familiar do these admonitions sound to you?

"Don't get angry."

"There's nothing to worry about."

"That isn't funny."

"There's no reason to feel bad."

"Control yourself—don't get excited."

"For God's sake, don't cry!"

Notice how each of these messages denies its recipient the right to experience a certain feeling. Anger isn't legitimate, and neither is fear. There's something wrong with finding certain situations humorous. You are silly for

173

feeling bad. Excitement isn't desirable—keep your emotions under contol. And finally, don't make a scene by crying.

As a parent I know that such admonitions are often nothing more than a coded request for some peace and quiet; but when repeated often enough, the message comes through lcud and clear that only a narrow range of emotions is acceptable to share or even to experience. Expressions of affection are fine within limits: A hug and kiss for mother and father is all right, though a young man probably ought to shake hands with Dad instead. Affection toward friends becomes less and less frequent as we grow older, so that even a simple statement of "I like you" is seldom heard between adults. Unhappiness is to be expected from time to time, but one certainly shouldn't become a bore by overdoing it.

The freedom to express one's feelings is further limited by the requirements of many social roles. Salespeople are taught to always smile at all customers, no matter how obnoxious. Teachers are portrayed as paragons of rationality, supposedly facing their field of expertise and their students with total impartiality; students are rewarded for asking "acceptable" questions and otherwise being submissive creatures.

Furthermore, we're discouraged from freely expressing certain emotions, depending on what sex we happen to be. Men don't cry and are rational creatures. They must be strong, emotionally as well as physically. Aggressiveness is a virtue ("The Marine Corps builds men"). Women are flighty, being prone to tears and other emotional outbursts. They are often irrational and intuitive. A certain amount of determination and assertiveness is appealing, but when faced with a man's resistance they ought to defer, lest they be accused of being a "bitch," or worse.

The result of all these restrictions is that many of us lose the ability to feel deeply. Much like a muscle withers away when it is unused, our capacity to recognize and act on certain emotions is reduced. After spending most of one's life being what society expects of a man, it's hard to cry, even when the tears are clearly inside. After years of denying your capacity to be angry, the ability to recognize that feeling takes real effort. For someone who has never acknowledged that it's possible to love one's friends, accepting this truth can be hard indeed.

And if *feeling* such emotions is difficult, it's easy to see why *sharing* them presents an even greater obstacle. Where does one find the courage to say "I'm lonesome" to a marriage partner of many years? How does a parent, boss, or teacher whose life has been built on the presumption of confidence and certainty say, "I'm sorry, I was wrong." How does a person who has made a life's work out of not relying on anyone suddenly say, "I want your friendship"? Changes like these make some of the earlier goals we've looked at in this book seem like child's play.

Benefits of Expressing Feelings Assertively Do we need to wear our feelings where everyone can read them? Probably not always. But unless you're a rare exception, it's likely that you could profit by sharing much more of how you feel with the important people in your life. There are several reasons why this is so.

First, sharing more of your emotions is healthy. As you read in Chapter 1, feelings that go unexpressed often show up later as psychosomatic illnesses—real ailments whose origins are psychological. The tense or angry 20th-century man suffering from stomach ulcers is so common as to be a stereotype. Migraine headaches, chronic back and neck pains, cardiac problems, insomnia, and even hemorrhoids can in many cases be traced back to the patients' inability to freely express emotions. You can verify the physical component of feelings for yourself by tuning into what happens to your body the next time you experience some strong emotion. Where does anger show up for you? In your stomach. In a clenched jaw? As a nervous tic or a pounding heart? What about fear, excitement, confusion, guilt? Once you realize how much better you feel after you've expressed these emotions fully and skillfully, the benefits of emotional expression are clear. For me, getting an emotion off my chest without demeaning anyone else brings enormous relief and satisfaction. I feel much calmer and stronger, both mentally and physically. When I contrast this to the wear and tear I experience when I don't express myself, there's no doubt about which state is healthiest. Isn't this also true for you?

Beyond the physiological benefits, another advantage to expressing your emotions fully is that you can reach greater intimacy with others. A friend of mine, reflecting on his marriage, affirmed this point. "For the longest time I held back a lot of feelings from Amy which I thought would hurt her. For instance, I didn't tell her when I was bored or angry or attracted to other women. By doing this I did spare her feelings, but by holding back I also felt more and more like a stranger to her. It finally got to the point where I was hiding so much of how I truly felt that instead of an honest, growing marriage, I felt like I was carrying on a charade with her. Finally I couldn't stand the experience of being isolated from the woman I had committed myself to spending my life with, and so I began to share all of the things that were going on inside me—the uncomfortable feelings as well as the pleasant ones. As we began to really talk about who we were again, we uncovered a lot of feelings which we had both been out of touch with. I won't say that this kind of sharing has made our life together easier—it's often hard for one of us to face how the other feels—but I can definitely say that I feel closer to Amy now than I have in a long time. Where before our marriage was based on a lot of pretending and avoidance, now we both know each other. And now that I can be honest with her, I'm experiencing more feelings of love all the time."

I think one reason that people like my friend are afraid to share how they're feeling is because they're not sure whether their relationships can survive such honesty. This fear results in thoughts like

—"If I tell him that I'm bored with our marriage, then maybe he'll leave me."

—"If I tell my friend that I'm hurt when she teases me about a certain subject, then perhaps she'll be offended and not like me any more."

—"If I tell my boss that I feel neglected and a little resentful when he ignores my suggestions, he might fire me."

While it's true that fears such as these *might* materialize, the consequences of not sharing the strong feelings are just as bad. When partners don't communicate, boring marriages don't change, friendships continue in hurtful patterns, and job conditions stay unpleasant. How long can such destructive patterns go on? Surely there comes a time when it's necessary either to share or to give up on the relationship.

Another reason we're reluctant to express our feelings to others is because we fail to recognize that this kind of honesty can result in benefits as well as pain. I have found this to be true again and again in my life. When I'm upset over the way one of my classes is going, sharing my feelings with the students most often allows us to figure out together what is wrong and correct it. Whenever I can summon up the courage to express my feelings of care or love or affection to my friends, I feel the quality of our relationship growing. Whenever I can let my wife know how I'm feeling, my self-respect increases, as do the chances for our marriage becoming stronger. Each of these benefits comes as a result of risking and discomfort, for feelings aren't always easy to share. But as poet Ric Masten puts it, "The height of my heights is directly proportionate to the depth of my lows." You can't have one without the other and while playing it safe only results in a predictable, boring sameness, honesty leads to an exciting, growthful, if tempestuous life.

Sharing Feelings: When and How? By now you might think that this book advocates totally spontaneous acting out of your feelings. This isn't so. The world would not be much better off if everyone erupted spontaneously with infantile outbursts of emotion. I do, however, think that we can strike a better balance between denying or downplaying our feelings on one hand and totally cutting loose with them on the other; and I think that to gain this balance most people will have to do a lot more sharing and a lot less censoring.

Here, then, are some guidelines you can use to help decide when and how to express your emotions in a complete and honest way that will give you the best chances for improving your relationships.

1. Recognize the Difference Between Feeling and Acting. When our daughter was an infant, she went through what seemed like endless periods of late-night crying. I remember moments in the wee hours of the morning when I was so tired that I felt like leaving home, with all its noise and confusion. Needless to say, I didn't follow through on this impulse.

Of course, I'd like to be the kind of parent who is totally patient, accepting, and rational, but I'm not. While I don't always want to act on my immediate feelings, I also don't want to ignore them so that they'll build up inside and some day consume me. For this reason I feel best when I can express what's happening for me and then decide whether or not I'll act on it.

For instance, I want to be able to acknowledge my nervousness in some new situations, even though I might not choose to show it. I want to accept it when I'm attracted to other women, even though I might not choose to act on my feelings. I want to get in touch with the boredom I sometimes experience in meetings and classes, even though I'll most likely resist falling asleep or walking out. In other words, just because I feel a certain way doesn't mean I'll always act it out.

This distinction is extremely important, for it can liberate you from the fear that acknowledging and sharing a feeling will commit you to some disastrous course of action. If, for instance, you say to a friend "I feel so angry that I could punch you in the nose," it becomes possible to explore exactly why you feel so furious and then to resolve the problem that led to your anger. Pretending that nothing is the matter, on the other hand, will do nothing to diminish your resentful feelings, which can then go on to contaminate the relationship.

2. Choose the Best Time and Place to Express Your Feelings.   When you do choose to share how you feel with another person, it's important to pick a time and place that's appropriate. Often the first flush of a strong feeling is not the best time to speak out. If you're awakened by the racket caused by a noisy neighbor, storming over to complain might result in your saying things you'll regret later. In such a case it's probably wiser to wait until you have thought out carefully how you might express your feelings in a way that would be most likely to be heard.

Even after you've waited for the first flush of feeling to subside, it's still important to choose the time that's best suited to the message. Being rushed, or tired, or disturbed by some other matter are probably all good reasons for postponing the sharing of your feeling. Often dealing with your emotions can take a great amount of time and effort, and fatigue or distraction will make it difficult to devote your energy to follow through on the matter you've started. In the same manner you ought to be sure that the recipient of your message is ready to hear you out before you begin your sharing.

3. Accept Responsibility for Your Feeling.   While you often experience a feeling in response to the behavior of others, it's important to understand that they don't *cause* your feelings. In other words, people don't make you sad, happy, and so on; you are responsible for the way you react. Look at it this way: It's obvious that you are more easily upset on some days than on others. Little things that usually don't bother you suddenly bring on a burst of emotion. Since this is true, it isn't the things or people themselves that

Do you experience the full range of your emotions? Do you express them in the most satisfying manner?

In the spaces below record a diary of your feelings for the next five to seven days. For each day first describe the events which surround the feeling, the emotion you experience, the manner in which you acted, and the consequences of your behavior.

After completing your diary, answer the following questions.

1. Does the range of emotions you experienced seem realistic considering the events you encountered? That is, do you seem to be either not experiencing or not expressing certain emotions?

2. Are you satisfied with the manner in which you communicated your emotions? If not, how would you go about expressing them more effectively?

Events surrounding the feeling	The feeling you experienced	The manner in which you expressed the feeling	The consequences of your behavior
I was rushing out of the house to a doctor's appointment. I was already late when W. a friend, walked by and wanted to talk about her latest romantic crisis (she always has one going).	Impatience	I was aware of shifting from one foot to another, looking away a lot, and fiddling with my car keys. I also smiled and tried to be polite by saying things like "yeah," "uh huh," and so on.	W. talked for five minutes before I could tear myself away. I was late to my appointment. Now I see that all I needed to do was tell her that I was in a hurry.
I was saying goodbye to my family after one of my rare visits.	Love and sadness that I don't see them more often.	I came right out and told them how I felt.	We were all a little choked up, but I'm glad I did it. They were really happy, and I was too.
At work Friday. I was looking forward to a quiet weekend of drinking beer and working in the garden. My boss asked me to work on some papers over the weekend.	Resentment	I said "I suppose so" in an exasperated tone and stomped off. I knew this was a bad response, so I waited until he had a free moment and told him that I'd been hoping for a chance to relax. There didn't seem to be a need to express my resentment, since by then it had pretty much evaporated.	He said that the work could wait, as long as it was done by Monday afternoon.

Events surrounding the feeling	The feeling you experienced	The manner in which you expressed the feeling	The consequences of your behavior

determine your reaction, but rather how you feel about them at a given time. If I'm especially harassed due to the press of unfinished work or because I'm late for an appointment, I may react angrily to the type of jokes a friend has been making at my expense for years. Can I really say that it's my friend who caused my upset? No, it's more correct to say that it's my own work habits or tardiness—in other words, something in me—that sets me off. The same principle holds true for other emotions: Unrequited lovers don't break our hearts; we allow ourselves to feel hurt, or rather, we simply *are* hurt. A large dose of alchohol doesn't make us sad or happy; those emotions are already within us.

It's important to make sure that your language reflects the fact that you're responsible for your feelings. Instead of "You're making me angry," say "I'm getting angry." Instead of "You hurt my feelings," say "I feel hurt when you do that." People don't make us like or dislike them, and pretending that they do denies the responsibility each of us has for our own emotions.

4. Share Your Feelings Clearly and Unambiguously. Either out of confusion or discomfort we sometimes express our emotions in an unclear way. Sometimes this means using many words where one will do better; "Uh, I guess what I'm trying to say is that I was pretty upset when I waited for you on the corner where we agreed to meet at 1:30 and you didn't show up until 3:00," instead of "I was angry when you were an hour and a half late." One key to making your emotions clear is to realize than you most often can summarize a feeling in a single word—hurt, glad, confused, excited, resentful, and so on. In the same way, with a little thought you can probably describe any reasons you have for feeling a certain way very briefly. Remember from Chapter 3 the importance of expressing your thought in a concise core statement.

In addition to excessive length, a second way in which you can confuse the expression of a feeling is to discount or qualify it—"I'm a *little* unhappy," "I'm *pretty* excited," "I'm *sort of* confused." Of course not all emotions are strong ones. We do experience degrees of sadness and joy, for example, but some communicators have a tendency to discount almost every feeling. Do you?

A third way to confuse the expression of an emotion is to send it in a coded manner. This most often happens when the sender is uncomfortable about sharing the feeling in question. Some codes are verbal ones, as when the sender hints more or less subtly at the message. For example, an indirect way to say "I'm lonesome" might be "I guess there isn't much happening this weekend, so if you're not busy why don't you drop by?" This indirect code does have its advantages: It allows the sender to avoid the self-disclosure of expressing an unhappy feeling, and it also serves as a safeguard against the chance of being rejected outright. On the other hand, such a message is so indirect that the chances of the real feeling being recognized are reduced. For this reason people who send coded messages stand less of a chance of having their emotions understood and their needs met.

5. Recognize the Difference Between Primary and Secondary Feelings. Many times the feeling we express isn't the only one we're experiencing. Consider the case of Heidi and Mike at a party. The conversation has turned to the subject of womens' figures, and Mike jokingly refers to Heidi's purchase several years earlier of a mail-order bust developer. Heidi is mortified and later confronts Mike angrily: "How could you? That was the most thoughtless, immature thing you could have said. I'm furious at you." While Heidi's anger is probably justified, she failed to share with Mike the emotion that preceded and in fact was responsible for her anger, namely the embarassment when a secret she hoped to keep private was exposed to others. If she had shared this primary feeling, Mike could have better understood her rage, and probably would have responded in a more constructive way. Anger often isn't the primary emotion, although it's the one we may express. In addition to embarrassment, it's often preceded by confusion, disappointment, frustration, or sadness. In each of these cases it's important to share the primary feeling as well as the anger that follows it.

6. Recognize That Your Emotions Are Related to Specific Situations. Make sure that both you and your partner understand that your feeling is centered on a specific set of circumstances, rather than being indicitive of the whole relationship. Instead of saying "I resent you," say "I resent you when you don't keep your promises." Rather than "I'm bored with you," say "I'm bored when you talk about your money."

Many communicators are afraid to express their feelings for fear they mean that the relationship has come to an end. Be aware that in the course of knowing anyone that you're bound to feel positive at some times and negative at others. By limiting your comments to the specific situation, you can express a feeling directly without feeling the relationship is jeopardized.

COPING ASSERTIVELY WITH CRITICISM

How do you respond to criticism? Take a moment before reading on to answer this question by recalling a few incidents from your life.

1. Describe a time when you were criticized by a family member.

_____

_____

_____

How did you respond to the criticism? What did you say and how did you feel? _____

_____

2. Describe a time when you were criticized by a friend or acquaintance. _____
_____
_____

How did you respond? _____
_____
_____

3. Describe a time when you were criticized at work or school. _____
_____
_____

How did you react? _____
_____
_____

It's likely that in these and other cases you respond to criticism in one of three ways. Perhaps you are one of the people who *withdraws* when judged negatively by others. Sometimes this withdrawal takes the form of accepting the attack silently, even though you don't agree with or appreciate it. In other cases the withdrawal is physical: you might leave the presence of the critic temporarily or even permanently if the criticism is harsh enough. While such a response does maintain peace and quiet, it takes a toll on your self-respect; for in addition to silently accepting the other's judgment of your behavior, you now must also suffer from the loss of self-esteem that comes from failing to stand up for your rights.

A second possible response to criticism is to *justify* yourself. While this alternative has the advantage of at least maintaining your self-respect, it has two drawbacks. First, the criticism you are resisting may be valid. Compulsive justifiers will defend against any attack and in so doing fail to learn much valuable information about themselves. A second shortcoming of justification is that the critic seldom accepts your explanation. "You can defend yourself all day long," the other might seem to say, "but I still think you're wrong." In such cases justification is hardly worth the effort.

A third typical response to criticism is to *counterattack*—to reduce the pressure on yourself by pointing out some fault of the speaker. While this strategy often shifts the spotlight away from your faults, it also has the undesirable consequence of generating ill will between you and the critic, thus weakening the relationship. In this sense counterattacking can sometimes result in your winning a battle and losing a friendship.

Given the fact that all these typical responses to criticism are unproductive, what is left? We do face criticism—both justified and unjustified—all the time, and we need to have some response ready when it comes. The following pages will give you two new alternatives—questioning and agreeing—to replace withdrawing, justifying and counterattacking. Once you have learned them, you'll be able to accept criticism assertively without threatening the rights of others. As an added bonus these responses will help you increase your self-esteem, learn more about yourself, and most likely strengthen your relationship with your critics. A tall order? Perhaps, but it's one you can realize by carefully reading and applying the following information.

A Case Study Jay and Patty have been together for three years. Their relationship has been a good one, although like most it has had its ups and downs. Tonight will prove to be one of the down periods. Jay and Patty have both had a difficult day at work, and Jay is also preoccupied by the recurring question of whether he ought to give up the rapid pace of city life and move to a quieter rural setting. In addition, he hasn't been feeling affectionate toward Patty lately, and although he knows by now that this usually passes after a few days, he's still bothered.

Patty has also noticed the drop in Jay's affection and is upset by it. Also, she has an item on her agenda that is incompatible with Jay's mood: She has lately become more and more excited about the thought of spending the holidays with her family and wants Jay to agree to such a visit. Watch the fireworks:

P: Now that you've had time to think about visiting my folks over the holidays, what do you say?

J: (*trying to be polite and attentive, although he doesn't want to discuss this matter*) Oh, I don't know.

P: Well, I'd really like you to decide tonight so I can phone Mom and Dad.

J: To tell you the truth I really don't feel like talking about it tonight.

P: (*persistently*) That's what you said last week. I can go by myself, but I know Mom and Dad would like to see you too. Anyway, I wish you'd quit avoiding a decision and give me your answer. (Note the criticism here that Jay is avoiding the decision.)

J: (*irritated*) Look, I'm just not in the mood to decide now. I've got a lot on my mind and I had a hard day at work.

P: (*now really angry and critical*) I swear, Jay you're really self-centered sometimes. I've had a hard day too, but I've been trying to get an answer out of you for a week now, and all you do is put me off. When you get moody, you think the whole world ought to stand still until you feel better.

J: Maybe there are more important things to me than whether or not to see your parents for two days. And don't talk to me about being moody. At least I try to keep it to myself when something is bothering me. That's a lot better than slamming doors and stomping around like you do!

We can leave the conversation at this point, being sure that matters will get worse between Jay and Patty before they get better. You can probably see the problem: Although her request seemed legitimate, once Patty started to criticize Jay, he became defensive and he counterattacked. This isn't to say that Patty's criticism was unjust or was the only cause of the fight. Certainly Jay's preoccupation with the job and his flagging affection were ingredients, as was fatigue resulting from both partners' days and perhaps even pressures exerted by Patty's parents. It is fair to say, however, that Patty's outburst of criticism provided the "critical mass" that led to the flareup and the subsequently spoiled evening. If Patty could manage to express her gripes in a less defense-arousing manner, she might stand a better chance of having her needs met. Of course it isn't fair to expect Patty to be a saint—from time to time she's bound to be critical: Even if she was able to withhold or rephrase her compliments, Jay is bound to be criticized by other people in his life. Therefore it's important for him to learn how to accept criticism more openly when it does come his way. These two goals, then—offering criticism in a nonantagonizing way and accepting it without defensiveness—will be the subject of the following pages.

Why Is Criticism So Hard to Accept? Why does criticism—even when it is kindly intended—so frequently lead to defensive exchanges such as the one you just read? There are at least two answers to this question. Looking at each of them should make it clear why your criticism arouses defensiveness in others and also explain why you become so upset when others attack you.

   We Become Defensive When Criticism Threatens a Shaky Public Image. To understand this principle, imagine that a particularly obnoxious preschooler approaches you and in a burst of juvenile aggression accuses you of being a "doo-doo head." How would you react? Probably with laughter, for while you might object to the youngster's choice of words, it's unlikely that you'd take the accusation seriously enough to defensively reply, "I am *not* a doo-doo head!" and then go on to protect your character against this assault. Even the thought of such a response is ridiculous, for few adults are so insecure that they feel compelled to justify themselves in the face of a child's obviously nonsensical remarks.

   In the same way you often (though not always) take in stride the remarks of adults when their criticism is obviously invalid. The grownup equivalent of "doo-doo head" might be the accusation that you've been lazy when in fact you've worked your hardest, or that you're incompetent even when everyone else admires your skill. We might describe your attitude in such situations as these by amending the old saying to read "Sticks and stones may break my bones, *but names I don't believe are true* will never hurt me."

   Another instance in which we usually aren't bothered by criticism is when we clearly agree with and accept another's critical remarks. For instance, imagine that you've just begun trying to learn some difficult skill that is totally new to you—say, electronic repair or an exotic foreign language. After a few minutes of instruction your teacher remarks that you really have a long way to go. It's likely that you would heartily agree with this judgment and resign yourself to a long and hard course of study. Since there is no dispute here, there is little likelihood of your reacting defensively.

Now consider the following scenes, which represent a different kind of situation. See if you would react as calmly to each of them as you did to the previous ones.

- —If you'd like to lose weight, imagine that a friend kids you about putting on a few pounds as you reach for a second helping of dessert.
- —If you're unhappy about being a smoker, picture a companion remarking about new research linking the habit to cancer each time you reach for a cigarette.
- —If you have a hard time saving money, imagine that you've just decided to spend your vacation this year traveling, even though you know the trip will put you into debt. Now a friend asks how you plan to pay for the holiday.
- —If you sometimes devote less than your full effort to your job, imagine that you have overslept one morning and upon arriving at work you see your boss glance at you and then look at the clock.

How did you picture yourself behaving in each of these cases? If you were able to identify with them, the image that came to mind as you responded to the other person's behavior probably involved a defensive reaction on your part. As you read earlier, such defensiveness is one of three forms: The first might have been withdrawal, whereby you resisted the criticism yet kept quiet to avoid a conflict. Your second possible defensive response could have been justification or rationalization: "I overslept because I was up so late thinking about how to do my job better," or "It's best to take the vacation now since it will cost more next year." On the other hand, your response to criticism might have been to strike back: "Don't give me a hard time about smoking. At least I don't drive like a maniac the way you do," or "Who are you to talk about overeating. I saw you gobble up those four slices of pizza!"

Whether your response to situations like these involves withdrawal, justification, or counterattack, it's clear that your behavior contained some element of defensiveness that didn't exist when the preschooler called you names or your instructor commented on your lack of experience. What's the difference? Why do you feel compelled to justify yourself in some situations and not others? While the deciding factor might first appear to have been an age gap with the child and tact with the teacher, a closer look will show that the reason has more to do with your attitude than the sender's. Since you know you aren't a doo-doo head, there's no need to protect yourself against such an accusation. And since you could freely admit your lack of knowledge about the skill you wanted to learn, it was easy to agree with the teacher that you have a long way to go. In other words, neither of these cases really involved a threat to your self-esteem. In the last four situations, however, you probably felt compelled to defend yourself against the judgments of others *to the extent that you perceived them to be true.* Do you feel a twinge of guilt when you overeat or smoke? Does the thought that you're spending beyond your means bother you? Do you sometimes feel guilty about devoting less than your full energy to a job? If the answer to any of these questions is affirmative, then the potential for responding defensively exists.

To understand this defensive response to criticism in more detail you need to recognize the existence of two views of ourselves that each of us possesses. The first is our *public image.* This is sometimes referred to as our character, the face we present to the world. Most often people try to project a favorable public image, reflecting honesty, attractiveness, dependability, and other virtues. In some cases, however, a communicator will perpetuate a negative public image. This might involve making statements and carrying out actions that suggest a lack of skill, of attractiveness, or of intelligence, to name a few traits. We perpetuate our public image in actions as well as words. We indicate our sophistication (or our attempts at it) with fashionable clothes and a knowing expression. We demonstrate our interest in others by an attentive glance and sympathetic nods. We advertise our easygoing nature with a casual laugh. All of our actions, verbal and nonverbal, tell others how we see ourselves.

In addition to a public image each of us also carries around a private self-image. As its name suggests, this private image consists of the views of ourselves we each hold and believe personally. The private image consists of the same categories as the public one, and in many cases the two are congruent. You might see yourself as a religious person or a science fiction fan, for instance, and have no reservations about expressing these convictions publicly. In other cases, however, we are not willing to share our private image with others or sometimes even to admit it to ourselves. Consider the scenes you just visualized. If you claim to be serious about controlling your weight and a companion points out your appetite for sweets, you have the choice of either admitting that you've strayed from your diet (and your principles) or of somehow protecting this public image of yourself as a self-disciplined dieter. Given the investment we often put into creating a favorable public image ("This time I'm *really* going to diet. I value my health too much to overeat any more."), it's understandable why we often have a tendency to perpetuate a falsehood. The same principle holds true for other situations. If you publicly claim to value your health, there is a need to justify physically damaging habits such as smoking. If you claim to be financially responsible, you need to protect this image from anyone who questions your decision to splurge on an unnecessary item. If you have an important stake in having others see you as a responsible employee, you need to have every one of your actions on the job fit that mold. In the same way, don't you find yourself proclaiming that you are *not* stubborn precisely at the moment when you are most closed-minded? Isn't it common to protest that you are paying attention when your mind has wandered? Do you ever insist in a petulant, juvenile voice that you are *not* acting childish? In cases like these we strive to maintain a public image that sometimes verges on perfection. Of course, the problem with such justification is the fact that few of us are totally open-minded, attentive, or adult, and thus we wind up in the ludicrous position of defending ourselves in situations that are really indefensible.

This striving for consistency, then, explains one reason why we react defensively to criticism. *When people's judgments conflict with the way we want to be seen, we tend to dispute their comments.* And since most of these defensive reactions are devoted to presenting ourselves in an unrealistically favorable light, it becomes apparent that *we often react defensively to precisely that criticism which is most true.*

See whether this principle holds for you. For the next few days pay attention to the occasions in which you react defensively to criticism. Are you protecting an inaccurate public image? Do you react most strongly to the criticism that strikes closest to home?

A period of self-observation is likely to prove that your defensiveness often serves to protect a shaky public image—but not always. You may find instances when another's criticism is hard to accept even though it's obviously wide of the mark. In fact, you might discover that you find that criticism from a certain person is always objectionable, while remarks on the same subject are easier to accept from others. The explanation for such a reaction lies in a second reason criticism is hard to accept:

We Become Defensive When the Critic Misidentifies Ownership of a Problem.   Psychologist Thomas Gordon created a model that explains this phenomenon. Consider your relationship with another person to be represented by the space inside this box.

Your relationship with another person

This relationship can be divided into three areas. The first section represents the area in which no problem exist.

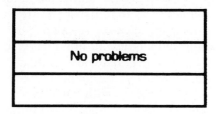

This area includes the situations in which your needs or wants and those of the other person are either the same or are compatible. For example:

—You want to be alone and so does your partner.
—You want to buy an encyclopedia and a salesperson wants to sell you one.
—You need some extra income and your boss wants someone to work overtime.
—You want to talk about a recent vacation and a friend wants to hear about it.

Obviously no relationship is entirely trouble-free. One common kind of difficulty occurs when *you own a problem*.

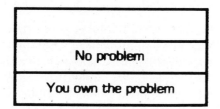

For instance:

—A neighbor's dog relieves itself on your front lawn.
—An instructor tells long stories that you find boring.
—Your family frequently offers you unsolicited advice about how to run your life.
—An acquaintance tells jokes that you find offensive.

It's important to understand that in each of these cases *you* are the one with unmet wants or needs, not the other person. The neighbor faces no difficulties when his dog defaces your lawn (and of course the dog has no problem either!). Your instructor probably is quite content to tell the same long-winded stories over and over. Your advice-giving relatives probably believe that they are fulfilling their responsibility by giving you advice.

Your joke-telling friend is enjoying the chance to be onstage and demonstrate her wit. In each of these instances realize that since you are the one who is bothered, you own these problems.

In contrast to the problems you own in a relationship are those situations in which the other person has unmet wants or needs—in other words, situations in which the *other owns the problem.*

The other owns the problem
No Problem
You own the problem

Sometimes the other person's problems arise from circumstances that have nothing to do with you.

—A friend doesn't feel like attending a party with you because he hasn't gotten much sleep lately and is tired.
—A supervisor snaps at you because she was just criticized by her boss.
—A stranger doesn't respond to your friendly overtures because he's just had a large investment go sour.
—A sales clerk is rude to you because she is suffering from a toothache.

Sometimes it's difficult to recognize that these unfriendly responses are a result of the other's problem; for we don't always know when someone is tired, has been harassed at work, is preoccupied with financial problems, or is in pain. And since we don't realize the source of problems like these, it's easy to be offended by the seemingly uncalled-for behavior of others.

In addition to the problems that have nothing to do with you, there are cases in which the other person has a problem that arises from your behavior. For instance:

—Someone seated near you in a restaurant is bothered by your cigarette smoke.
—A relative is upset because you forgot his birthday.
—Your partner wants to be alone with you, and you are leaving to visit other friends.
—A friend wants to discuss a problem with you, and you're too busy or preoccupied to help.

It should be clear that although all of these last four situations do involve you, in each of them the problem still belongs to the other person. You are content enough to be smoking; it's your neighbor that is bothered. You weren't hurt by the forgotten birthday; it was your relative who felt neglected. You have no need for intimacy; it is your partner who craves it. You don't need to talk out a problem; it's your friend who is in need of counseling.

What does all this have to do with criticism, which after all is our main topic here? Quite a bit. A major reason we act defensively is because others incorrectly accuse *us* of having a problem that is really *theirs*. Recalling the argument between Jay and Patty should illustrate this point. Remember that the conversation began to heat up when Patty accused Jay of being self-centered—in other words, when she said to him, "You have a problem." While it's certainly true that Jay was preoccupied and moody, the fact is that Patty spoke primarily because she wanted to help *herself*, not Jay—in other words, because she had a problem.

In the same way it's frequently true that we resent criticism because others incorrectly blame us, when in fact it's they who have the problem. Think of the following accusations and realize how likely they are to cause defensiveness:

> —"You talk too much."
> —"You are cheap."
> —"You ought to be more considerate."
> —"You aren't listening to me."

Even when these accusations are true, they're especially hard to accept when the speaker fails to acknowledge that the reason for bringing them up is to express an unmet want or need that happens to be made worse by your behavior. In the next chapter you will learn a method for expressing your complaints to others in a way that clearly acknowledges your ownership of a problem. For now it's sufficient to explain that one reason we become so defensive in the face of criticism is because the other person is incorrectly accusing us of having a problem when quite the opposite is true.

Realization of this fact can help you face criticism and still keep your composure. The next time someone says "You have a problem" by accusing you of being inconsiderate, selfish, loud, or whatever, you can keep calm by understanding that it is really they who are upset.

METHODS FOR COPING WITH CRITICISM

While it's important to understand how you've reacted defensively to criticism in the past, such insights don't guarantee that you'll handle yourself more effectively in the future. It's difficult to keep cool when another person incorrectly but vehemently accuses you of having a problem when in fact it's theirs. In other instances you'll find yourself defending a public image, even while a voice inside whispers that the criticism is valid.

For situations like these you need to learn some alternatives to defensiveness: There are honest, nonmanipulative ways of dealing with criticism without feeling the need to justify yourself or to counterattack. There are two such methods, each of which at first appears to be almost childishly simple, yet in practice has proved over and over to be among the most valuable assertive skills many communicators have learned.

When Criticized, Seek More Information This response makes good sense when you realize that it's foolish to respond to a critical attack until you understand what the other person has said. Even comments that upon first consideration appear to be totally unjustified or foolish often prove to contain at least a grain of truth, and sometimes much more.

Many readers object to the idea of asking for details when they are criticized. Their resistance grows from confusing the act of *listening openmindedly* to a speaker's comments with *accepting* them. Once you realize that you can listen to, understand, and even acknowledge the most hostile comments without necessarily accepting them, it becomes much easier to hear another person out. If you disagree with a speaker's objections, you will be in a much better position to explain yourself once you understand the critic. On the other hand, after carefully listening to the other's remarks, you might just see that they are valid, in which case you have learned some valuable information about yourself. In either case you have everything to gain and nothing to lose by hearing the critic out.

Of course, after years of instinctively resisting criticism, this habit of hearing the other person out will take some practice. To make matters more clear, here are several ways in which you can seek additional information from your critics.

Ask for Specifics.   Often the vague attack of a critic is practically useless, even if you sincerely want to change. Abstract accusations such as "You're being unfair" or "You never help out" can be difficult to understand. In such cases it is a good idea to request more specific information from the sender. "What do I *do* that's unfair?" is an important question to ask before you can judge whether the accusation is correct. "When haven't I helped out?" you might ask prior to agreeing with or disputing the accusation.

In seeking additional information it's helpful to recall the method introduced in Chapter 3 which you used to define problems behaviorally and to establish clear goals:

—Ask *who* besides you the criticism involves. "To whom am I rude?" "Which guests did I ignore?" "Exactly who thinks I ought to apologize?"

—Find out in what *circumstances* the objectionable behavior occurs. "When don't I listen to you?" "When did you first begin to feel embarrassed around me?" "Exactly when do you think I'm not handling the ball like you told me?"

—Understand the *specific behavior* that bothers your critic. "What do I do that makes it difficult for you to understand me?" "How do I act when you think I'm not being affectionate enough?" "Exactly what parts of the painting don't you like?"

If you already solicit specifics by using these questions and are still accused of reacting defensively, the problem may be in the *way* you ask. Again, as you read in Chapter 3, your tone of voice, facial expression, posture, and other nonverbal clues can give the same words radically different connotations. For example, think of how you could use the words "Exactly what are you talking about?" to communicate either a genuine desire to know or your belief that the speaker is crazy. It's important to request specific information only when you genuinely want to learn more from the speaker, for asking under any other circumstances will only make matters worse.

Guess about Specifics. On some occasions even your sincere and well-phrased requests for specific details of another's criticism won't meet with success. Sometimes your critics won't be able to define precisely the behavior they find offensive. In these instances you'll hear such comments as "I can't tell you exactly what's wrong with your sense of humor—all I can say is that I don't like it." In other cases your critics may know the exact behaviors they don't like but for some reason they seem to get a perverse satisfaction out of making you struggle to figure it out. At times like this you hear such comments as "Well, if you don't know what you did to hurt my feelings, I'm certainly not going to tell you!"

Needless to say, failing to learn the details of another's criticism when you genuinely want to know them can be a frustrating experience. In instances like these you can often learn more clearly what is bothering your critic by *guessing* at the specifics of a complaint. In a sense you become both detective and suspect, with the goal being to figure out exactly what "crime" you have committed. Like the technique of asking for specifics, guessing must be done with goodwill if it's to produce satisfying results. You need to convey to the critic that for both of your sakes you're truly interested in finding out what is the matter. Once you have communicated this intention, the emotional climate generally becomes more comfortable, since in effect both you and the critic are seeking the same goal.

Here are some typical questions you might hear from someone guessing about the details of another's criticism:

—"So you object to the language I used in writing the paper. Was my language too formal?"
—"O.K. I understand that you think the outfit looks funny. What is it that's so bad? Is it the color? Does it have something to do with the fit? The fabric?"
—"When you say that I'm not doing my share around the house, do you mean that I haven't been helping enough with the cleaning?"

Paraphrase the Speaker's Ideas. Another strategy for learning more about criticism is to draw out confused or reluctant speakers by paraphrasing their thoughts and feelings. This is actually another use of the active listening technique you learned in Chapter 7. As you read there, paraphrasing is especially useful in assisting others in solving their problems; and since people generally criticize you because your behavior creates some problem for them, the method is especially appropriate.

One advantage of paraphrasing is that you don't have to come up with any guesses about the specifics of your behavior that might be offensive. By clarifying or amplifying what you understand critics to be saying, you'll learn more about their objections. A brief dialogue between a disgruntled customer and an especially talented store manager using paraphrasing might sound like this:

C: The way you people run this store is disgusting! I just want to tell you that I'll never shop here again.

M: *(reflecting the customer's feeling)* It seems that you're quite upset. Can you tell me your problem?

C: It isn't *my* problem, it's the problem your salespeople have. They seem to think it's a great inconvenience to help a customer find anything around here.

M: So you didn't get enough help locating the items you were looking for, is that it?

C: Help! I spent twenty minutes looking around in here before I even talked to a clerk. All I can say is that it's a hell of a way to run a store.

M: So what you're saying is that the clerks seemed to be ignoring the customers?

C: No. They were all busy with other people. It just seems to me that you ought to have enough help around to handle the crowds that come in at this hour.

M: I understand now. What frustrated you the most was the fact that we didn't have enough staff to serve you promptly.

C: That's right. I have no complaint with the service I get once I'm waited on, and I've always thought you had a good selection here. It's just that I'm too busy to wait so long for help.

M: Well, I'm glad you brought this to my attention. We certainly don't want loyal customers going away mad. I'll try to see that it doesn't happen again.

This conversation illustrates two advantages of paraphrasing. First, the critic often reduces the intensity of her attack once she realizes that she's being heard. Often criticism grows from the frustration of unmet needs—which in this case was partly a lack of attention. As soon as the manager genuinely demonstrated his interest in her plight, the customer began to feel better, and she was able to leave the store in a relatively calm mood. Of course this sort of active listening won't always mollify your critic, but even when it doesn't, there's still another benefit that makes the technique worthwhile. In the above conversation, for instance, the manager learned some valuable information by taking time to understand the customer. He discovered that there were certain times when the number of employees was insufficient to help the crowd of shoppers. He also learned that the delays that occurred at these times seriously annoyed at least some shoppers, thus threatening a loss in business. This knowledge is certainly important, and by reacting defensively to the customer's complaint the manager would have kept himself from learning it. As you read earlier, even apparently outlandish criticism often contains at least a grain of truth, and thus a person who is genuinely interested in improving would be wise to hear it out.

Ask about the Consequences of Your Behavior. As a rule people complain about your actions only when some need of theirs is not being met. One way to respond to this kind of criticism is to find out exactly what troublesome consequences your behavior has on them. You'll often find that actions that seem perfectly legitimate to you cause some difficulty for your critic; once you have understood this, comments that previously sounded foolish take on a new meaning.

A: You say that I ought to have my cat neutered. Why is that important to you?
B: Because at night he picks fights with my cat, and I'm tired of paying the vet's bills.

C: Why do you care whether I'm late to work?
D: Because when the boss asks where you are. I feel obligated to make up some story so you won't get in trouble, and I don't like to lie.

E: Why does it bother you when I lose money at poker? You know I never gamble more than I can afford.
F: It's not the cash itself. It's that when you lose you're in a grumpy mood for two or three days, and that's no fun for me.

Solicit Additional Complaints. Although the idea might at first sound outlandish, once you've understood one complaint it's often beneficial to see if there is anything else about your behavior that bothers your critic. Soliciting additional complaints can be a good idea for the simple reason that if you can learn one valuable lesson from a single criticism, you ought to double your knowledge by hearing two.

Of course, it isn't always wise to seek additional gripes. There are three conditions that should be met before doing so. First, you should be sure that you understand the first complaint before tackling another one in the same sitting. Resolving the complaint sometimes means agreeing to the other's demands for change, but in other circumstances it can mean hearing out the other's request and promising to think about it. In still other instances the critic really doesn't expect you to change; in such cases resolution can simply mean that you've taken the time and spent the effort to truly understand the criticism.

You can see how solicitation of additional criticism works by returning to the conversation between the store manager and a disgruntled customer.

M: I can promise you that I'll see what I can do about having more employees on hand during busy periods. While you're here, I'd like to know if you can think of any other ways we could improve our operation.
C: What? You really want to know what else I think you're doing wrong?

M: Sure. If we're not aware of ways we could do better, we'll never change.

C: Well, the only other thing I can think of is the parking situation. A lot of times I'll come by and have to wait several minutes for a delivery truck to unload before I can get into the lot from the south side. I wish you could have the trucks park somewhere else or unload at a quieter hour.

M: That's a good point. We can't always control when the drivers from other companies will show up, but I can sure give their dispatchers a call and see what can be done. I want to say that I appreciate your thoughts. Even when we have our bad days around here, it's important to us that we do everything we can to make this a good place to shop.

Sometimes soliciting and understanding more information from a critic isn't enough. What do you do, for instance, when you fully understand the other person's objections and still feel a defensive response on the tip of your tongue? You know that if you try to protect yourself, you'll wind up in an argument; on the other hand, you simply can't accept what the other person is saying about you. The solution to such a dilemma is outrageously simple:

When Criticized, Agree with the Speaker   But, you protest, how can you honestly agree with comments that you don't believe are true? The following pages will answer this question by showing that *there's virtually no situation in which you can't honestly accept the other person's point of view and still maintain your position.* To see how this can be so, you need to realize that there are four different types of agreement, each of which you can express in different circumstances.

1. **Agree with the Truth.**   This is the easiest type of agreement to understand, though not always to practice. You agree with the truth when another person's criticism is factually correct:

> —"You're right, I am angry."
> —"I suppose I was being defensive."
> —"Now that you mention it, I did get pretty sarcastic."

Agreeing with the facts seem quite sensible when you realize that certain matters are indisputable. If you agree to be somewhere at four and don't show up until five, you *are* late, no matter how good your explanation for tardiness is. If you've broken a borrowed object, run out of gas, or failed to finish a job you started, there's no point in denying the fact. In the same way, if you're honest you will have to agree with many interpretations of your behavior, even when they're not flattering. You do get angry, act foolishly, fail to listen, and behave inconsiderately. Once you rid yourself of the myth of perfection, it's much easier to acknowledge these truths.

But if it's so obvious that the descriptions others give of your behaviors are often accurate, why is it so difficult to accept them without being defensive? The answer to this question lies in a confusion between agreeing with the *facts* and accepting the *judgment* that so often accompanies them. Most critics don't merely describe the action that offends them, they also evaluate it; and it's this evaluation that we resist.

—"*It's silly* to be angry."
—"*You have no reason* for being defensive."
—"*You were wrong* to be so sarcastic."

It's judgment like these that we resent. By realizing that you can agree with—and even learn from—the descriptive part of many criticisms and still not accept the accompanying evaluations, you'll often have a response that is both honest and nondefensive. A conversation between a teacher and a student illustrates this point.

TEACHER: "Look at this paper! It's only two pages long and it contains twelve mis-
spelled words. I'm afraid you have a real problem with your writing.
STUDENT: You're right. I know I don't spell well at all.
T: I don't know what's happening in the lower grades. They just don't seem to be
turning out people who can write a simple, declarative sentence.
S: You're not the first person I've heard say that.
T: I should think you'd be upset by the fact that after so much time in English
composition classes you haven't mastered the basics of spelling.
S: You're right. It does bother me.

Notice that in agreeing with the teacher's comments the student did not in any way demean himself. Even though there might have been extenuating circumstances to account for his lack of skill, the student didn't find it necessary to justify his errors because he wasn't saddled with the burden of pretending to be perfect. By simply agreeing with the facts he was able to maintain his dignity and avoid an unproductive argument.

Of course, in order to reduce defensiveness it's important that your agreements with the facts are honest ones admitted without malice. It's humiliating to accept descriptions that aren't accurate, and maliciously pretending to agree with only lead to trouble. You can imagine how unproductive the above conversation would have been if the student had spoken the same words in a sarcastic tone. Only agree with the facts when you can do so sincerely. While this won't always be possible, you'll be surprised at how often you can use this simple response.

At this point you might accept the idea that agreeing with criticism is fine, but insisting that it is so by itself isn't an adequate response to your critic. For instance, once you've admitted to another that you are defensive, habitually late, or sarcastic, you can expect the other to ask what you intend to do about this behavior.

Questions like these are fair ones. In most cases it would be a mistake simply to understand another's criticism, to agree with the accusations, and then to go on behaving precisely as before. Such behavior makes it clear that you have no concern for the speaker. The message that comes through is, "Sure, now I understand what I've done to bother you. You're right, I have been doing it and I'll probably keep on doing it. If you don't like the way I've been behaving, that's tough!" Such a response might be appropriate for dealing with people you genuinely don't care about—manipulative solicitors, abusive strangers, and so on—but it is clearly not suitable for people who matter to you.

Before reading on, then, understand that responding nondefensively to criticism is only the *first step* in resolving the conflicts that usually prompt another's attack. Because it is such an important step it's worthy of an extended treatment here; but by itself it won't help you satisfactorily manage many of the interpersonal problems you face. In order to fully manage your conflicts, you'll need to learn the skills described in Chapter 9. For now, it's sufficient to practice the coping skills of questioning and agreeing with criticism.

Agree with the Odds. Sometimes a critic will point out possible unpleasant consequences of your behavior.

> —"If you don't talk to more people, they'll think you're a snob."
> —"If you don't exercise more, you'll wind up having a heart attack one of these days."
> —"If you run around with that crowd, you'll probably be sorry."

Often comments such as these are genuinely helpful suggestions that others offer for your own good. In other cases, however, they are really devices for manipulating you into behaving the way your critic wants you to. For instance, "If we go to the football game, you might catch cold" could mean "I don't want to go to the football game." "You'll probably be exhausted tomorrow if you stay up late" could be translated as "I want you to go to bed early." Chapter 9 will have more to say about such methods of indirect aggression, but for now it is sufficient to say that such warnings often generate defensiveness. A mother-son argument shows what I mean.

MOTHER: I don't see why you want to ride that motorcycle. You could wind up in an accident so easily. (*Stating the odds for an accident*)

SON: Oh, don't be silly. I'm a careful driver, and besides you know that I never take my bike on the freeway. (*Denying the odds*)

M: Yes, but every time I pick up the paper I read about someone being hurt or killed. There's always a danger that some crazy driver will miss seeing you and run you off the road. (*States the odds for an injury*)

S: Oh, you worry too much. I always look out for the other driver. And besides, you have a lot better maneuverability on a motorcycle than in a car. (*Denies the odds for an injury*)

M: I know you're careful, but all it takes is one mistake and you could be killed. (*States the odds for being killed*)

S: Somebody is killed shaving or taking a shower every day, but you don't want me to stop doing those things, do you? You're just exaggerating the whole thing. (*Denies the odds for being killed*)

From this example you can see that it's usually counterproductive to deny another's predictions. You don't convince the critic, and your mind stays unchanged as well. Notice the difference when you agree with the odds (though not the demands) of the critic.

M: I don't see why you want to drive that motorcycle. You could wind up in an accident so easily. (*States the odds for an accident*)

S: I suppose there is a chance of that. (*AGREES with the odds*)

M: You're darned right. Every time I pick up the newspaper I read about someone being hurt or killed. There's always a danger that some crazy driver will miss seeing you and run you off the road. (*States the odds for an injury*)

S: You're right, that could happen (*AGREES with the odds*), but I don't think the risk is great enough to keep me off the bike.

M: That's easy for you to say now. Some day you could be sorry you didn't listen to me.

S: That's true. I really might regret driving the bike some day. (*AGREES with the odds*)

Notice how the son simply considers his mother's predictions and realistically acknowledges the chance that they might come true. While responses such as this might at first seem indifferent and callous, they can help the son to avoid the pitfall of indirect manipulation. Suppose the conversation was a straightforward one in which she was simply pointing out the danger of motorcycle riding to her son. He acknowledged that he understood her concern and even agreed with the possibility that her prediction could come true. If, however, her prediction was really an indirect way of saying "I don't want you to ride any more," then the son's response would force her into making her demand clear, thus allowing him to deal with it openly. At this point they might be able to figure out a solution that lets the son satisfy his need for transportation and excitement and at the same time allows the mother to alleviate her concern.

In addition to bringing hidden agendas into the open for resolution, agreeing with the odds has the added advantage of helping you become aware of some possible consequences of your actions that you might not have previously considered. Instead of blindly denying the chance that your behavior is inappropriate, agreeing with the odds will help you take an objective look at whether your course of action is in fact the best one. After such a look you might agree with your critic that the odds are such that you really should change your behavior.

Agree In Principle. Often criticism comes in the form of abstract ideals against which you're unfavorably compared.

—"I wish you wouldn't spend so much time on your work. Relaxation is important too, you know."

—"You shouldn't expect so much from your kids. Nobody's perfect."

—"What do you mean, you're not voting? The government is only going to get better when people like you take more of an interest in it."

—"You mean you're still upset by that remark? You ought to learn how to take a joke better."

In such instances it's entirely possible for you to accept the principle upon which the criticism is based and still continue to behave as you have been doing. This apparent inconsistency is reasonable for two reasons. First, no abstract statement applies to every instance of human behavior. For instance, while relaxation is important, there are occasions where it is appropriate to throw yourself totally into your work for a period of time. While it is unfair to put excessive demands on one's children, in some cases it becomes necessary for them to behave in an exceptional manner. As the Bible says, there is a time for every purpose, and what might usually be right isn't always so.

A second reason why you might agree in principle with a criticism but not change your behavior is precisely because people *are* inconsistent. Not being totally rational, we often do things that aren't in our best interests or those of another person. Again the myth of perfection needs debunking: Since you're not a saint, it's unrealistic to expect that you'll always behave like one. As an author and teacher of assertive communication, I can relate to this principle. There are occasions when I find myself behaving in a very unassertive manner: Failing to define my problems and goals behaviorally, expecting myself to improve in some way all at once instead of changing in gradual steps, and (ironically enough) becoming defensive in the face of criticism. In the face of such situations my inner dialogue often goes something like this:

TOP DOG: Boy, are you a hypocrite. Here you are, the expert on assertiveness, and you can't even take a little criticism yourself. Do as I say, not as I do, eh?

UNDER DOG: (*whining*) Well, it's not just my fault, you know. I do the best I can, but sometimes other people are so obnoxious that . . . Wait a second. You're right. (*Agreeing with the principle.*) I probably ought to be able to accept criticism better, but I guess I still haven't managed to totally master everything I teach. Maybe after a little longer I'll get better. I sure hope so for everybody's sake!

Agree with the Critic's Perception. What about times when there seems to be no basis whatsoever for agreeing with your critic? You've listened carefully and asked questions to make sure you understand the objections, but the more you listen, the more positive you are that they are totally out of line: There is no truth to the criticism, you can't agree with the odds, and you can't even accept the principle the critic puts forward. Even in these cases there's a way of agreeing—this time not with the critics' conclusions, but with their right to perceive things their way.

A: I don't believe you've been all the places you were just describing. You're probably just making all this up so we'll think you're hot stuff.

B: Well, I can see how you might think that. I've known people who lie to get approval.

A: I want to let you know right from the start that I was against hiring you for the job. I think the reason you got it was because you're a woman.

B: I can understand why you'd believe that with all the antidiscrimination laws on the books. I hope that after I've been here for a while you'll change your mind.

A: I don't think you're being totally honest about your reasons for wanting to stay home. You say that it's because you have a headache, but I think you're avoiding Mary and Walt.

B: I can see why that would make sense to you since Mary and I got into an argument the last time we were together. All I can say is that I do have a headache.

Responses such as these tell critics that you're acknowledging the reasonableness of their perception, even though you don't choose to accept it yourself or change your behavior. This copying style is a valuable one, for it lets you avoid the debates over who is right and who is wrong which can turn an exchange of ideas into an argument. Note the difference in the following scenes between Amy and Bob.

Disputing the Perception:

AMY: I don't see how you can stand to be around Josh. The guy is so crude that he gives me the creeps.

BOB: What do you mean, crude? He's a really nice guy. I think you're just touchy.

A: Touchy! If it's touchy to be offended by disgusting behavior, then I'm guilty.

B: You're not guilty about anything. It's just that you're too sensitive when people kid around.

A: Too sensitive, huh? I don't know what's happened to you. You used to have such good judgment about people. . . .

Agreeing with the Perception:

A: I don't see how you can stand to be around Josh. The guy is so crude that he gives me the creeps.

B: Well, I enjoy being around him, but I guess I can see how his jokes would be offensive to some people.

A: You're damn right. I don't see how you can put up with him.

B: Yeah. I guess if you didn't appreciate his humor, you wouldn't want to have much to do with him.

Notice how in the second exchange Bob was able to maintain his own position without attacking Amy's in the least. This acceptance is the key ingredient for successfully agreeing with your critics' perceptions: When it is present, you make it clear that in no way are you disputing their views of the matter. And since you have no intention of attacking your critics' views, they are less likely to be defensive.

A SAMPLE DIALOGUE

On page 183 you saw how the typical defensive reaction to criticism ruined any chance for effective communication between Jay and Patty. Let's take another look at their conversation to see how it might have gone if both partners had practiced the coping skills of seeking information and agreeing with criticism.

As you'll recall, Jay and Patty had both had hard days at work. Also, Jay is preoccupied with the question of whether he might be happier moving from the city to a more rural location and Patty wants an answer from him on whether he is willing to visit her parents over the holidays. In addition, both of them are bothered by the fact that Jay hasn't been very affectionate toward Patty lately.

P: Now that you've had time to think about visiting my folks over the holidays, what do you say?

J: (*trying to be polite and attentive, though he doesn't want to discuss this matter*) Oh, I don't know.

P: Well, I'd really like to decide tonight so I can phone Mom and Dad.

J: To tell you the truth, I really don't feel like talking about it tonight.

P: (*persistently*) That's what you said last week. I can go by myself, but I know Mom and Dad would like to see you too. Anyway, I wish you'd quit avoiding a decision and give me your answer. (*Note the criticism here: "You're avoiding the decision."*)

J: You're right. I suppose I have been avoiding a decision about whether I want to go. (*AGREEING with the truth*) I've had a lot on my mind, and to tell you the truth, I just haven't felt like worrying about one more thing.

P: Well, I really wish you would decide soon.

J: (*in a genuinely interested tone of voice*) Why does it bother you that I haven't decided yet? (*ASKING about the consequences of his behavior*) After all, the holidays are still two months off.

P: It's just that I hate to bother you about it. I feel like a nag every time I bring it up, so if you could decide once and for all, neither of us would have to worry about it any more.

J: Oh, I get it. You think I resent it when you keep asking me (*paraphrasing the speaker*)

P: Well, partly. It's more that I'm just tired of asking. It seems like it wouldn't be such a big deal for you to decide so that I don't have to keep hassling about it.

J: I can see why it would seem like an easy decision to you. (*AGREEING with Patty's perception*) Listen, is that all that's bothering you, or is there anything else?

P: (*hesistantly*) I suppose everything else is okay. . . (*Blurts out*) It's just that things haven't been very good between us lately.

J: I've kind of felt that way too. Does it have anything to do with my worrying about whether I want to move to the country? (*GUESSING about specifics*)

P: (*accusingly*) No. To tell you the truth, you just haven't been very affectionate lately.

J: I know, and it bothers me too. (*AGREES with the truth*)

P: Well, I wish I knew what it was all about. I just can't help thinking that you don't care about me any more.

J: I can see why it looks that way. (*AGREES with Patty's perception*) I do care . . . it just seems that I get into these moods once in a while.

P: It just seems to me that if one person really cares about another person, he should show it physically.

J: I know. It seems like that to me too. (*AGREES in principle*) All I can say is that I still do care, and this has me as confused as you.

P: Well, I sure hope we can figure it out. I'm really afraid that if this kind of thing keeps up, it might be a sign that we don't have a future together.

J: I suppose that's a possibility." (*AGREES with the odds*) But I sure know that I want us to stay together. I'll tell you what: If things don't get better soon, maybe I'll talk to Ben. Once he mentioned that he and Sally went through something like this but that they saw a counselor and worked it out. At least it's worth a try.

ADVANTAGES OF COPING ASSERTIVELY WITH CRITICISM

Notice that while Jay and Patty didn't solve their problems in this dialogue, they did accomplish a great deal. This is especially clear when you compare this conversation with their first one as described on page 183. By looking at what occurred here, several advantages of coping assertively with criticism become apparent.

The first benefit of such coping is that it reduces defensiveness. Where before Jay and Patty wound up in an argument within a few sentences, this time they were able to carry on a civil conversation. This change is mostly due to a new attitude that comes with questioning and agreeing with the critic: If you are occupied in genuinely trying to understand what the other person objects to about your behavior, you won't feel the need or have the time to protect yourself by withdrawing or counterattacking.

In addition to making criticism easier for you to accept, these assertive techniques also have the effect of calming down even the most excited critic. Criticism often grows out of the frustration of not being heard or respected, and your questions and agreement are a clear signal that you consider the other person's viewpoint interesting and valid. Thus, by following the suggestions here you're helping both yourself and the critic, even if you carry on with the original behavior that brought about the criticism.

A third advantage of responding to criticism by questioning and agreeing is that you can learn a great deal about yourself. Since it's true that we often resist those criticisms that are most true, asking questions and agreeing with another's objections will allow you to consider the merits of that point of view. Once you've taken the time to do so, you may well find that the original criticisms are, in fact, valid. Thus, acknowledging criticism nondefensively can help you change for the better.

In addition to learning more about yourself, the behaviors described here can help you understand your critic better. In the conversation above, for example, Jay learned that Patty was just as bothered as he was about the lack of affection in their relationship. Where before he had felt alone with his concern, at least he discovered how Patty felt on the issue.

A final benefit of questioning and agreeing with your critic is that it often sets the stage for resolving your conflicts. The cooperative atmosphere that comes with such behavior makes it clear that you and the other person are not adversaries, that you are both interested in seeking a solution to the problem. It's clear that an attitude like this makes the chances for finding an answer to your difficulties much greater than does a combative, defensive climate.

▶ Test your understanding of these methods for assertively coping with criticism. Below is a list of three complaints you have probably heard more than once in your life. For each one indicate how you might use the questioning and agreeing techniques described in the text.

As you read each comment, try to visualize a specific person from your life speaking it. Picture the place, time, and the circumstances that prompted the comment. As you write your responses, get a clear image of yourself speaking the words in an assertive manner.

SAMPLE CRITICISM: "Sometimes I think you don't take me seriously. It seems like everything I say goes in one ear and out the other."
A. Questioning responses
    1. Ask for specifics "I'd understand what you mean better if you could give me some examples of when I seem to be ignoring you."
    2. Guess about specifics "Are you talking about our political discussion at the party?
    3. Paraphase the speaker's ideas "It sounds like you're mad at me because you think I'm just humoring you. Is that it?"
    4. Ask for the consequences of your actions "Why does it matter whether I take you seriously or not?"
    5. Ask for more complaints "Is it just my not taking you seriously that's upsetting you, or is there something else too?"
B. Agreeing responses
    1. Agree with the truth "Well, I suppose you're right. Sometimes I don't pay attention to what you say, mostly when I'm tired or mad."
    2. Agree with the odds "I suppose you're probably right. I'm sure I don't always give you my full attention."
    3. Agree in principle "You're right. The decent thing would be for me to always pay attention to you. If I was a better communicator, I'd probably do it more."
    4. Agree with the perception "I can see why you might think that I'm not listening when I say I'll do something and then don't."
STATEMENT #1: "You know, you're sure sensitive to criticism. You shouldn't be so touchy—it'll only get you in trouble."
A. Questioning responses

    1. Ask for specifics _____

_____

_____

    2. Guess about specifics _____

_____

_____

3. Paraphrase the speaker's ideas _____

_____

_____

4. Ask for the consequences of your actions _____

_____

_____

5. Ask for more complaints _____

_____

_____

B. Agreeing responses

1. Agree with the truth _____

_____

_____

2. Agree with the odds _____

_____

_____

3. Agree in principle _____

_____

_____

4. Agree with the perception _____

_____

_____

STATEMENT #2: "You're going to have to do a better job around here. I just don't think you're trying your hardest."

A. Questioning responses

1. Ask for specifics _____

_____

_____

2. Guess about specifics _____

_____

_____

3. Paraphrase the speaker's ideas _____

_____

_____

4. Ask for the consequences of your actions _____

_____

_____

5. Ask for more complaints _____

_____

_____

B. Agreeing responses

   1. Agree with the truth _____

_____

_____

   2. Agree with the odds _____

_____

_____

   3. Agree in principle _____

_____

_____

   4. Agree with the perception _____

_____

_____

STATEMENT #3: "You've certainly been in a lousy mood lately. Sometimes you're awfully hard to live with."

A. Questioning responses

   1. Ask for specifics _____

_____

_____

   2. Guess about specifics _____

_____

_____

3. Paraphrase the speaker's ideas _____

_____

_____

4. Ask for the consequences of your actions _____

_____

_____

5. Ask for more complaints _____

_____

_____

B. Agreeing responses

1. Agree with the truth _____

_____

_____

2. Agree with the bdds _____

_____

_____

3. Agree in principle _____

_____

_____

4. Agree with the perception _____

_____

_____

You can also practice managing criticism by trying the following exercise, based on the work of Smith.

Join with a partner and decide which of you will take the role of critic. The other partner then becomes the coping recipient. The critic begins by pointing out some fault—real or imagined—about the recipient, who in turn uses one or more of the techniques described in this chapter to respond. The critic then escalates the attack by either amplifying the original complaint or finding a new one. This process goes on for a period of three or four minutes, during which the only responses the recipient can make are limited to those listed above. Upon completing this half of the role-playing, the partners switch positions and repeat the procedure.

This activity can become quite humorous as the criticisms become more and more outlandish, but the point is still clear: You can listen to and respond to the attacks of another person without becoming defensive or abusive yourself.

AFTER COPING WITH CRITICISM, WHAT?

The preceding pages have dealt with improving your initial response to another's criticism. As such they have focused on the first few sentences you'll speak after being judged. A detailed treatment of this brief period is worthwhile, considering the potential for trouble that exists at this time. A defensive response to another's comment—perhaps a justification, a sarcastic remark, or a burst of anger—can begin a spiral of conflict that usually ruins any chance of satisfying communication. The consequences of a defensive outburst can extend beyond a single conversation, for in the heat of argument accusations are made and threats tossed about that can plague both speaker and target for years to come. Given the seriousness of mishandling criticism, it's fair to say that the ability to cope calmly and nondefensively is a prerequisite to effective communication.

Notice the word *prerequisite;* as you've read earlier, handling criticism constructively is only the first step in resolving conflicts happily. Remember that other people usually criticize you because *they* have a problem—because they aren't getting something they want or need. You can use the information-seeking responses you've learned here to find out about others' problems in greater detail; the agreeing replies you've practiced will help acknowledge your role in them. Once you've accomplished these steps, however, the need still exists to *resolve* the problem so that the other doesn't need to criticize you any longer. Chapter 9 is devoted to the resolution of such problems.

SUMMARY

Our society downplays the recognition and expression of many feelings. This emotional inhibition prevents us from enjoying many benefits: better physical health, increased intimacy with others, and the growth of interpersonal relationships. The decision of whether to express a particular feeling at a given time should be based on several factors: Recognition that sharing a feeling does not require acting on it, consideration of the appropriateness of the time and place, assumption of responsibility for the emotion, recognition of the need for stating it clearly and unambiguously, distinguishing between primary and secondary feelings, and recognition that a given feeling is limited to a specific situation.

Criticism is usually hard to accept because it threatens a weak public image and because it misidentifies the ownership of a problem as belonging to the recipient and not the speaker. There are two recommended methods of coping with criticism—requesting further information and agreeing with the critic. Following these methods results in several benefits: You learn more about yourself, become less defensive, and at the same time disarm the critic.

It is important to realize that learning details of the criticism and agreeing with the critic are only the first steps in resolving interpersonal conflict. Additional skills will be introduced in Chapter 9.

Expressing feelings.

9

Satisfying Personal Needs: Managing Conflicts, Making Requests, and Saying No

THE NATURE OF CONFLICT

What conflicts do you face in your life? Take a few moments now to describe four examples from your recent experience. Don't read on until you have completed this step.

Conflict #1 _____

_____

_____

Conflict #2 _____

_____

_____

Conflict #3 _____

_____

_____

Conflict #4 _____

_____

_____

These examples probably illustrate the fact that conflicts can take place with a wide range of people on a variety of subjects and in numerous settings. Sometimes they involve those with whom you are most intimate—spouse, parents, children, lovers, friends—and at other times they involve total strangers. They can take place on the job, at home, or in unfamiliar places. Sometimes they deal with highly important issues—your career, the future of your relationships, or your personal rights—and in other instances they seem to revolve around such insignificant matters as whether the newspaper is delivered on your doorstep or in the bushes, who gets to read the comics or front page first, or whether to coffee you are served in a restaurant is warm. Sometimes your conflicts can result in feelings of anxiety or pain, while in other instances they engender reactions of bitterness, anger, competitiveness, excitement, or even sometimes a kind of joyful relief. Sometimes these reactions are intense enough to block out awareness of anything else in your life, and in other cases they are so weak that they are barely noticeable. Sometimes the effects of a conflict are negligible, being forgotten by the participants almost immediately, and in other cases the residue lasts for years or even a lifetime.

In spite of these widely varying circumstances all of the conflicts you described above, as well as every other one in your life, share a common element—the existence of one or more sets of apparently incompatible needs.[1] Sometimes these needs are easily recognized; in other cases they are difficult to detect. In any case, to the degree that they go unmet the conflict has little chance of being resolved, and in fact it often can grow to even greater proportions.

Precisely because people's needs are frequently incompatible, it is im-

---

[1] Many communicators abuse the word "need" by also applying it to situations where "want" would be a more appropriate term. ("I *want* you to be quiet" vs. "I *need* you to be quiet.") While recognizing this distinction, in the interests of brevity "need" will be used here to cover all instances in which the speaker indicates any sort of desire.

portant to recognize that conflicts are inevitable. In Chapter 2 you read about the myth of perfection—the unrealistic idea that a successful communicator ought to have no faults. Relationships suffer from this same myth. Husbands and wives enter marriage believing in the fairy tale idea that they will live happily ever after. Parents expect their children to behave perfectly, and kids expect their folks to be ideal too. Unsatisfied job-seekers look for the perfect occupation. Lonesome people seek the totally fulfilling friendship. Expectations such as these are bound to go unmet because no person or group can always satisfy all your needs. A far more realistic attitude to take in approaching a relationship is that both good times and conflicts are bound to occur.

While conflicts may be inevitable, they do not need to go unresolved. Given the right attitude and a bit of knowledge it's possible to settle many of the conflicts you experience in a way that is satisfying to everyone involved. By the end of this chapter, then, you'll see clearly that it isn't the *existence* of conflicts that is in itself troublesome, but rather the way in which such matters are handled. The following pages will introduce you to several methods for dealing with problems. Understanding the characteristics of each is an important first step toward effective conflict resolution.

STYLES OF CONFLICT

There are four ways in which people can act when their needs are unmet. Each one has very different consequences, which I can best explain by sharing a problem of mine. As I write these words I am sitting in the study of a house that my wife and I bought recently. Outside my window, in the middle of the street, sit two small dogs who bark almost constantly and chase most of the cars that drive by. Because of this barking I find it difficult to concentrate. It is clear that I won't be able to stand this situation much longer, and so I am faced with the decision of what to do. By describing my available choices the differences between nonassertive, directly aggressive, indirectly aggressive, and nonassertive behaviors should become more clear.

Nonassertive Behavior There are two ways in which nonasserters manage a conflict. Sometimes they ignore their needs. For instance, faced with the dogs a nonassertive person would try to forget their barking by closing the window and trying to concentrate even harder. Another form of denial would be to claim that no problem exists—that a little barking never bothered anyone. To the degree that it's possible to make one's problems disappear by ignoring them, such an approach is probably advisable. In many cases, however, it simply isn't realistic to claim that nothing is wrong. For instance, if your health is being jeopardized by the cigarette smoke from someone nearby, you are clearly punishing yourself by remaining silent. If you need to learn more information from a supervisor before undertaking a project, you reduce the quality of your work by pretending that you understand it all. If you claim that an unsatisfactory repair job is acceptable, you are paying good money for nothing. In all these and many more cases, simply pretending that nothing is the matter when your needs continue to go unmet is clearly not the answer.

A second nonassertive course of action is to acknowledge that one's needs are not being met but simply to accept the situation, hoping that it might clear up without any action on your behalf. I could, for instance, wait for the neighbor who owns the barking dogs to move. I could wait for the dogs to be run over by a passing car or die of old age. I could hope that my neighbor will realize how noisy the dogs are and do something to quiet them. Each of these occurrences is a possibility, of course, but it would be unrealistic to count on one of them to solve my problem. And even if by chance I was lucky enough for the dog problem to be solved without my taking action, that I couldn't expect to be so fortunate in other parts of my life.

In addition, while waiting for one of these eventualities, I would undoubtedly grow more and more angry at my neighbor, making a friendly relationship between us impossible. I would also lose a degree of self-respect, since I would see myself as the kind of person who can't cope with even a common everyday irritation. Besides, how can I justify myself as the author of a book on assertive behavior if I can't even assert myself? Clearly, nonassertion is not a very satisfying course of action—not for me in this case, and not for you in most instances.

Direct Aggression   Where the nonasserter underreacts, a directly aggressive person overreacts. The usual consequences of aggressive behaviors are anger and defensiveness on the one hand and hurt and humiliation on the other. In either case aggressive communicators build themselves up at the expense of others.

I could handle the dog problem with direct aggression by abusively confronting my neighbor, calling her names and threatening to call the dogcatcher the next time I see her hounds running loose. Since the town in which I live has a leash law, I would be within my legal rights to do so, and I would gain my goal of bringing peace and quiet to the neighborhood. Unfortunately, my direct aggression would have other, less productive consequences. My neighbor and I would probably cease to be on speaking terms, and I would expect a complaint from her the first time I violated even the smallest legal technicality. Since I expect both of our families to live in the neighborhood for a long time, this state of hostilities isn't very appealing.

Indirect Aggression   In several of his works psychologist George Bach (1968, 1970, 1974) describes behavior that he terms "crazymaking." Crazymaking occurs when a people have feelings of resentment, anger, or rage they are unable or unwilling to express directly. Instead of keeping these feelings to themselves, the crazymakers send these aggressive messages in subtle, indirect ways, thus maintaining the front of kindness. This amiable façade eventually crumbles, however, leaving the crazymaker's victim confused and angry at having been fooled. The recipient of the crazymakers can either react with aggressive behavior of his or retreat to nurse his hurt feelings. In either case indirect aggression seldom has anything but harmful effects on a relationship.

I could respond to my neighbor and her dogs in several crazymaking, indirectly aggressive ways. One strategy would be to complain anonymously to the city pound and then, after her dogs have been hauled away, express my sympathy. Or I could complain to everyone else in the neighborhood, hoping that their hostility would force the offending neighbor to quiet her dogs or face being a social outcast. A third possibility would be to strike up a friendly conversation with the owner and casually remark about the terrible neighborhood I had just left, in which noisy dogs roamed the streets, uncontrolled by their thoughtless owners. (Or perhaps I could be more subtle and talk about noisy children instead!)

There are a number of shortcomings to such approaches as these, each of which illustrates the risks of indirect aggression. First, there is the chance that my crazymaking actions won't work: My neighbor might simply miss the point of my veiled attacks and continue to ignore the barking. On the other hand she might get my message clearly, but either because of my lack of sincerity or out of sheer stubbornness, she might simply refuse to do anything about my complaining. In either case it's likely that in this and other instances indirect aggression won't satisfy my unmet need.

Even when indirect aggression proves successful in the short run, a second shortcoming lies in its consequences over the longer range. I might manage to intimidate my neighbor into shutting up her mutts, for instance, but in winning that battle I could lose what would become a war. As a means of revenge, it's possible that she would wage her own campaign of crazymaking by such tactics as badmouthing my sometimes sloppy gardening to other neighbors or by phoning in false complaints about my allegedly loud parties. It's obvious that feuds such as this one are counterproductive and outweigh the apparent advantages of indirect aggression.

In addition to these unpleasant possibilities, a third shortcoming of indirect aggression is that it denies the people involved a chance of building any kind of honest relationship with each other. As long as I treat my neighbor as if she were an obstacle to be removed from my path, there's little likelihood that I'll get to know her as a person. While I must confess that this thought doesn't bother me now, possibly because I've been attempting to manipulate her and thus haven't given myself the chance to find out that she is an interesting, cooperative person. Even if I never care to become closer to my neighbor, the principle that indirect aggression prevents intimacy holds true in other important areas of life. To the degree that I try to manipulate my wife and children, they won't know the real me. The fewer of my needs I share directly with my co-workers, the less chance we have of becoming true friends and colleagues. The same principle holds for my friends, students, and those people I hope to meet in the future: Indirect aggression denies closeness.

Assertion Assertive people handle conflicts skillfully by expressing their needs, thoughts, and feelings clearly and directly, but without judging others or dictating to them. They have the attitude that most of the time it is possible to resolve problems to everyone's satisfaction. Possessing this attitude and the skills to bring it about doesn't guarantee that assertive communicators will always get what they want, but it does give them the best chance of doing so. An additional benefit of such an approach is that whether or not it satisfies a particular need, it maintains the self-respect of both the asserters and those with whom they interact. As a result, people who manage their conflicts assertively may experience feelings of discomfort while they are working through the problem. They usually feel better about themselves and each other afterward—quite a change from the outcomes of unassertiveness and aggression.

An assertive course of action in my case would be to wait a few days to make sure that the noise and car chasing of the dogs is not just a fluke. If things continue in the present way, I will introduce myself to my neighbor and explain my problem. I will tell her that although she might not notice it (she works all day), the dogs often play in the street and run barking after cars. I will tell her why this behavior bothers me: It keeps my three-year-old daughter from her naps and makes it hard for me to do my work. I'll point out that I don't want to keep my feelings to myself and become resentful toward her, nor do I want to be a grouch and call the pound. Rather than behaving in these ways, I will tell her that I've come to see what kind of solution we can find that will satisfy both of us. This approach may not work, and I might then have to decide whether it is most important to me to avoid her bad feelings or to have peace and quiet. But the chances for a happy ending are best with this assertive approach, and no matter what happens, I can keep my self-respect by behaving directly and honestly.

Managing conflicts assertively is probably the most challenging skill described in this book. It requires the greatest amount of goodwill and it demands a commitment to follow the methods described in the following pages, especially when your old destructive habits seem so much more natural. On the other hand, conflict management is probably the most important talent you can develop, for it is this skill that keeps relationships together and allows them to grow in the face of the irritations, misunderstandings, and clashing of incompatible needs that are bound to occur between people.

STYLES OF COMMUNICATION

	Nonassertive	Directly Aggressive	Indirectly Aggressive	Assertive
Approach to Others	I'm not O.K., You're O.K.	I'm O.K., You're not O.K.	I'm O.K., You're not O.K. (But I'll let you think you are.)	I'm O.K., You're O.K.
Decision Making	Let others choose.	Chooses for others. They know it.	Chooses for others. They don't know it.	Chooses for self.
Self-Sufficiency	Low	High or low	Looks high but usually low	Usually high
Behavior in Problem Situations	Flees, gives in	Outright attack	Concealed attack	Direct confrontation
Response of Others	Disrespect, guilt, anger, frustration	Hurt, defensiveness, humiliation	Confusion, frustration, feelings of manipulation	Mutual respect
Success Pattern	Succeeds by luck or charity of others	Beats out others	Wins by manipulation	Attempts "Win–Win" or "No-Lose" solutions

Adapted with permission from Phelps, S., and N. Austin, *The Assertive Woman,* San Luis Obispo, CA Impact, 1974, page 11 and Gerald Piaget, American Orthopsychiatric Association, 1974.

▶   Check your understanding of the various styles of conflict management by examining the four communication situations below. Either by yourself or in a small group, write four responses for each: Nonassertive, directly aggressive, indirectly aggressive, and assertive. Describe the probable consequences of each.

EXAMPLE: Three weeks ago your friend borrowed an article of clothing, promising to return it soon. You haven't seen it since, and the friend hasn't mentioned it.
Nonassertive response Say nothing to the friend, hoping she will remember and return the item.
Probable consequences of this response There's a good chance I'll never get the item back. I would probably resent the friend and avoid her in the future so I won't have to lend anything else.

Directly aggressive response <u>Confront the friend and accuse her of being inconsiderate and</u> <u>irresponsible. Say that she probably ruined the item and is afraid to say so.</u>

Probable consequences. <u>My friend would get defensive and hurt. Even if she did intentionally</u> <u>keep the item, she'd never admit it when approached this way. We would probably avoid each</u> <u>other in the future.</u>

Indirectly aggressive response <u>Drop hints about how I loved to wear the borrowed item. Cas-</u> <u>ually mention how much I hate people who don't return things. Gossip about the incident to</u> <u>others.</u>

Probable consequences <u>My friend would be embarrassed by my gossip. She might ignore my</u> <u>hints. She'll most certainly resent my roundabout approach, even if she returns the article.</u>

Assertive response <u>Confront the friend in a noncritical way and remind her that she still</u> <u>has the item. Ask when she'll return it, being sure to get a specific time.</u>

Probable consequences <u>The friend might be embarrassed when I bring the subject up, but since</u> <u>there's no attack it'll probably be okay. Since we'll have cleared up the problem, the relationship</u> <u>can continue.</u>

1. Someone you've just met at a party criticizes a mutual friend in a way you think is unfair.

   Nonassertive response _____

   _____

   _____

   _____

   Directly aggressive _____

   _____

   _____

   _____

   Indirectly aggressive _____

   _____

   _____

   _____

   Assertive _____

   _____

   _____

   _____

2. A fan behind you at a ballgame toots a loud air horn every time the home team makes any progress. The noise is spoiling your enjoyment of the game.

   Nonassertive response _____

   _____

_____

_____

Directly aggressive _____

_____

_____

_____

Indirectly aggressive _____

_____

_____

_____

Assertive _____

_____

_____

_____

3. Earlier in the day you asked the person with whom you live to stop by the store and pick up snacks for a party you are having this evening. He/she arrives home without the food, and it's too late to return to the store.

Nonassertive response _____

_____

_____

_____

Directly aggressive _____

_____

_____

_____

Indirectly aggressive _____

_____

_____

_____

Assertive _____

_____

_____

_____

4. You are explaining your political views to a friend who has asked your opinion. Now the friend obviously isn't listening: You think to yourself that since the person asked for your ideas, the least he/she can do is pay attention.

Nonassertive response _____

_____

_____

_____

Directly aggressive _____

_____

_____

_____

Indirectly aggressive _____

_____

_____

_____

Assertive _____

_____

_____

_____

Now that you understand these four types of responses, return to the personal conflicts you described on pages 209–210 and decide in which manner you handled each. Based on these examples and other incidents you can recall, how would you say you behave when your needs are unmet—nonassertively, with direct aggression, with indirect aggression, or assertively? After you have formed your own opinion, explain these concepts to one or more friends and see how they classify you. Are you satisfied with your present manner of handling conflicts? If not, consider how you can apply the methods described in this chapter to your life.

ASSERTIVE PROBLEM SOLVING

The remainder of this chapter will give you a method that you can use to meet your needs assertively. The beauty of this approach is that it works on such a wide variety of situations: You can use it to make requests of others comfortably and directly, to stand up for your personal rights, to share complaints with others and hopefully resolve your conflicts, and even to say no to undesirable requests.

Because the information that follows is so important, it is absolutely essential that you read it carefully and practice every exercise as it is described, either by yourself or in an assertiveness building group. The methods you will learn are definitely effective, but they will only work the best when they are used skillfully. Be prepared to read each section individually and become confortable with it before going on. This process may take a fair amount of time, but the rewards you gain as a result will be well worth your investment.

"I" Language: Own Your Problem   Recall from Chapter 8 that there are two kinds of problems—those you own and those that belong to others. A problem is yours whenever your needs go unmet. Whether you want to return an unsatisfactory piece of merchandise, to complain to a noisy neighbor because your sleep is being disturbed, or to request a change in working conditions from your employer, the problem is yours. Why? Because in each case *you* are the person who is dissatisfied, while the other person's needs are all being met. You are the one who has paid for the defective article; the merchant who sold it to you has the use of your good money. You are the one who is losing sleep as a result of your neighbors' activities; they are content to go on as before. You are the one who is unhappy with your working conditions, not your boss. In other words, the distinguishing characteristic of problems you own is that the circumstances prompting the conflict are primarily troublesome to you, thus leading you to speak out on them.

In contrast to these situations are those in which you are content, but the other person has an unmet need—in other words, when the other owns the problem. It would be accurate to say that other people own a problem when they are bothered by your table manners or sense of humor, are offended by your failure to keep a promise, or are unhappy with your performance on the job. Every case in which others have a problem is identifiable by the fact that one or more of their needs are unmet, while yours are all being satisfied.

When the matter of problem ownership is presented in this manner, it is obvious that you have no need to speak out about problems that are owned by others, for these matters simply aren't any concern of yours. For instance, the world is filled with millions of selfish, inconsiderate, dishonest people, yet if this fact bothers you at all, it's only in an abstract way. It is only when the behavior of one of these unsavory characters begins to affect you in some way that you feel a need to speak out. In spite of this fact many communicators make the critical mistake of misidentifying their problems as belonging to others, and in so doing diminish the chances for resolving their conflicts effectively.

In the following situations speakers mistakenly imply that the other person has a problem when in fact the unmet need is their own.

—A late sleeper accuses a group of noisy, playful neighborhood children of being ill behaved. (Translation: "You have a problem: You're inconsiderate.")

—A customer who tries to return an article he purchased is turned down because he doesn't have a sales slip. He fumes that the store personnel know nothing about "the proper way to run a business." (Translation: "You have a problem: You don't know how to do your work properly.")

—A husband becomes upset when his wife decides to enroll in a class that meets two evenings per week and accuses her of not caring for him. (Translation: "You have a problem: You don't pay enough attention to me; you're not a good wife.")

In each of these cases the problem really belonged to the speakers, for the unmet needs were theirs.

—The sleeper needed more rest.
—The customer needed to return the item without finding the sales slip.
—The husband needed to spend the evenings in question with his wife.

▶ In order to manage your conflicts constructively, it is vital for you to recognize that the only time you initiate a conflict is when some need for yours is not being met. To verify this principle, describe below four incidents in which you either thought about or actually did judge or criticize another person's behavior. Describe your problem in each incident—in other words, state the need that prompted you to speak out.

EXAMPLE
Your complaint or criticism <u>I criticized my friend in an indirectly aggressive manner by mentioning that she must be quite busy since she hasn't dropped by to see my new place as she promised.</u>
Your unmet need that prompted the comment <u>I had two unmet needs here: (1) I enjoy socializing with her, and (2) I need some reassurance that my friendship is still important to her.</u>

CONFLICT #1

Your complaint or criticism _____

_____

_____

Your unmet need that prompted the comment _____

_____

_____

CONFLICT #2

Your complaint or criticism _____

_____

_____

Your unmet need that prompted the comment _____

_____

_____

CONFLICT #3

Your complaint or criticism _____

_____

_____

Your unmet need that prompted the comment _____

_____

_____

CONFLICT #4

Your complaint or criticism _____

_____

_____

Your unmet need that prompted the comment _____

_____

_____

In completing the previous exercise it's likely that you recalled at least one incident in which you inaccurately blamed another person for a problem that was really yours. If you did make this mistake, the consequences of such an act should be clear to you. As you read in Chapter 8, people don't like to be criticized, even when the evaluation is correct; and when the blame is incorrectly fixed, the odds that they will become defensive are even greater. Of course, once someone becomes defensive, the likelihood of having your needs met is drastically reduced. The two following colloquys, between mother and son and parking lot attendant and customer, follow this pattern.

MOTHER: Are those your dishes in the sink?
SON: Yeah.

M: I don't know what's wrong with you. If I've told you once, I've told you a thousand times to clean up the kitchen after you have a snack. Why don't you listen to me? (*Translation: "You have two problems: You don't listen to me and you don't clean up the kitchen like you should." Notice that even though both accusations are true, they are the mother's problems and don't bother the son in the least.*)

S: Aw Jeez! What's the big deal about a few dishes in the sink? You sure get uptight about little things, Mom. (*Now that he has been attacked, the son accuses his mother of having a problem.*)

M: Listen, Buster, I don't need any lectures from you about being uptight: The only thing you worry about is listening to what I tell you and then doing it.

S: (*sullenly*) If there was anything worthwhile to listen to, I might do it.

CUSTOMER: Hey! That's no way to drive my car. You ought to be a little more careful with other people's property. (*Translation: "You have a problem: You're irresponsible."*)

PARKING LOT ATTENDANT: (*defensively*) Did you see me hit anything?

C: No, but when you drive that fast in a crowded lot, it's just a matter of time. (*Translation: "You have a problem: You're headed for an accident."*)

ATTENDANT: (*sarcastically*) Listen, sir, I've worked in this lot for two years and I've never even scratched a bumper.

C: Don't get smart with me or I'll see to it that your manager hears about this.

A: Go ahead and complain. The manager is my brother-in-law, and compared to him I drive like a little old lady.

Exchanges like these clearly don't do any good. They create ill feelings and usually leave the complainers further away than ever from getting what they want. Yet as both these incidents suggest, complaints are often legitimate: Parking lot attendants do speed, and children have been know to forget their cleanup obligations. In the same ways salespeople are often not helpful, husbands and wives often act in objectionable ways, friends disappoint you, and in countless other ways you find the behavior of others unsatisfying. Failing to speak up in situations like these is not usually the answer. On the other hand, the examples you just read make it clear that aggressive complaining doesn't pay off either. What is the alternative?

By now the answer to this question might be clear: *The first step in assertive conflict resolution is to clearly identify the problem as yours.* By doing so you reduce the likelihood that the other person will become defensive, for you have in no way been an attacker. In addition, a clear statement of your problem may be news to the other people, who have never realized how their behavior affected you.

To be most effective your statement of ownership should contain three elements:

—A description of the specific behavior that presents a problem for you.

—An outline of the concrete, observable consequences of this problem.

—A description of the feelings you experience as a result of the problem.

You can share this information by using an easily memorized formula devised by Thomas Gordon.

"I have a problem. When you _____
(specific behavior)'

_____ happens, and I feel _____ "
(specific consequences)   (your feelings)

If the upset mother you just read about had used this formula, instead of blaming her son she could have said to him, "I have a problem. When you leave your dishes in the sink after I've cleaned up the kitchen (*behavior*), I have to come back in and wash them (*consequences*), which makes me very tired and upset (*feeling*)."

In the same way, the irate customer in the parking lot could have explained himself by declaring "I have a problem. When you drive my car fast enough to make the tires squeal (*behavior*), I complain (*consequences*) because I'm worried (*feeling*) about a possible accident."

This formula works in virtually all situations in which you have an unmet need:

—"I have a problem. When you play your stereo set this loud after midnight (*behavior*), I can't sleep and all the dogs in the neighborhood start barking (*consequence*). I guess you can imagine how upset I get when that happens (*feeling*)."

—"I have a problem. When you say you'll be here for our date at six and don't show up until after seven (*behavior*), the dinner gets ruined, we're late for the show we planned to see (*consequences*), and I feel hurt because it seems like I'm just not that important to you (*feeling*)."

Sometimes this message makes more sense if you arrange the behavior that bothers you, its consequences, and your feelings in a different order. In other cases you might use different words to indicate that you have a problem. The important thing is that all these elements are present and that the other person understands them.

—"I have to tell you that I get upset (*feeling*) when you make jokes about my bad memory in front of other people (*behavior*). In fact, I get so angry that I find myself bringing up your faults to get even (*consequences*)."

—"The reason I haven't invited Jason over to play with Erika (*consequences*) is because I'm really afraid (*feeling*) that he'll lose his temper and start throwing things at her again (*behavior*)."

—"The employees want to let management know that we've been having a hard time lately with the short notice you've been giving when you need us to work overtime (*behavior*). That probably explains some of the grumbling and lack of cooperation you've mentioned (*consequences*). Anyhow, we wanted to make it clear that this policy has really got a lot of the workers feeling pretty resentful (*feeling*)."

Notice that whatever the order of words, the effect of each message is to *describe* the sender's problem, not to *evaluate* the other's behavior. As a result, there is a maximum of "I" language—sharing and explaining—and a minimum of "you" language—judging, blaming, name calling, and criticizing. Also realize that at no time do you ask for a change in the other's behavior. The time for such requests will come soon enough, but you can't expect people to change before they clearly understand your reasons for asking.

The most important ingredient in the whole process of sending "I" messages is a genuine recognition that the problem is truly yours. Beyond this, it's essential that your description of the troublesome behavior be as specific as possible. For instance, instead of mentioning the other person's inattention, describe what they actually *do* in detail—interrupt you in mid-sentence, wander away before you've finished talking, or forget something you've just said. The same need for specificity applies to your description of the consequences that follow from the other's behavior. Don't simply say that you are inconvenienced; describe the ways in which you are put out. Finally, be sure that the other person understands the full intensity of your feelings. If you are getting upset, don't mention that you've been "a little bothered"; be sure to let the other person know how strongly you feel.

Of course there is no guarantee that "I" language will always reduce defensiveness or cause others to change their actions to suit you. Sometimes they will understand your predicament and perhaps even sympathize. In other instances people simply won't care *what* difficulties you face; they might in effect say "All right, so you have a problem. What's it to me?"

Don't worry too much about these situations. There are methods you will learn in a few pages that will help you deal with them. For the time being realize that if you can truly believe that any complaint you have with another person is your problem, and if you learn to describe these problems according to the formula outlined here, you will notice a tremendous increase in the number of conflicts you successfully resolve. To help you achieve this goal, be sure to complete the following exercises before reading on.

▶ Write an "I have a problem" response for each of the situations below. Remember to include in your answer a description of the <u>specific behavior</u> that causes or constitutes your behavior, and a clear indication of the intensity of your <u>feelings</u> on the matter. Label each of these elements in parenthesis.

SAMPLE SITUATION: For some time you have felt that an old friend is angry at you. This person hasn't suggested that you get together in a long time, and every time you try to suggest a date you get a cool response.

    Your statement <u>There's something that has been bothering me and I want to share it with</u> <u>you. I'm afraid that you're angry with me for some reason (feeling). I say that because you</u> <u>haven't invited me to get together with you for almost three months, and every time I call you</u> <u>say that you're busy (behavior). I'm worried that if things go on this way our friendship will be</u> <u>over, and I'd hate to see that (consequences)."</u>

    Situation #1: An acquaintance has lately become involved in a local fund-raising drive and has asked you several times to join in the effort by doing some door-to-door soliciting. You've politely said that you aren't interested, but the acquaintance has continued to insist that you help.

    Your statement _____

_____

_____

_____

_____

_____

_____

    Situation #2: You have enrolled in a class you find interesting. The only problem is that the instructor often disgresses from the subject at hand by telling long and (to you) uninteresting stories about his travels. You want to spend your time learning more about the stated topic.

    Your statement _____

_____

_____

_____

_____

_____

_____

    Situation #3: For several years you have been eating at a local restaurant. The food has been good, the atmosphere pleasant, and the service friendly and attentive. Lately, however, the place has changed. The new waiters haven't seemed to care about you, the place hasn't seemed as clean as before, and the food is often mediocre. You have decided to give the restaurant one last chance, and as you are eating a tasteless stew, the owner approaches you and asks you if everything is all right.

Your statement _____

_____

_____

_____

_____

_____

Once you have completed the statements above and are satisfied that you understand how to use the "I have a problem" formula, turn to the personal conflicts you described on pages 209 and 210. In the spaces below describe how you could apply this new method if you chose to share your problem with the other person or people involved. As before, make sure you clearly identify the problem as your own and that your descriptions of the troublesome behavior, its consequences, and your resulting feelings are detailed.

Conflict #1 _____

_____

_____

_____

_____

_____

Conflict #2 _____

_____

_____

_____

_____

Conflict #3 _____

_____

_____

_____

_____

_____

Conflict #4 _____

_____

_____

_____

_____

_____

Now that you have considered how you might share your problem by using the "I have a problem" format, the question becomes whether you should go ahead and actually approach others in this way. Of course, asserting yourself is the goal of this book, but whether you should do so in a instance depends on several factors. First, you should be sure that you introduce the "I" language into your life at an appropriate rate. Remember the principle of shaping you read about in Chapters 4, 5, and 6: The way to change an old habit is by *gradually* increasing your new target behavior. Don't make the mistake of overusing this new formula. Begin by slowly, surely introducing it into your life.

A second consideration to ponder before approaching others in this new way is your chance for success in a particular situation. There are some aggressive people who will either scoff at or ignore your problems. In these cases you will need to use the more forceful methods described in the following pages. In choosing to use "I" language, then, be sure to select people who are most likely to be receptive. The third point to consider is the matter of timing. It's not always wise to approach the other person immediately upon recognizing a problem: If your partner is tired, upset, or preoccupied, it might be wise to arrange for a talk at a time when you will have a better chance of being understood. A final point to consider before using this formula is whether you're comfortable with it. If the method doesn't feel natural to you, reinforce your understanding of it by using the behavior-rehearsal methods described in Chapter 4. If you are fortunate enough to be enrolled in an assertiveness-training group, you have an excellent setting to practice this behavior with the other members. Even if you are reading this book on your own, you can use the technique of covert behavior rehearsal (see pages 77–80) to sharpen your skill.

Repeated Assertion: Persist until Understood While the "I have a problem" approach often proves successful in stating your complaints, there are times the other person won't clearly receive even the most effectively expressed message. Suppose, for instance, that you share the following problem with a friend:

— "I've been bothered by something lately and I want to share it with you. To be honest, I'm uncomfortable (*feeling*) when you use so much profanity (*behavior*). I don't mind an occasional 'damn' or 'hell,' but the other words are hard for me to accept. Lately I've found myself avoiding you, and that's no good either (*consequences*), so I wanted to let you know how I feel."

When you share your feelings in this nonevaluative way, it's likely that the other person will understand your position and possibly try to change behavior to suit your needs. On the other hand there are a number of less satisfying responses that could be made to your comment:

— "Listen, these days everyone talks that way. And besides, you've got your faults too, you know!" (*Your friend becomes defensive, rationalizing and counterattacking.*)
— "Yeah. I suppose I do swear a lot. I'll have to work on that some day." (*Gets the general drift of your message but fails to comprehend how serious the problem is to you.*)
— "Listen, if you're still angry about my forgetting to pick you up the other day, you can be sure that I'm really sorry. I won't do it again." (*Totally misunderstands.*)
— "Speaking of avoiding, have you seen Chris around lately? I wonder if anything is wrong with him." (*Gets discomfited at your frustration and changes the subject entirely.*)

In each of these cases it's obvious that your friend either didn't accurately understand what you were saying or wasn't willing to acknowledge your concern. Since there's little likelihood of resolving problems that aren't faced, it's essential at such times that you persist in delivering your message until it's received. The method for such persistence has most clearly been termed *repeated assertion*.

Repeated assertion simply means stating your important message over and over until you are sure that the other person has received it accurately. Sometimes the most effective method of repeated assertion is simply to repeat the same phrase again and again until the other person is forced to acknowledge it. This technique is especially effective when you sense that others are deliberately evading giving you a direct response. See how the student handles the professor.

STUDENT: I'm having a problem understanding the material that will be on the coming test. I'm concerned about doing my best, and I'd like to go over some points with you. When can we get together?

PROFESSOR: Have you reread all the chapters in the text? I'm sure that you'll find everything you need to know there.

S: I've already done that, and I still am confused. When can we get together? (*Repeated assertion.*)

P: Well, this is a very busy time for me. I have several committee meetings in the next week, and I do teach other classes, you know.

S: I understand that, and I'm willing to meet whenever you can find the time. When can we get together? (*Repeated assertion.*)

P: Normally I would suggest my office hour, of course, but unfortunately this Tuesday I have a dental appointment at that time.

S: I see. If the office hour wouldn't work for you, I could see you any time between now and Tuesday. I'm on campus almost all day, and tomorrow I'll be here in the evening. When can we get together? (*Repeated assertion.*)

P: Well, I suppose I could come in early on Monday morning. Can you be at my office around eight?

S: Sure. I'll see you then.

Notice that in this scene the student wasn't sidetracked by the professor's problems with staff meetings, classes, and dental appointments. The main issue was finding a time to meet, and she persisted until she reached her goal. As another advocate of persistence points out (Smith, 1975), most people have only so many no's in their bag, and all you need is one yes. Of course, while you're persisting it's important to remain calm and genuinely interested in having your need understood, rather than simply punishing the other person in an indirectly aggressive manner.

While the key element of repeated assertion is the persistent statement of your message, it isn't always necessary to use exactly the same words every time. In instances where you do choose diffeent language to repeat your problem, be sure that in every case you make your message clear. The following conversation is between husband and wife.

HUSBAND: *I've been bothered lately by the amount we spend on food.* I was noticing that it's gone up to almost half again what we spent last year, and it's cutting into the money we wanted to set aside for our vacation. Have you noticed what I mean?

WIFE: (*defensively*) I can't help it if prices keep going up. I wish you wouldn't blame me for the state of the economy. It's not my fault, you know.

H: I didn't say it was your fault—don't get me wrong. I was just saying that *I'm worried because the extra money spent there might keep us from taking the vacation.* (Repeated assertion.)

W: Yes, I suppose we could have to cut the trip short if we can't save enough. (*Misunderstanding the seriousness of the problem.*)

H: No, it's worse than that. At the rate we're going we won't even have enough saved to get us there, let alone take care of our lodging and meals. *That's why I'm worried about the food budget.* (Repeated assertion.)

W: I didn't realize it was that serious. I wonder what we can do about it?

While sheer persistence won't in itself solve your problems, it is clearly an important step in reaching that goal; for if the other person doesn't understand what's bothering you, you almost certainly won't resolve the problem.

Many times communicators fail to persist in delivering their message for fear they'll be considered pushy or obnoxious. While this is always a possibility, if you can politely but firmly use repeated assertion to make your "I have a problem" message clear, it is likely that the other person will understand the importance of your message and appreciate why you are trying so hard to get it across. And even in those cases where the other person does think less of you, this is sometimes the price you have to pay for respecting yourself.

You can sharpen your skill at repeated assertion by practicing the following scenes. If you are in an assertiveness-building group, the best method is to split into trios and decide which member will be the asserter, which will be the recipient of the assertive message, and which will be the coach. By shifting roles for each of the following scenes, each person can receive practice in the technique.

If you are reading the book by yourself, use covert behavior rehearsal (see Chapter 4) to visualize yourself using repeated assertion in each of the situations. Remember to keep your image as clear and detailed as possible for maximum effectiveness.

In each example begin by sharing your predicament through the "I have a problem" format you learned earlier. Then continue the dialogue by assuming that the other person either becomes defensive as a result of your comments, misunderstands the extent of your feelings or the seriousness of the consequences you describe, totally misunderstands you, or changes the subject.

Situation #1: You have been feeling dizzy for almost two days, and have finally decided that you need to see a doctor. You have never felt this way before, and are becoming more worried. The receptionist informs you that the soonest she can fit you in for an appointment is a week from now. You want to see the doctor today.

Situation #2: For several months you have been carpooling to work or school with a neighbor. At first the arrangement worked well: By alternating rides you saved on gasoline money and gained companionship. Lately, however, your fellow rider has been phoning at the last minute to cancel the day's drive. Sometimes the excuse is illness, sometimes an appointment, and in other cases it is mechanical trouble, in which case you have taken over her turn for driving. These cancellations have occurred often enough now that you feel the need to speak up about them. When you now confront her with your problem, she doesn't seem to give a direct answer to your statement.

Situation #3: You have an extreme physical reaction to cigar smoke— watering eyes, a cough, and nausea. When you see a new guest to your home pull out a five-inch stogie, you explain your condition to the smoker using the "I have a problem" format. He responds by saying that once you become used to the aroma you'll hardly notice it, and also insists that it's no worse than the cigarettes you smoke.

Request Making   Up to this point in a conflict your entire effort has been directed toward stating your problem clearly and repeating your assertion until you are sure the other person understands. While this process is sometimes time-consuming and frustrating, it's worth the energy since you can't expect the other person to change without learning why the issue at hand is so important to you. Once you've completed this step, you're ready actually to request some change from the other.

The first thing to realize here is that requests by themselves often aren't effective. In some cases it's necessary to accompany them with a *description of your needs*. Needs and requests are quite different: We make requests to satisfy needs.

—You ask (or want to ask) talkers in a movie theater to be quiet because you need to hear the dialogue.
—You ask friends to social engagements because you need companionship.
—You ask questions in a class or lecture because you need to satisfy your curiosity (or because you need to pass an exam).
—You ask for a refund in a store because you need a more satisfactory item than the one you purchased.

There are two reasons it is important to precede many requests with a statement of your need for making them. First, such a statement will help the other person understand why the request is important to you. Once you make your need clear, there's a greater chance that the other person will help you satisfy it. For instance, when a stranger approaches you and requests some spare change, you probably would be reluctant to comply; however, your attitude might change when the "panhandler" turns out to be a responsible citizen who needs to report a fire from a coin telephone. If a friend asks that you and the other guests leave a party early, your feelings of hurt and resentment might switch to empathy when you learn that she is feeling ill and needs to go to bed.

There is another reason it is important to preface your requests with a description of your needs. Often there is a better way to solve your problem than the one you suggest, and if the other people know the need behind your request, they can propose alternate and perhaps better ways of meeting it. A traveler might ask an inhabitant of a city for the names of some interesting local attractions, explaining that he's new in town, only to find that the resident is hospitable enough to conduct an informal sightseeing tour. In the same way, you might ask a co-worker to cover for you at work so that you can do some necessary shopping and learn that the colleague already has the items you need or can suggest a more convenient place to get them. In a few pages you'll read more about how to satisfy the needs of both parties in a conflict; for now, it's sufficient to understand the importance of stating the reason for you request.

You have already described the needs for each of the conflicts you described on pages 209 and 210. Now take a few moments to think about how you could share these needs with the people involved. Either rehearse a statement you could make with other members of your assertiveness-building group or practice your remarks covertly.

Once you've made your needs clear, it's time to ask the other person to change. At this point it's important to realize that there are several ways of delivering such messages.

The most indirect way is to *hint* at what you want. For example, if you wanted to borrow a few dollars from a friend, you could mention all the expenses you've had lately and talk about how hard it is to make ends meet. If you know that a friend is having a party in the future and you'd like to go, you could casually ask if she had been doing anything interesting lately and remark about your dull social life. Hints such as these are the least threatening way for a person to make requests because they don't involve any risk of direct rejection: Since you never really asked, you can't be turned down. They also have the advantage of making it easy for the other person to refuse, and as such they help unassertive communicators decline without anxiety. On the other hand, hints have several disadvantages. Sometimes they are so indirect that the other person misses them entirely, leaving you no better off than before. In other instances the importance of your request is diminished by the subtlety of its expression, so that people won't take an important need of yours as seriously as you intended it. A final disadvantage of such indirect requesting is that, like most unassertive acts, it often diminishes your self-respect. The thought that comes is "I can't even ask for what I want."

If hinting is the unassertive way of making requests, *demanding* is its aggressive counterpart. Rather than asking, the demander orders the other person to comply. "Shut off that damn music!" the demander shouts. "Don't tell me about your problems, I want you to be a little more affectionate," the insistent husband or wife might hurl at a mate. The results of such aggressive behavior are clear: While such speakers might be able to intimidate others into meeting their needs, often such insistence will only stiffen people's resistance. In any case the demander's inconsistency usually meets with resentment and hurt.

In contrast to the extremes of demanding and hinting lies the assertive course of directly *asking* for what one wants. The advantages of this style make it the usual first choice for meeting needs. By asking the other to change, you make it clear that you are taking responsibility for your thoughts and feelings while allowing the other person a choice of how to behave. Thus, asking demonstrates an attitude of equality and respect between the parties. In addition, a direct request is the clearest way of stating what you want. When accompanied with a statement of your needs, it not only shows how you would like the other person to behave, but also explains why this change is important to you.

▶ Take another look at the conflicts you described on pages 209 and 210. For each one decide how you would like the other person to change and describe how you could make the request by hinting, demanding, and asking assertively.

SAMPLE CONFLICT

Hint "I'm glad you're here. I was beginning to wonder whether I had written the wrong date on my calendar."

Demand "You're going to have to show up on time from now on. I'm sick of waiting around for you."

Ask "From now on I'd like you to show up within a few minutes of the time we agree on."

CONFLICT 1

Hint _____

_____

_____

Demand _____

_____

_____

Ask _____

_____

_____

CONFLICT 2

Hint _____

_____

_____

Demand _____

_____

_____

Ask _____

_____

_____

CONFLICT 3

Hint _____

_____

_____

Demand _____

_____

_____

Ask _____

_____

_____

CONFLICT 4

Hint _____

_____

_____

Demand _____

_____

_____

Ask _____

_____

_____

You can practice your skill in making requests by completing the following tasks.

1. Approach three strangers and ask each one for directions. It doesn't matter whether you already know where to go; the idea here is to become accustomed to asking for what you want.
2. Over the telephone, ask assistance from your local department of motor vehicles on how to transfer ownership of a used car. Remember to use repeated assertion until you are sure you understand the procedure.
3. Request help from the staff of your local library in finding some ob-

scure fact you've always wanted to know—other places in the world that have the same climate as your home, population characteristics of Tasmania, how an air conditioner works, and so on.

4. Ask a friend's advice on how you could improve your appearance. Make it clear that you really want to know.

After making your request, it's often important to describe the consequences that will most likely follow if the other person accepts your proposal, as well as outlining what will probably happen if he/she fails to do so. Stating these consequences helps your partner see the advantages of cooperating with you and the drawbacks of failing to do so.

—"I hope that from now on you'll let me know when you're mad at me instead of keeping it to yourself. If you do, there's a pretty good chance that we can talk about it and work out a solution. As for not telling me, there's no way I can change if I don't know what you want from me."

—"I'd like to finish this whole matter right now by getting a cash refund. I'm sure you've got better things to do than spend your time worrying about a few dollars, and I know I do; so if you can give me the money I'll be on my way. On the other hand, the matter is important enough to me that if we can't settle it now, I'll have to talk to the district sales manager, which will probably result in a lot of aggravation for everybody."

—"In the future I hope you'll come to me with any questions before you type a final copy. If you do that, I can clear up the confusion then and you'll only have to do the job once. If you guess about what you think I want and it turns out to be wrong, you'll only have to do it again, which will cost both of us a lot of unnecessarily wasted time."

In describing the consequences of complying with your request, you enter a tricky area. With the wrong attitude your descriptions will come across as threats and will most likely result in the other person becoming defensive. Realize that what you're doing here is not threatening; rather, you're simply predicting the future as accurately as you can. Make it clear at this point that you want a solution as much as the other person does; that there will be advantages for *both* of you if your proposal is accepted, and drawbacks for both if it's rejected.

▶ In the following spaces describe the consequences that will follow the acceptance or the rejection of the requests you outlined on pages 233 and 234. Phrase your description in a way to demonstrate your nonthreatening attitude and genuine desire to find a solution that's satisfying for both parties.

SAMPLE CONFLICT: "If you can show up on time from now on, I know it will be better for

(continued)

both of us: We won't have to rush so much, and we won't fight over being late. On the other hand, I'm afraid that if we do continue to run late, I'll probably get angrier and angrier."

CONFLICT 1 _____

_____

_____

_____

_____

CONFLICT 2 _____

_____

_____

_____

_____

CONFLICT 3 _____

_____

_____

_____

_____

CONFLICT 4 _____

_____

_____

_____

_____

Negotiate a Solution Now you've made your request in as assertive a manner as possible. You've prefaced it with a description of your need so that the other person understands how important it is to you. You've asked for what you want instead of aggressively demanding your way or unassertively hinting. Finally, you've described both the benefits that both of you will enjoy if your request is met and the problems that are likely to occur if it is rejected.

At this point your partner can respond in two ways. The first is to accept your proposal, in which case most of your problems will be over. On the other hand you may find that the other person rejects your request. At this time don't mistakenly assume that all your efforts are wasted. While it is possible that the other's no is not negotiable, there is still a good chance of resolving the problem in a way that satisfies both partners. The key to success in such cases is recognition that the other person may reject your solution while still acknowledging your need.

Shortly after she turned fifteen, Julie experienced her first taste of the classic parent–teenager conflict. For several months Julie had been going out steadily with Gary, an eighteen-year-old from a nearby town. Julie's mother and father thought highly of their daughter's friend, although they were worried about problems that might arise out of the age difference between him and their daughter. They shared their concern with Julie, predicting that since most of Gary's friends were also older, there would be times when their activities would be out of the league of a fifteen-year-old high school sophomore. At that time Julie assured her parents that both she and Gary understood this and that they were willing to adapt their behavior in an appropriate way when the time came.

The first test came when Gary's best friend and his fiancée announced their upcoming wedding in a city over a hundred miles from Julie's home. Gary and Julie approached her parents with the proposal that they drive to the distant town with several other friends. After attending the wedding and reception the group planned to rent two motel rooms—one for the males and the other for the females—where they would spend the night, returning home the next day.

As soon as they heard this plan, Julie's parents announced that it was unacceptable to them. While they might have agreed if their daughter was older, they stated that in their opinion it just wasn't appropriate for a fifteen-year-old girl to spend the night unescorted in the presence of her boyfriend. Julie responded to this statement with dismay, pleading that there was nothing to worry about and accusing her parents of not trusting her.

At this point most families would have reached an impasse, with both parents and child standing firm on their demand. The typical outcome in such situations is a win-lose one: Either the parents get their way, leaving Julie heartbroken and resentful, or Julie prevails, in which case her parents would be worried while their daughter was away and feel that they had abdicated their responsibility after she returned home. Clearly, neither of these alternatives is particularly desirable. Fortunately for everyone concerned, this family was skilled in the art of negotiating no-lose solutions (Gordon, 1970). By following their behavior in this situation, you can learn the steps in this process and see how it can apply to your own life.

Define Each Party's Needs. Next to defining problem ownership incorrectly, mistakenly focusing only on requests and neglecting needs is the biggest drawback to effective problem solving. In the present example Julie's request was to spend the night in a motel. Following the advice already given in this chapter, Julie didn't merely stop here. She went on to explain her needs behind such a request. First and foremost she needed ("wanted" would have been a more appropriate term) to enjoy what looked to be an exciting time at the wedding. She insisted that the issue of where she slept was really not very important to her, although the thought of being on her own for twenty-four hours did sound like fun. Her second need had to do with the trust of her parents. She was bothered by the fact that in spite of her assurances they didn't seem to believe that she could behave responsibly on the trip.

Julie's parents responded by stating their needs in the situation. The first one they described was a feeling of responsibility for their daughter's welfare. They stated that this responsibility included several factors. The first was a knowledge of exactly where and with whom Julie would be while away from home. Neither they nor Julie had met anyone other than Gary who would be attending the wedding,, and they felt uncomfortable sending their daughter off to a distant city with strangers. They asured her that while all the people involved were probably trustworthy and responsible, they needed to be certain of this fact. Their second need had to do with Julie's inexperience. While they knew that she was a responsible girl, they also were aware that the large quantity of champagne available at the reception might create a situation that would affect her judgment. Knowing that it was impossible to insist that she and her companions would remain teetotalers at such a festive occasion, they feared that Julie might overestimate her alcoholic limit and in so doing lose her usual good judgment. Their fear in this regard centered on two areas—riding in a car with an intoxicated driver, and becoming overly affectionate with Gary. Although Julie assured her parents that they needn't worry on either account, they insisted that their need for reassurance on these matters was very important. They needed to be satisfied before they would agree to the trip.

Once they had reached the stage of making their needs clear, the task for Julie and her parents became to find a solution that would satisfy everyone. How could Julie enjoy the wedding and her parents trust while they could be assured that she was with responsible people and was protected from any lapses in her judgment? In an attempt to answer this question the family moved on to the second step of no-lose problem solving.

Brainstorm Possible Solutions. The idea here is to generate a number of potential solutions that will satisfy everyone's needs, so that you can choose the best one. In their haste to resolve a problem to suit themselves many people become so committed to the first solution they propose that they fail to think about other courses of action that might be more advantageous. To avoid this problem, your goal at this point should be to develop a list of solutions that *might* work. This list should be tentative—many items on it will probably be unworkable. Don't be bothered by this fact as you think of ideas: Simply record everything that comes to mind, realizing that you will have time later to eliminate the bad suggestions. As you make this list, realize that your efforts here should be cooperative. Don't be concerned whether a suggestions belongs to one party or the other—simply jot them down as they occur, regardless of whose they are. If you make one suggestion that triggers a modification on the part of your partner, that's fine—just write both down. After all, if you can find an answer that meet's everyone's needs, it doesn't matter who developed it.

Julie and her parents brainstormed a number of possible solutions that might satisfy their needs:

1. Julie and Gary stay in town and enjoy themselves locally.
2. Julie attends the reception but afterward spends the night at her aunt and uncle's home in the city of the wedding.
3. Julie phones her parents to verify her condition during the reception, before driving to the motel, and upon arrival there.
4. Julie's parents meet the friends of Gary's who will be attending the wedding.
5. Julie, Gary, and their friends find transportation from the reception and a place to stay that is enjoyable and safe.

Choose the Best Alternative. After generating your list of possible solutions, the next step is to pick the best one and modify it so that it suits everyone's needs as much as possible.

Upon reviewing their list, Julie and her parents found several items to be unsatisfactory. Suggestion 1 was clearly out of the question for Julie, who saw the wedding as a major event in her social calendar. Item 2 was also unacceptable for her, since the act of staying with her relatives symbolized attachment to the family apron strings Julie wanted to untie for the occasion. Julie was agreeable to the third suggestion, for she thought she could make the phone calls without attracting attention to herself as a "mama's girl." However, it didn't satisfy the parents' need of knowing the people their daughter would be spending so much time with. The fourth suggestion didn't satisfy all of the parents' concern either, for while they would know more about Julie's companions, they would have no guarantee of how everyone might behave under the festive conditions of the reception and its aftermath.

The final item sounded appealing to both Julie and her parents, although they were at a loss as to who might provide such enjoyable and safe transportation and lodging. The deadlock seemed unbreakable until Julie asked Gary to join the conversation in hope that he could offer a suggestion. After being informed of the situation, Gary had an idea: His older brother and sister-in-law, both in their middle twenties, would also be attending the wedding. Both were schoolteachers, and thus seemed responsible enough to Julie's parents. At the same time they were young enough to be acceptable as companions for the trip. Gary thought that they might be willing to keep an eye on Julie at the reception and stay at the same motel afterward. Since they lived in the same town as did Julie's family, perhaps they could meet each other before the trip to get acquainted and verify the arrangements. This plan sounded fine to Julie and Gary and also appealed to the parents. When Gary proposed the idea to his brother and sister-in-law, they also agreed, and the problem was resolved to everyone's satisfaction.

Evaluate Your Solution in a Checkup Meeting. Even the best-conceived plans often turn out to be flawed in practice. Since these imperfections are to be expected, it's usually a good idea to meet with the other person involved after your solution has been in effect for a while to see if any modifications are necessary.

The only problem involving Julie and Gary's trip to the wedding occurred on the return journey. The car they were traveling in broke down and required repairs that delayed their homecoming by several hours. Since Julie's parents were still apprehensive about her trip in spite of their agreement, this delay led to considerable worry on their part. After sharing their concern with their daughter, all agreed that in the future Julie would phone home as soon as possible after any major change in plans occurred, to let her parents know that she was all right.

No-lose solutions often seem simple in retrospect, but they take a considerable amount of skill and goodwill to implement. As you read earlier, the biggest hurdle to overcome is the tendency to believe that one party in a conflict must be a loser. This attitude leads partners to defend their original proposal against any reservations the other person might have, believing that any modification would be a defeat. Simply believing that satisfaction of one's needs is the ultimate goal, and further that it's possible to get what you want while at the same time helping the other person, can make a world of difference in your conflicts. Of course good intentions alone will not solve problems. A second point to keep in mind is the importance of cooperatively generating a list of possible solutions without critically evaluating any of them at that point. Nothing stifles creativity so much as criticism: Often a farfetched idea leads to a second and more realistic one, and any defensiveness or reservation to speak out can squelch what might be the ideal solution to your problem. Finally, remember the importance of following up on your solutions after they have had a chance to work for a while. It often happens that the most valuable ideas come after both parties have had a chance to experience their plan in action and see how it can be improved.

CHECKLIST FOR ASSERTIVE CONFLICT MANAGEMENT

You can use the following list as a guideline to ensure that you approach the inevitable conflicts in your life in a manner that gives the best chance of producing satisfying results for both partners.

There are two ways to use the list—either as a diagnostic tool by which you can analyze unproductive communication styles in your previous conflicts, or as a step-by-step guideline you can follow while actually working through a problem.

—Identify ownership of the problem
—Present the problem to the other person using "I" language
    —describe the behavior that bothers you
    —outline the consequences of the other's behavior on you
    —express your feelings that result from the other's behavior
—Persist until you are sure the other person hears and understands you
    —use "repeated assertion"
—Make your request assertively
    —preface the request with a need
    —when appropriate, ask—don't hint or demand
    —describe the consequences of accepting and rejecting your proposal
—Negotiate a no-lose solution if necessary
    —restate your needs and learn those of the other party
    —brainstorm possible solutions
    —choose the best alternative
    —plan a checkup meeting to evaluate progress

SAYING NO

As the pages you have just read suggest, there are many situations in which it's best to negotiate a no-lose solution when you're faced with an undesirable request. In other cases, however, it is essential to simply and unequivocally say no when asked for certain things.

The most common time to say no is when your relationship with the person doing the requesting isn't important to you. In such cases it simply isn't worth the considerable effort that is usually required to negotiate a no-lose solution. Times when you would not care to meet the other's needs might include the following:

—A door-to-door solicitor interrupts your sleep to seek contributions for a cause you do not support.

—A co-worker who never repays her obligations asks you for a few dollars "until Monday."

—A stranger with several grocery items asks permission to move in front of you in the checkout line when you are already late for an appointment.

A second occasion for unequivocally saying no is when your dignity or an important personal principle is jeopardized. Breaking the law, embarrassing others, or breaking personal commitments would all fall into the category of nonnegotiable principles. You might, for instance, refuse outright to agree with the following proposals:

—A business associate proposes that you sign receipts making it possible for him to cheat on his income tax.

—A group of friends invites you to join in gossip about an absent third person.

—Your host at a party urges you to break your diet by enjoying a rich dessert.

In addition to times you don't care about others and cases in which your personal principles are at stake, a third instance in which saying no is appropriate takes place with people who matter to you, but over issues that aren't important enough to merit strenuous no-lose negotiations. Sometimes a request is undesirable enough to necessitate your refusal, but not so important that your unqualified no will jeopardize a relationship. For instance:

—A friend casually invites you to a party when you feel like staying home.

—Your employer asks you to work late on a noncritical project when you already have other plans.

—A neighbor asks you to help move some furniture when you are occupied with a chore of your own.

While most of the situations don't seem of much importance, many people have an incredibly difficult time saying no when faced with them. This difficulty stems from two of the myths you were introduced to in Chapter 2. Some communicators resist saying no because of the myth of acceptance, believing that it's necessary for them to gain the approval of others in everything they do. When saddled with this burden, every no increases the risk of disapproval and thus jeopardizes one's chance of being universally loved. Of course, there are problems that come with this striving for acceptance: First, by compromising ideals and inconveniencing oneself, one loses self-respect. It is hard to feel good about yourself when you know you constantly bend to the wishes of others. A second consequence of seeking total acceptance by never saying no is that you often wind up in a double bind, where it is impossible to please two people who have conflicting needs. If one friend wants you to be serious and another wants you to act playfully, you are in trouble. If two hosts invite you to parties on the same date and the person with whom you live wants you to stay home, you are in a difficult situation. Trying to win acceptance from everyone can be an exhausting and discouraging goal.

A second myth that prevents communicators from saying no is the myth of perfection, the idea that you can and should try to meet everyone's needs. You have probably know people who fit this description. They are constantly subordinating their own needs to those of others—doing favors, lending money, running errands, and generally solving the problems others have created for themselves. Sometimes these people are regarded as selfless martyrs, but just as often others see them as doormats or suckers who constantly let others take advantage of them. In addition to the wear and tear that comes with trying to be perfect and the ridicule that often results from these efforts, these martyrs often build up a reservoir resentment toward others: "Why should I always be the good guy?" But they never express these sentiments directly, since to do so would detract from their perfect nature. As a result of these unexpressed feelings, saints often turn into indirect aggressors, complying with every request that is made of them, yet punishing those who do the asking by later criticizing, gossiping, or other crazymaking activities.

Since there are clearly times when it's important to say no, you need to learn how to do so. The first step is to realize that there are several ways of delivering such a message.

The first way is to say no with abuse. ("I don't have time to do your chores. If you want the furniture moved, hire someone to do the job.") This directly aggressive course of action includes criticizing, complaining, and ridiculing. Needless to say, while such behavior will get you out of complying with the request, the unpleasant feelings it generates makes it unacceptable as an alternative.

The unassertive way to say no is to offer an unsound excuse, by claiming that the refusal is really not a matter of choice but is due to circumstances beyond one's control. ("I would help you move tomorrow, but I have to do some work around the house.") Sometimes such excuses are outright lies, which can be embarrassing when they are detected. In other cases the extenuating circumstances are true, but they could be changed if you really wanted to comply.

An indirectly aggressive way to refuse is to agree to comply and then fail to do so. This course of action has the short-term advantage of making you seem compliant and thus avoid the discomfort of saying no; in the long run, of course, it can only cause trouble.

In contrast to these generally unsatisfactory ways of declining requests stand two assertive alternatives. The first is to accompany your no with an explanation. Unlike excuses, explanations make it clear that you accept responsibility for your refusal rather than blaming the choice on some outside force. ("Today isn't a good day for me to help you—I have several things I want to do around here.") Your explanation has the advantage of letting the other person know the reason behind your choice. On the other hand, there will be occasions when a simple no unaccompanied by any other comment is the most appropriate response. This will be especially suitable for use with strangers or people you don't care about. This simple, unadorned refusal is based on the principle that you are under no obligation to explain yourself to others, though you may choose to do so.

Like other types of messages, you can't always expect others to understand or to accept your refusal the first time you offer it. On many occasions you will need to use the technique of repeated assertion introduced on page 228 to make your intentions clear. This is especially true when others seek your compliance by trying to make you feel guilty or otherwise manipulate you. Just remember that in these cases all you need do is to repeat your message calmly over and over until the other person gets the point. Notice that there is no need to accompany your refusal with aggressive abuse or unassertive excuses. A simple series of no's with one explanation is sufficient, as is illustrated by the following confrontation between a door-to-door solicitor and a householder.

SOLICITOR: Good afternoon. I'm from the Save the Rutabegas Foundation, and I'd like to talk with you about a matter that concerns every citizen.
HOUSEHOLDER: I'm very busy now, and I'm not interested.
S: Did you realize that the rutabega is an endangered species?
H: No, and I'm not interested.
S: Surely you're concerned at the thought that special-interest groups are waging a deliberate campaign to take away your freedom of choice to enjoy one of nature's finest foods.
H: I'm really not interested.
S: Well, before I go I'd just like to leave this envelope with you. It explains our cause and gives you a way to send in a few dollars if you see fit.
H: No, thank you. I'm not interested.

In addition to saying no, there is another alternative you can use when faced with an undesirable request: You can withhold your decision until you have thought about how to respond. Many communicators find themselves agreeing with others simply because they have been caught off guard. At the moment they cannot think of any logical reason for refusing, yet they also can't think of anything to say to the requester. As a consequence, they say yes almost as a reflex. Although it seems so obvious that it hardly needs saying, it's important that you remember that you are under no obligation to answer most requests immediately. "I'd like to think about it" is a perfectly acceptable response.

The following exercises offer good practice in declining unwanted requests. Practice them either with a partner or on your own using covert behavior rehearsal.

Identify a personal possession that is precious to you. Imagine or act out a scene in which another person attempts to borrow that item using flattery, trickery, humiliation, helplessness, guilt, and any other devices available. Your job is to refuse the request in the most assertive and persistent manner possible.

Once you have completed this phase, go on to imagine that the other person is now trying to take away a personal trait that you value (honesty, helpfulness, goodwill, etc.) by asking you to carry out an act contrary to your principles. Again, the other persons are using all the tactics at their disposal, and your task is to stand your ground without becoming aggressive or unassertive.

A second activity involves a partner escalating the demands after you have initially agreed to a certain course of action. For instance, if you have agreed to water his plants for a weekend, the partner increases the demand by insisting that you do so for a week, then a month, and so on—until you are assertive enough to stand your ground and refuse. Repeat the same process with a borrowed item (first asking the loan of your car for an hour and escalating to a month), and finally with a matter of principle (asking you to tell a "white lie" and then moving on to more serious falsehoods).

SAMPLE DIALOGUE

To make the principles in this chapter clearer, here is a dialogue between two communicators using the principles of assertive communication to resolve a conflict. Anna and Margo have been friends since their college days. Since then they have lived in the same town and continued to share common interests. They play tennis and attend adult education classes together. They travel in the same circle of friends, have similar families, and share many views about their role in society. Their friendship extends into the area of doing favors for each other. When one is sick, the other cooks meals. They babysit for each other's children, and when one is involved in a project, the other has always helped out in any way she could.

In the past year Anna has started to build an increasingly successful business as an interior decorator. Working out of her home, she has been able to secure several residential jobs, and she is now aiming toward some large commercial projects. As her business has continued to grow, Anna has experienced a new problem with Margo. Before, the two woman would happily spend hours on end trading ideas; Anna often has little time available for such pastimes now. Because the practice of dropping by each other's home to chat has always been a part of their relationship, Anna has been reluctant to speak up about her problem so far. Today, however, the issue had come to a head. Anna is frantically trying to meet a deadline, and Margo has just stopped in to chat and seems prepared to spend the whole afternoon.

MARGO: . . . Anyway, I wanted you to come down to the village with me this afternoon to take a look at the new bank there. It's really designed well, and I thought you might get some ideas for your projects from it.

ANNA: (*uncertainly*) Er, that's a good idea. I'd like to do that. (*NONASSERTION: The only thing Anna wants to do this afternoon is to finish her work.*)

M: Great. And afterward I thought it might be fun to stop off at Swensen's for an ice cream sundae. It's time for our once-a-week splurge, eh?

A: (*speaking sarcastically as she suddenly begins to resent Margo's role as social director when there is so much to do*) Gee, that would be wonderful. And after we do that, why don't we go window-shopping? Then we could play a few sets of tennis, go to the gym, and drop by the college to see if there are any new classes. After all, this old project doesn't matter as much as blowing a whole afternoon! (*INDIRECT AGGRESSION*)

M: Hey, what's the matter? I just thought it would be fun to fool around a bit.

A: (*her voice a mixture of anger and despair at losing her temper and being so far behind*) Can't you see that I don't have time to waste like you do? It would really be nice if I could just drop everything, but I have a job to do. I would think you'd understand that without my having to spell it out in black and white. (*DIRECT AGGRESSION*)

M: (*shaken but trying unsuccessfully to keep back her tears*) I didn't realize that I was bothering you. I'm sorry. I should have known that I've been a pest—it won't happen again. (*Stumbles toward the door*)

A: Wait! I'm sorry, Margo. I'm so frazzled now that I'm saying things I don't really mean—or at least saying them in the wrong way. I should have told you a long time ago that I've been having a problem with our visiting. You know that I enjoy being with you more than almost anybody. . . . It's just that when I'm wrapped up in a project and you drop by unexpectedly wanting to play, I wind up going along when I should stay home and work. When that happens, I feel so guilty and distracted that I'm not very good company. And what makes matters worse, I've taken to blaming you when it's really my fault for not speaking up. How could you know what's bothering me—you're not a mind reader. (*Anna uses "I" LANGUAGE to acknowledge ownership of her problem and to identify Margo's troublesome behavior, its consequences, and her feelings.*)

M: (*now more upset than before—she didn't realize how long her friend had felt this way*) I see. I wish I had known that your job was more important than our friendship. As I said, it won't happen any more.

A: No, Margo. You didn't understand what I was trying to say. Our friendship is more important than I could ever say, and I don't want to do anything to harm it. It's only the times when you drop by unexpectedly and I'm up against a deadline that messes me up. That's when I visit with you when I shouldn't and then feel so guilty and resentful. I know that it's my problem, and I want to do something to clear it up. (*REPEATED ASSERTION*)

M: (*now somewhat reassured that Anna still cares about her*) Well, what do you think ought to be done?

A: The thing I need is to be undisturbed when I'm rushing to make a deadline. I guess the best thing for me would be if you would call ahead before you come over so I could tell you if I'm busy. If you did that, I could tell you that I was up to my ears and it would save us scenes like this. Then when I did say that I was free, we could have a good time, knowing that there was no job lurking in my conscience. (*Anna STATES HER NEEDS, MAKES A REQUEST, and DESCRIBES THE CONSEQUENCES of complying and failing to do so.*)

M: Gee, I don't really like the idea of having to phone ahead. Somehow that takes all the spontaneity out of my dropping by, and that's half the fun. How about if you just tell me when you're busy and I'll leave? (*Margo SHARES HER NEED, and they begin to BRAINSTORM POSSIBLE SOLUTIONS*)

A: Here's another idea: I could set aside one or two days a week for our time together, and we could do our visiting then. That way I'd know exactly when to work and when to play." (*more BRAINSTORMING*)

M: Hmmm. That's not too spontaneous either. Listen: You've said before that this decorating business is wearing you down. Why don't you just take a few months off and see how important it really is? That would solve our problem.

A: No, that won't work. The job is too important to give up. I'm sure there's a solution that will let me work and keep up our friendship too. (*Anna gives an unequivocal NO WITH EXPLANATION when faced with abandoning her important values*)

M: Okay. I didn't realize it was that important. How about letting *me* know when you're busy? I can stay away then, and when I don't hear from you, I'll know that it's okay to come over.

A: That sounds good. Let's try it for a month or two and see if it works. But look: Even if it doesn't, let's try to figure something out. I haven't liked myself lately for not talking to you about this, and I don't want to let things get bad again. (*The friends CHOOSE THE BEST SOLUTION AND PLAN A CHECKUP MEETING TO EVALUATE PROGRESS*)

M: (*relieved*) Neither do I! Let me know when you finish this job so we can celebrate our new regime!

SUMMARY

Any conflict can be looked on as consisting of one or more sets of apparently incompatible needs. Because people's needs can be expected to differ frequently, it is realistic to expect that conflicts will be inevitable in any relationship. The key to successful communication is not to avoid such problems, but to handle them skillfully when they do occur.

There are four ways in which people act when their needs are not met. The first is nonassertively, when the individual ignores the need or denies its importance. The second response is direct aggression, in which the person with the problem attacks the other with criticism or blame. The third possible response is indirect aggression, in which the individual expresses hostility in a more subtle manner. The final type of response is assertion, a mode of behavior that has the greatest chance of meeting with success and strengthening the relationship.

Assertive problem-solving consists of four steps. First, it is essential to identify the problem as one's own by using "I" language. The second step is to ensure that the other person has correctly received the message; this can be achieved by using the technique of repeated assertion when necessary. The third stage calls for making one's request directly, prefacing it with a statement of needs and following it with a description of the likely consequences of compliance and noncompliance. Finally, it is important to negotiate a no-lose solution to the problem, one that satisfies the needs of both parties.

There are some cases in which no negotiation is possible and where a simple no, possible accompanied by an explanation, is called for. These include situations in which the relationship is not important to the initiator, times when one's dignity or important personal principles are involved, and cases where the relationship will not be jeopardized by a failure to negotiate a solution. People generally fear saying no at such times because of adherence to two irrational beliefs: (1) the idea that it is important to be universally accepted; (2) the myth that it is always possible to satisfy everyone's needs. In many cases others will not accept the first refusal of a request. When this occurs, it is important to use repeated assertion to make one's message clear. Finally, it is important to realize that one need not always answer a request as soon as it is made: In some situations it is more desirable simply to state that one needs more time to think about the proposal.

Owning the problem.

"Who's next?"—handling conflicts skillfully.

Appendix I

Possible Assertive Goals

This list contains a number of common assertive goals. Examining it can help you select and clarify your own assertive target behaviors.

The list is divided into four categories, each of which deals with some aspect of assertive communication. As you read the items, place a check next to the ones that you might work on with profit. Upon completing this step, you can specify several personal targets by combining elements from several categories. For instance, you might decide to work on saying no in a loud, firm voice to strangers who approach you in public places to solicit contributions.

As you define each goal, record it in Appendix II.

If you are interested in seeking more information about an item on the list, refer to the index for the appropriate page references.

A. *People* with whom you want to behave more assertively
——parents
——children
——spouse

——other relatives
——co-workers
——supervisor
——subordinates
——strangers
——neighbors
——friends
——instructors
——salespeople
——physician
——hired help (plumber, etc.)

——other _____

——other _____

B. *Settings* in which you would like to behave more assertively
——home
——work
——school
——parties
——public places
——stores
——restaurants
——unfamiliar places (when lost, etc.)
——in a group

——other _____

——other _____

C. *Emotional moods* during which you want to communicate more assertively
——angry
——rushed
——tired
——happy
——sad
——confused
——affectionate
——hurt
——defensive

D. *Subjects* you would like to discuss more assertively
——finances
——sex

——politics
——religion
——obscenity
——parent-child communication

——other _____

——other _____

E. *Skills* you would like to acquire or improve
——saying no to unwanted requests
——starting conversations
——carrying on conversations
——terminating conversations
——asking questions
——asking for help
——coping with criticism
——offering criticism
——stating needs
——expressing feelings verbally (specify the feeling)
——expressing feelings nonverbally (specify the feeling)
——making introductions
——standing up for personal rights
——expressing personal opinions
——giving compliments
——receiving compliments
——using "I" language
——defining problem ownership
——negotiating no-lose solutions
——projecting consequences
——increasing eye contact
——selecting appropriate distance for communication
——improving facial expression
——improving gestures
——improving posture
——improving body orientation
——speaking with appropriate volume
——speaking at appropriate rate
——improving vocal fluency (reducing "um," "er," etc.)
——speaking with appropriate tone
——speaking with appropriate inflection
——speaking in complete sentences
——expressing ideas concisely, in single core sentences
——reducing use of verbal qualifiers

Appendix II

Personal Assertive Goals

Use the spaces below to record the specific ways in which you would like to behave more assertively. It is important to write out each goal as you think of it. By doing so and keeping all your target behaviors in one place, you will be better able to consolidate any similar objectives into broader categories and then to establish priorities for reaching them.

In writing out your personal goals, be sure to follow the format indicated. First describe the person or people involved. Next describe the circumstances in which you want to communicate more effectively: The times and places, if they are significant, as well as your emotional mood or any other factors that set these occasions apart from other ones. Finally, be sure to describe the specific, desirable way in which you want to behave. If you have any problems answering these questions, see Chapter 3.

ASSERTIVE GOAL 1

People involved _____

The circumstances in which I want to behave more assertively _____

_____

_____

_____

The specific way in which I want to behave _____

_____

_____

_____

ASSERTIVE GOAL 2

People involved _____

_____

The circumstances in which I want to behave more assertively _____

_____

_____

_____

The specific way in which I want to behave _____

_____

_____

_____

ASSERTIVE GOAL 3

People involved _____

_____

The circumstances in which I want to behave more assertively _____

_____

_____

_____

The specific way in which I want to behave _____

_____

_____

_____

ASSERTIVE GOAL 4

People involved _____

_____

The circumstances in which I want to behave more assertively _____

_____

_____

_____

The specific way in which I want to behave _____

_____

_____

_____

ASSERTIVE GOAL 5

People involved _____

_____

The circumstances in which I want to behave more assertively _____

_____

_____

_____

The specific way in which I want to behave _____

_____

_____

_____

ASSERTIVE GOAL 6

People involved _____

_____

The circumstances in which I want to behave more assertively _____

_____

_____

_____

The specific way in which I want to behave _____

_____

_____

_____

ASSERTIVE GOAL 7

People involved _____

_____

The circumstances in which I want to behave more assertively _____

_____

_____

_____

The specific way in which I want to behave _____

_____

_____

_____

ASSERTIVE GOAL 8

People involved _____

_____

The circumstances in which I want to behave more assertively _____

_____

_____

_____

The specific way in which I want to behave _____

_____

_____

_____

ASSERTIVE GOAL 9

People involved _____

_____

The circumstances in which I want to behave more assertively _____

_____

_____

_____

The specific way in which I want to behave _____

_____

_____

_____

ASSERTIVE GOAL 10

People involved _____

_____

The circumstances in which I want to behave more assertively _____

_____

_____

_____

The specific way in which I want to behave _____

_____

_____

_____

ASSERTIVE GOAL 11

People involved _____

_____

The circumstances in which I want to behave more assertively _____

_____

_____

_____

The specific way in which I want to behave _____

_____

_____

_____

ASSERTIVE GOAL 12

People involved _____

_____

The circumstances in which I want to behave more assertively _____

_____

_____

_____

The specific way in which I want to behave _____

_____

_____

_____

ASSERTIVE GOAL 13

People involved _____

_____

The circumstances in which I want to behave more assertively _____

_____

_____

_____

The specific way in which I want to behave _____

_____

_____

_____

ASSERTIVE GOAL 14

People involved _____

_____

The circumstances in which I want to behave more assertively _____

_____

_____

_____

The specific way in which I want to behave _____

_____

_____

_____

ASSERTIVE GOAL 15

People involved _____

_____

The circumstances in which I want to behave more assertively _____

_____

_____

_____

The specific way in which I want to behave _____

_____

_____

_____

ASSERTIVE GOAL 16

People involved _____

_____

The circumstances in which I want to behave more assertively _____

_____

_____

_____

The specific way in which I want to behave _____

_____

_____

_____

ASSERTIVE GOAL 17

People involved _____

_____

The circumstances in which I want to behave more assertively _____

_____

_____

_____

The specific way in which I want to behave _____

_____

_____

_____

ASSERTIVE GOAL 18

People involved _____

_____

The circumstances in which I want to behave more assertively _____

_____

_____

_____

The specific way in which I want to behave _____

_____

_____

_____

ASSERTIVE GOAL 19

People involved _____

_____

The circumstances in which I want to behave more assertively _____

_____

_____

_____

The specific way in which I want to behave _____

_____

_____

_____

ASSERTIVE GOAL 20

People involved _____

_____

The circumstances in which I want to behave more assertively _____

_____

_____

_____

The specific way in which I want to behave _____

_____

_____

_____

ASSERTIVE GOAL 21

People involved _____

_____

The circumstances in which I want to behave more assertively _____

_____

_____

_____

The specific way in which I want to behave _____

_____

_____

_____

ASSERTIVE GOAL 22

People involved _____

_____

The circumstances in which I want to behave more assertively _____

_____

_____

_____

The specific way in which I want to behave _____

_____

_____

_____

ASSERTIVE GOAL 23

People involved _____

_____

The circumstances in which I want to behave more assertively _____

_____

_____

_____

The specific way in which I want to behave _____

_____

_____

_____

ASSERTIVE GOAL 24

People involved _____

_____

The circumstances in which I want to behave more assertively _____

_____

_____

_____

The specific way in which I want to behave _____

_____

_____

_____

ASSERTIVE GOAL 25

People involved _____

_____

The circumstances in which I want to behave more assertively _____

_____

_____

_____

The specific way in which I want to behave _____

_____

_____

_____

Appendix III

Self-Modification Progress Charts

The following charts are the heart of your Assertiveness-Building Project, as described in Chapter 6. They will provide a summary of exactly how you want to communicate and show where you stand in relation to your goal. In addition to measuring your progress, the charts will help you diagnose and remedy problems that may occur during your project. For samples of completed progress charts see Appendix IV.

To complete your chart, follow these steps:
1. Establish a behaviorally clear communication target (see pages 55–63, 112–113). Record it in the appropriate space on your chart.
2. Record a baseline period, during which you measure the frequency with which you engage in your target behavior before trying to change (pages 113–123).
3. Establish intermediate goals, which you will use to gradually increase the frequency of your target behavior. Be sure to set your first intermediate goal just slightly above your baseline frequency, and to make the space between goals modest enough to ensure your success (pages 123–130). If your intermediate goals consist of separate ele-

ments (pages 127–128), use the supplementary chart in this appendix to record your progress on the intermediate goals and the main chart to record the frequency of your target behavior. See the sample supplementary chart in Appendix IV.

4. List a number of reinforcers you can use to increase the frequency of assertive behaviors (pages 131–144). These reinforcers should fall into two categories:
   a. Rewards you can give yourself for each individual assertive act (required)
   b. Rewards for reaching each intermediate goal (optional)

   Remember to consider token and multiple reinforcers.

▶ SELF-MODIFICATION PROGRESS CHART

TENTATIVE INTERMEDIATE GOALS*   REINFORCERS*

1. _____   _____
2. _____   _____
3. _____   _____
4. _____   _____
5. _____   _____
6. _____   _____
7. _____   _____
8. _____   _____

Frequency of Target Behaviors
Described in (c) Below

Days

Target

a. The person or people involved _____
    _____

b. The circumstances in which I want to behave more assertively _____
    _____

c. The specific behavior(s) I want to increase _____
    _____

*Projects following the elements approach should use the Supplementary Progress Chart on the next page to record intermediate goals and reinforcers.

► SUPPLEMENTARY PROGRESS CHART
(Sample in Appendix IV)

1. Use this chart in projects with intermediate steps consisting of separate elements. (See pages 127–128.)

2. As you work on each element, describe it in the leftmost clear space above the graph, and record your progress immediately below.

3. Along with each intermediate goal, describe the reinforcer you will use to increase its frequency.

4. In addition to working on the intermediate goals listed below, remember to keep recording the frequency of your ultimate target on the Self-Modification Progress Chart. As you master each intermediate goal, you should begin to see improvement on your final target.

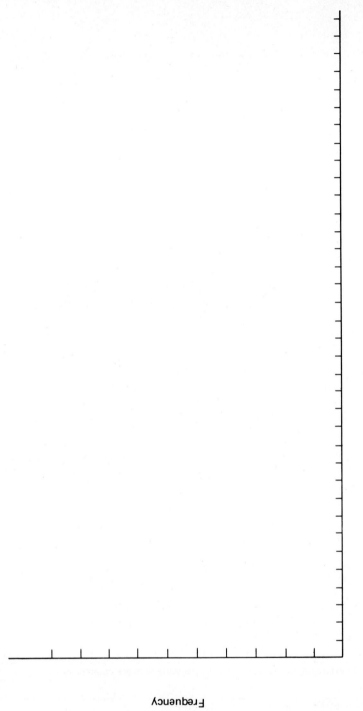

Frequency

Days

Appendix IV

Sample Self-Modification Progress Charts

The following charts illustrate how to record progress during your self-modification project. Notice that each chart clearly

a. describes the target behavior
b. records baseline data for a reasonable period of time
c. sets a realistic final goal
d. establishes manageable intermediate goals
e. specifies reinforcers to be awarded for achieving goals

As you examine these charts, pay close attention to the one that follows the method of counting behaviors you have selected after reading pages 113–116.

SELF-MODIFICATION PROGRESS CHART
Duration Method with Token Reinforcers

TENTATIVE INTERMEDIATE GOALS*	REINFORCERS*
1. 5 minutes	Each conversation in which I reach the present
2. 6 minutes	Intermediate goal earns 1 point
3. 7 minutes	5 points = one hour swimming
4. 8 minutes	10 points = weekend boating
5. 9 minutes	15 points = new lens for camera
6. 10 minutes	20 points = trip to visit J. L.
7.	
8.	

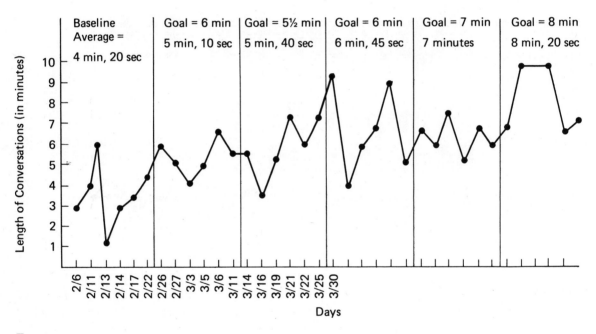

Target

a. The person or people involved   *people I meet who seem interesting.*

b. The circumstances in which I want to behave more assertively   *when at parties or other occasions where conditions permit an extended conversation (quiet enough with sufficient time).*

c. The specific behavior(s) I want to increase   *increase length of conversations to 10 minutes or longer.*

SELF-MODIFICATION PROGRESS CHART
Percentage Method

TENTATIVE INTERMEDIATE GOALS*

1. 30% _____
2. 40% _____
3. 50% _____
4. 60% _____
5. 70% _____
6. _____
7. _____
8. _____

REINFORCERS*

Each time I express an opinion I earn one of the following:

Watch 15 minutes of T.V. news _____
10 minutes reading TIME magazine _____
Pre-bedtime snack _____
Ride bike to park _____
_____
_____
_____

NOTE: Expressing my opinions 70% of the time is about right for me. Sometimes it's best to keep my mouth shut!

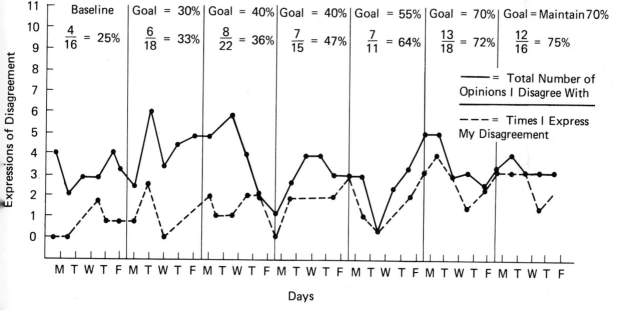

Days

Target

a. The person or people involved _supervisors and colleagues at work._

b. The circumstances in which I want to behave more assertively _when I disagree with them about how to do a job._

c. The specific behavior(s) I want to increase _to express my opinion clearly._

271

SELF–MODIFICATION PROGRESS CHART
Elements Approach (also see next page)

TENTATIVE INTERMEDIATE GOALS*	REINFORCERS*
	See next page

1. Start interview with open-ended question
2. Ask at least 20 questions per hour
3. Keep eye contact when asking questions
4. Allow subject to talk without interrupting
5. Ask for clarification when confused
6.
7.
8.

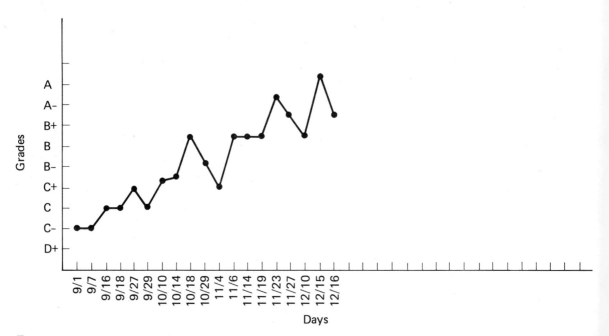

Target

a. The person or people involved *subjects I'm assigned to interview in my journalism class.*

b. The circumstances in which I want to behave more assertively *while arranging and conducting interviews.*

c. The specific behavior(s) I want to increase *the grade I receive on articles for my journalism class.*

SUPPLEMENTARY PROGRESS CHART

1. Use this chart in projects with intermediate steps consisting of separate elements. (See pages 127–128).

2. As you work on each element, describe it in the leftmost clear space above the graph, and record your progress immediately below.

3. Along with each intermediate goal, describe the reinforcer you will use to increase its frequency.

4. In addition to working on the intermediate goals listed below, remember to keep recording the frequency of your ultimate target on the Self-Modification Progress Chart. As you master each intermediate coal, you should begin to see improvement on your final target.

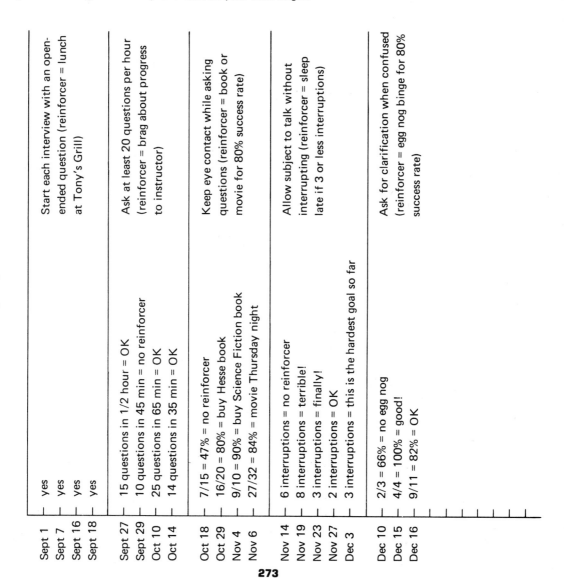

Frequency

Start each interview with an open-ended question (reinforcer = lunch at Tony's Grill)

Ask at least 20 questions per hour (reinforcer = brag about progress to instructor)

Keep eye contact while asking questions (reinforcer = book or movie for 80% success rate)

Allow subject to talk without interrupting (reinforcer = sleep late if 3 or less interruptions)

Ask for clarification when confused (reinforcer = egg nog binge for 80% success rate)

Sept 1	yes
Sept 7	yes
Sept 16	yes
Sept 18	yes
Sept 27	15 questions in 1/2 hour = OK
Sept 29	10 questions in 45 min = no reinforcer
Oct 10	25 questions in 65 min = OK
Oct 14	14 questions in 35 min = OK
Oct 18	7/15 = 47% = no reinforcer
Oct 29	16/20 = 80% = buy Hesse book
Nov 4	9/10 = 90% = buy Science Fiction book
Nov 6	27/32 = 84% = movie Thursday night
Nov 14	6 interruptions = no reinforcer
Nov 19	8 interruptions = terrible!
Nov 23	3 interruptions = finally!
Nov 27	2 interruptions = OK
Dec 3	3 interruptions = this is the hardest goal so far
Dec 10	2/3 = 66% = no egg nog
Dec 15	4/4 = 100% = good!
Dec 16	9/11 = 82% = OK

Selected References

Adler, R. and Towne, N. *Looking Out/Looking In: Interpersonal Communication,* 2d ed. New York: Holt, Rinehart and Winston, 1978.

Alberti, R. and Emmons, M. *Your Perfect Right,* 2d ed. San Luis Obispo, Calif.: Impact, 1974.

Aronson, E. *The Social Animal.* New York: Viking Press, 1972.

Bach, G. and Goldberg, H. *Creative Aggression.* New York: Doubleday, 1974.

—— and Deutsch, R. *Pairing.* New York: Avon, 1970.

—— and Wyden, P. *The Intimate Enemy.* New York: Avon, 1968.

Bernstein, D. and Borkovec, T. *Progressive Relaxation Training.* Champaign, Ill.: Research Press, 1973.

Bodner, G. "The Role of Assessment in Assertion Training." *Counseling Psychologist,* 5, no. 4 (1975), 90–96.

Cotler, S. and Guerra, J. *Assertion Training: A Humanistic-Behavioral Guide to Self-Dignity.* Champaign, Ill.: Research Press, 1976.

Dunbar, F. *Mind and Body: Psychosomatic Medicine.* New York: Random House, 1947.

Ellis, A. *Humanistic Psychotherapy: The Rational-Emotive Approach.* New York: Julian Press, 1973.

——. *Reason and Emotion in Psychotherapy.* New York: Lyle Stuart, 1962.

—— and Harper, R. *A New Guide to Rational Living.* Englewood Cliffs, N.J.: Prentice-Hall, 1975.

Fensterheim, H. and Baer, J. *Don't Say Yes When You Want to Say No.* New York: David McKay, 1975.

Flowers, J., Cooper, C., and Whitley, J. "Approaches to Assertion Training." *Counseling Psychologist,* 5, no. 4 (1975).

Franks, C. (ed.) *Behavior Therapy: Appraisal and Status.* New York: McGraw-Hill, 1969.

Gordon, T. *The Basic Modules of the Instructor Outline for Effectiveness Training Courses.* Pasadena, Calif.: Effectiveness Training Associates, 1971.

——. *Parent Effectiveness Training.* New York: Peter H. Wyden, 1970.

Hall, E. *The Hidden Dimension.* Garden City, N.Y.: Doubleday, 1969.

——. *The Silent Language.* Greenwich, Conn.: Fawcett Books, 1959.

Hersen, M. and Bellack, A. "Assessment of Social Skills" in Ciminero, A., Calhoun, K., and Adams, H. (eds.). *Handbook for Behavioral Assessment.* New York: Wiley, 1977.

Jakubowski, P. and Lacks, P. "Assessment Procedures in Assertion Training." *Counseling Psychologist,* 5, no. 4 (1975), 84–90.

Kranzler, G. *You Can Change How You Feel.* Eugene, Ore.: Cascade Press, 1974.

Langer, E. and Abelson, R. "The Semantics of Asking a Favor: How to Succeed in Getting Help Without Really Dying." *Journal of Personal and Social Psychology,* 24 (1972), 26–32.

Lazarus, A. and Fay, A. *I Can if I Want To.* New York: William Morrow, 1975.

McCroskey, J. "The Implementation of a Large-Scale Program of Systematic Desensitization for Communication Apprehension." *Speech Teacher,* 21, no. 4 (1972), 225–264.

McQuade, W. and Aikman, A. *Stress.* New York: E. P. Dutton, 1974.

Mahoney, M. and Thoresen, C. *Self-Control: Power to the Person.* Monterey, Calif.: Brooks/Cole, 1974.

Marquis, J., Morgan, W. and Piaget, G. *A Guidebook for Systematic Desensitization,* 4th ed. Palo Alto, Calif.: Veterans' Administration Hospital, 1974.

Moriarty, T. "A Nation of Willing Victims." *Psychology Today,* 8, no. 11 (April 1975), 43–50.

Mulac, A. and Sherman, A. "Behavioral Assessment of Speech Anxiety." *Quarterly Journal of Speech,* 60, no. 2 (1974), 135–143.

Osborn, S. and Harris, G. *Assertive Training for Women.* Springfield, Ill.: Charles C Thomas, 1975.

Paul, G. and Shannon, D. "Treatment of Anxiety through Systematic Desensitization in Therapy

Groups." *Journal of Abnormal and Social Psychology, 71* (1966), 124–135.

Perls, F. *Gestalt Therapy Verbatim.* Lafayette, Calif.: Real People Press, 1969.

Phillips, G. "Reticence: Pathology of the Normal Speaker," *Speech Monographs, 35* (1968), 39–40.

———. "The Reticent Syndrome: Some Theoretical Considerations about Etiology and Treatment." *Speech Monographs, 40* (1973), 220–230.

Powell, J. *Why Am I Afraid to Tell You Who I Am?* Chicago: Argus Communications, 1969.

Rathus, S. "Principles and Practices of Assertive Training: An Eclectic Overview." *Counseling Psychologist, 5,* no. 4 (1975), 9–19.

Rimm, D. and Masters, J. *Behavior Therapy: Techniques and Empirical Findings.* New York: Academic Press, 1974.

Sawrey, W. "An Experimental Investigation of the Role of Psychological Factors in the Production of Gastric Ulcers in Rats." *Journal of Comparative Physiological Psychology, 49* (1956), 457–461.

Selye, H. *The Stress of Life.* New York: McGraw-Hill, 1956.

Shelton, J. and Ackerman, J. *Homework in Counseling and Psychotherapy.* Springfield, Ill.: Charles C Thomas, 1974.

Sherman, A. "Real-Life Exposure as a Primary Therapeutic Factor in the Desensitization Treatment of Fear." *Journal of Abnormal Psychology, 79,* no. 1 (1972), 19–28.

Smith, M. *When I Say No, I Feel Guilty.* New York: Bantam, 1975.

Suinn, R. "Body Thinking: Psychology for Olympic Champs." *Psychology Today, 10,* no. 2 (1976), 38–43.

Watson, D. and Tharp, R. *Self-Directed Behavior: Self-Modification for Personal Adjustment,* 2d ed. Monterey, Calif.: Brooks/Cole, 1977.

Wolf, S. *The Stomach.* Oxford: Oxford University Press, 1965.

Wolfe, J. and Fodor, I. "A Cognitive/Behavioral Approach to Modifying Assertive Behavior in Women." *Counseling Psychologist, 5,* no. 4 (1975).

Wolpe, J. *The Practice of Behavior Therapy,* 2d ed. Elmsford, N.Y.: Pergamon Press, 1973.

———. *Psychotherapy by Reciprocal Inhibition.* Stanford, Calif.: Stanford University Press, 1958.

——— and Lazarus, A. *Behavior Therapy Techniques.* Elmsford, N.Y.: Pergamon Press, 1966.

Wood, J. *What Are You Afraid Of?* Englewood Cliffs, N.J.: Prentice-Hall, 1975.

Zimbardo, P., Pilkonis, P., and Norwood, R. "The Silent Prison of Shyness." Unpublished manuscript, Stanford University, 1974.

———., ———., and ———. "The Social Disease Called Shyness." *Psychology Today, 8,* no. 12 (1975), 69–72.

Zunin, L. and Zunin, N. *Contact: The First Four Minutes.* New York: Ballantine Books, 1972.

Index

DUPLICATED ACTIVITIES

The best way to learn most new skills is with the help of an expert. Since communicating effectively is no exception to this principle, you can expect to make the greatest progress if you receive advice and comments from a professional who can praise you for a job well done and offer suggestions when you might profit by them.

Because you might not have access to such a professional, this feature of *Talking Straight* offers you the chance to ask questions and share your progress with a person knowledgeable in the field of assertiveness training, and receive feedback which can help you to better express yourself most effectively.

The activities which follow are duplicates of most of the exercises in the body of this book. If you feel the need, you are invited to complete and detach the sections of your choice and send them to *Talking Straight* Feedback; Holt, Rinehart and Winston; 383 Madison Ave.; New York, NY 10017. The publisher will forward them to a trained communication consultant, who will look over your progress, offer comments, and return the activity to you. Mail as many activities as you need advice with, but be sure and send each one soon after you have completed it. The point of this feedback is to provide information which you can use to modify your behavior if necessary, so don't proceed too far in the book until you have received your comments. They may cause you to change your approach.

From pages 30–32

▶ No one is born unassertive. Once you realize that your present style of communication is a result of past learning, you will see that it is possible to learn more rewarding ways of self-expression.

Turn to the list of unassertive behaviors you recorded on page 18. Pick the three items there that seem to be the biggest problems for you now. Complete the spaces below for each.

EXAMPLE: a) The behavior   When angry with my family or friends, I either keep the feeling to myself or express it indirectly by hinting, grumbling, or sulking.

b) How it was learned and perpetuated
  ☒ I have never learned better alternatives
  ☒ I have been rewarded for behaving unassertively
  ☐ I have been punished for behaving assertively
  ☐ I have believed in irrational myths

c) Explanation   I grew up in a household where nobody seemed to share angry feelings directly. Some of my friends did come from families where anger was outwardly expressed, but in extremely aggressive ways which I found unappealing. Therefore, I have had no close models for being assertive. Also, now when I do sulk, hint, or grumble, I often get my way, so this indirect aggression has been reinforced.

From pages 30–32

1. a) The behavior _____

_____

_____

   b) How it was learned and perpetuated
   - ☐ I have never learned better alternatives
   - ☐ I have been rewarded for behaving unassertively
   - ☐ I have been punished for behaving assertively
   - ☐ I have believed in irrational myths

   c) Explanation _____

_____

_____

2. a) The behavior _____

_____

_____

   b) How it was learned and perpetuated
   - ☐ I have never learned better alternatives
   - ☐ I have been rewarded for behaving unassertively
   - ☐ I have been punished for behaving assertively
   - ☐ I have believed in irrational myths

   c) Explanation _____

_____

_____

3. a) The behavior _____

_____

_____

   b) How it was learned and perpetuated
   - ☐ I have never learned better alternatives
   - ☐ I have been rewarded for behaving unassertively
   - ☐ I have been punished for behaving assertively
   - ☐ I have believed in irrational myths

   c) Explanation _____

_____

_____

From page 34:

▶ What role does the self-fulfilling prophecy play in shaping your communication? Turn to the list of communication problems you've made on page 18 and recall any instances in which you thought about yourself in a manner that made these events occur when they might otherwise not have happened; in other words, where you behaved in accordance with the self-fulfilling prophecy. List three such instances here, indicating for each one a description of how you behaved, the other person or people involved, and the circumstances in which the behavior occurred.

EXAMPLE: I was recently invited to a party at which I didn't know anyone but the host. I went, even though I was sure I'd have a terrible time. Because of my expectation, I didn't try to meet anyone. Looking back, I can see that I may have created my own miserable situation.

1. _____

_____

_____

_____

2. _____

_____

_____

_____

3. _____

_____

_____

_____

Duplicated page 52 appears on the reverse side of this page.

From page 52:

▶ Whether your problems in stating a core idea clearly are due to embarrassment or hazy thinking, the point is the same. An assertive message must be brief and to the point. Take a few minutes to organize your thoughts and feelings on each of the following subjects into one concise sentence.

a. Describe one dissatisfaction you presently have with the behavior of a friend or acquaintance. _____

_____

_____

b. List one personal belief that you suspect others might dispute.

_____

_____

_____

c. Write one expression of gratitude or appreciation you feel toward another person, including your reasons for feeling as you do. _____

_____

_____

From pages 41–43:

▶   This exercise will help you to identify the situational nature of your communication and to define your personal assertive goals more clearly. Review the list of personal unassertive behaviors you made on page 18. From that information choose three important areas of communication from your life and describe your strengths and weaknesses in each area. Since recording the problems on page 18, you may have become aware of some other ways in which you would like to behave more assertively. If this is so, you may substitute such problems for one or more of the items on page 18.

Remember, if you seriously want to improve your own communication, you must do each exercise in this book before reading on.

EXAMPLE: a. Type of communication Expressing anger
             b. My strengths in this area When it's really important, I express my anger directly to my friends and family instead of holding it inside or being indirectly or directly aggressive.
             c. My weaknesses in this area I often get angry at poor service in stores, restaurants, and government offices. When this happens, I don't say anything and wind up with an upset stomach.

1. a. Type of communication _____

       _____

      b. My strengths in this area _____

       _____

       _____

       _____

      c. My weaknesses in this area _____

       _____

       _____

       _____

2. a. Type of communication _____
      b. My strengths in this area _____

       _____

       _____

From pages 41–43

    c. My weaknesses in this area _____

_____

_____

_____

3. a. Type of communication _____

_____

    b. My strengths in this area _____

_____

_____

_____

    c. My weaknesses in this area _____

_____

_____

_____

From pages 54–55:

▶ Write behavioral definitions for three communication problems; either ones you listed on page 18 or ones you discovered as a result of the checklist immediately above. If you have any difficulty defining the problem behaviorally, begin a diary in which you record your behavior in the situations you have specified. When you are ready, answer the questions below.

Remember, it is important that you complete this exercise before proceeding.

EXAMPLE: a) The people involved in my problem Guests visiting my home.
b) The circumstances in which my problem occurs When I am tired or have something more important to do than keep talking with my guest.
c) The problem behavior I continue to talk to the guests as if I had nothing else to do. I respond to their statements, and deny that I'd like them to go when they suggest that it may be time to leave.

1. a) The people involved in my problem _____

_____

b) The circumstances in which my problem occurs _____

_____

_____

_____

c) The problem behavior _____

_____

_____

_____

2. a) The people involved in my problem _____

_____

b) The circumstances in which my problem occurs _____

_____

_____

_____

c) The problem behavior _____

_____

_____

_____

3. a) The people involved in my problem _____

_____

b) The circumstances in which my problem occurs _____

_____

_____

_____

c) The problem behavior _____

_____

_____

_____

From pages 60–61:

▶ Take a moment now to think of models who skillfully handle each of the situations you described on pages 54–55. The models you choose can be either real or symbolic. For each problem, note the name of the model you have selected and describe the <u>specific</u> behaviors this person exhibits that you would like to master.

EXAMPLE:

The model <u>My friend Cecily</u>

The behaviors your model exhibits that you would like to master <u>When she is tired or busy and guests seem to be staying, she explains without apologizing why she needs to do something else. Usually she doesn't have to do anything else: people understand and leave.</u>

Model 1

The model _____

The behaviors your model exhibits that you would like to master _____

_____

_____

_____

Model 2

The model _____

The behaviors your model exhibits that you would like to master _____

_____

_____

_____

Model 3

The model _____

The behaviors you model exhibits that you would like to master _____

_____

_____

_____

From pages 68–70:

▶ From the list of assertive goals you have recorded in Appendix II, pick three that you would like to work toward. Decide how you could break each one into a series of subgoals, and list your plans below. Before you begin writing, you might find it useful to discuss possible approaches with a friend or instructor, in addition to previewing the material on shaping in Chapter 6, if necessary.

EXAMPLE: I want to take the initiative in my social life by inviting friends to activities instead of waiting for them to make the plans.

    step a. Casually invite R. (carpool partner) to drop by my place on our way home from work.

    step b. Invite J. (a neighbor) to go to the nursery shopping for garden supplies.

    step c. Invite J. over for lunchtime salad prepared from my garden.

    step d. Invite W. over for dinner.

    step e. Invite W., V., and S. with their families over for weekend party.

Goal 1. _____

_____

_____

    step a. _____

_____

    step b. _____

_____

    step c. _____

_____

    step d. _____

_____

    step e. _____

_____

Goal 2. _____

_____

_____

    step a. _____

_____

step b. _____

_____

step c. _____

_____

step d. _____

_____

step e. _____

_____

Goal 3. _____

_____

_____

step a. _____

_____

step b. _____

_____

step c. _____

_____

step d. _____

_____

step e. _____

_____

From page 83:

▶ Describe two communication situations in which you find yourself fearful or anxious.
EXAMPLE: Who the situation involves: Smokers. Mostly strangers, but friends, too.
The circumstances in which it occurs: When the person's smoke is blowing in my face, especially at crowded parties and meetings and when I'm eating.
The way you behave: I feel nauseated and have the urge to either leave or ask the smoker to
put his cigarette out. I imagine that if I did either, the smoker and everyone else would think I
was obnoxious and rude, so I keep quiet.

SITUATION #1
  Who the situation involves: _____

_____

_____

  The circumstances in which it occurs: _____

_____

_____

  The way you behave: _____

_____

SITUATION #2
  Who the situation involves: _____

_____

_____

  The circumstances in which it occurs: _____

_____

_____

  The way you behave: _____

_____

_____

From pages 92–93:

▶ Use the space below to dispute any irrational beliefs which might be causing communication anxiety for you. Begin by applying the form below to the situations you listed on page 83. Or, if you prefer, use it with any other unpleasant emotions associated with your communication.

EXAMPLE: a. The activating event and the emotional consequences which follow The last time we were together my friend T. made the remark that she thought I was a tightwad. For a couple of days since then I've felt depressed and apprehensive about seeing her.

b. Your self-talk concerning the event I guess I interpreted her remark to mean that she didn't like the way I handle my finances with friends, and further that she didn't think much about me as a friend because of the way I've treated her. Since I care about her a great deal, I'm depressed at the loss of her friendship.

c. Dispute any irrational ideas I suppose my interpretation was catastrophic. It's accurate to say that she doesn't approve of the way I handle money, but I don't think that will jeopardize our friendship. She's told me often that she values me a lot, and I know that she'll accept me in spite of what she sees as my tight-fistedness.

Situation 1

a. The activating event and the emotional consequences which follow _____

_____

_____

_____

b. Your self-talk concerning the event _____

_____

_____

_____

_____

_____

c. Dispute any irrational ideas _____

_____

_____

_____

_____

_____

Situation 2

a. The activating event and the emotional consequences which follow_____

_____

_____

_____

b. Your self-talk concerning the event_____

_____

_____

_____

_____

_____

c. Dispute any irrational ideas_____

_____

_____

_____

_____

_____

From page 97:

▶ ANXIETY SITUATION CARDS

1. Cut along the lines.
2. Describe one specific situation in your anxiety hierarchy on each card.
3. Rank orders cards from least to most threatening.
4. Assign a SUDS number to each in the space provided.
5. Write additional situation cards as necessary to keep SUDS level increases gradual.
6. Number each card in the space provided.

From pages 135–144:

► REINFORCEMENT CHECKLIST

There are many ways you can reinforce yourself for practicing a new communication behavior. The list obviously isn't complete: But by suggesting a large number of common reinforcers it will cause you to think of other items that are especially pleasant for you. Use the list as follows:

1. As you move through each category, check any item that might serve as a reinforcer for you. In the space provided fill in any specific details that describe your potential reinforcer more fully. For instance, under the category of "visiting friends" you might list one or two special names; under "reading" you could describe a particular book or a type of reading you enjoy.
2. When you think of a possible reinforcer that is not included on this list, immediately describe it in one of the spaces provided at the end of each section.

When you have finished this page, you should have a catalog of possible reinforcers you can use for your self-modification project.

A. Material Reinforcers

    1. Foods

        a. Snacks _____

        b. Favorite meals or dishes _____

        c. Beverages _____

        d. Dining out _____

        e. _____

        f. _____

    2. Clothing

        a. _____

        b. _____

        c. _____

        d. _____

    3. Hobby Items

        a. Sports equpment _____

        b. Puzzles _____

        c. Photographic equipment _____

        d. Tools _____

        e. Camping gear _____

        f. Musical (instruments, music, etc.) _____

g. _____

h. _____

4. Personal Appearance

    a. Hair styling _____

    b. Cosmetics _____

    c. Jewelry _____

    d. _____

    e. _____

5. Home Decoration and Improvement

    a. Furniture _____

    b. Photographs of paintings _____

    c. Plants and flowers _____

    d. Appliances _____

    e. Music equipment (speaker, records, etc.) _____

    f. _____

    g. _____

6. Books and Magazines

    a. Fiction _____

    b. Current events _____

    c. Art _____

    d. Humor _____

    e. School _____

    f. _____

    g. _____

7. Transportation (car, bicycle, motorcycle, etc.)

    a. Repairs _____

    b. Accessories _____

    c. _____

    d. _____

8. Savings (set aside a specified amount for each assertive act or goal reached)

    a. For specific object _____

    b. For general savings _____

9. Other Material Reinforcers

    a. _____

    b. _____

    c. _____

    d. _____

    e. _____

    f. _____

    g. _____

B. Social Reinforcers

  10. Receiving Compliments from Others

    a. _____

    b. _____

    c. _____

    d. _____

  11. Receiving Affection

    a. _____

    b. _____

    c. _____

    d. _____

  12. Hearing Jokes

    a. _____

    b. _____

  13. Visiting with Friends

    a. _____

    b. _____

    c. _____

    d. _____

  14. Visiting with Relatives

    a. _____

    b. _____

    c. _____

    d. _____

15. Talking on the Telephone

    a. _____

    b. _____

    c. _____

16. Meeting New People

    a. _____

    b. _____

    c. _____

17. Receiving Surprise Gifts

    a. _____

    b. _____

    c. _____

18. Saying "I told you so"

    a. _____

    b. _____

    c. _____

19. Giving Parties

    a. _____

    b. _____

20. Attending Parties

    a. _____

    b. _____

21. Going on Dates

    a. _____

    b. _____

    c. _____

22. Flirting

    a. _____

    b. _____

    c. _____

23. Sex

    a. _____

b. _____

c. _____

d. _____

24. Other Social Reinforcers

a. _____

b. _____

c. _____

d. _____

e. _____

f. _____

g. _____

C. Activity Reinforcers

25. Traveling

a. Driving _____

b. Vacationing _____

c. Visiting new place near your home _____

d. Sightseeing _____

e. _____

f. _____

g. _____

26. Exercise

a. Cycling _____

b. Tennis _____

c. Golf _____

d. Swimming _____

e. Football _____

f. Baseball _____

g. Basketball _____

h. Bowling _____

i. Skiing _____

j. Running _____

k. Hiking or taking walks _____

l. Horseback riding _____

m. _____

n. _____

o. _____

p. _____

q. _____

27. Television or Radio

    a. _____

    b. _____

    c. _____

28. Reading

    a. Fiction _____

    b. Current events _____

    c. History _____

    d. Humor _____

    e. School _____

    f. Biography _____

    g. _____

    h. _____

    i. _____

29. Going to Movies, Plays or Concerts

    a. _____

    b. _____

    c. _____

30. Looking at Attractive Men or Women

    a. _____

    b. _____

    c. _____

31. Hobbies

    a. Sewing _____

    b. Crafts _____

    c. Collecting _____

d. Art _____

e. Puzzles _____

f. _____

g. _____

h. _____

32. Dancing

a. _____

b. _____

c. _____

33. Picnicking and Camping

a. _____

b. _____

c. _____

34. Gardening

a. _____

b. _____

c. _____

35. Playing Cards or Gambling

a. _____

b. _____

36. Listening to Music

a. Live _____

b. Recorded, at home _____

c. In the car _____

d. _____

37. Cooking

a. Your own favorite foods _____

b. For others _____

c. _____

d. _____

38. Smoking

a. _____

b. _____

39. Free time

   a. Time to "waste" without guilt _____

   b. _____

   c. _____

40. Bathing

   a. Bubble bath _____

   b. Showering _____

   c. Sauna _____

41. Sleeping

   a. Oversleep in morning _____

   b. Naps _____

   c. _____

   d. _____

42. Other Activity Reinforcers

   a. _____

   b. _____

   c. _____

   d. _____

   e. _____

   f. _____

   g. _____

3. List the reinforcers here that have met the above criteria and that you are satisfied would be most effective in your self-modification project.

_____

_____

_____

_____

4. Now transfer some or all of these items to your Self-Modification Progress Chart. Indicate which ones you will use to reinforce single instances of desired behaviors and which you will earn for reaching intermediate goals. For examples, see the sample Progress Charts in Appendix IV.

From pages 156–159:

▶ Test your ability to distinguish between the various levels of communication about which you've just read. In the spaces following the example list three genuine personal responses for each category.

SAMPLE TOPIC: The author and his writing.
  a. Facts
   1. This is the second book I've written.
   2. The first one was a text on interpersonal communication.
   3. Thanks to my efforts I was able to take a trip to Canada this past summer. I may even have enough money left over to repair my leaky roof before the rains come.
  b. Opinions
   1. I think it's been worth the effort to write the books.
   2. I think I've become a better instructor as a result of the research involved in my writing.
   3. I'm not very efficient when it comes to dividing my time between writing and fooling around.
  c. Feelings
   1. I'm flattered and proud that a first-rate company thought enough of my work to publish it.
   2. I'm getting nervous about whether I'll finish this manuscript before the publisher's deadline.
   3. Right now I'm tired of writing and think I'll spend the rest of this sunny day at the beach.

1. TOPIC: Assertiveness training
  a. Facts

   1. _____

   _____

   _____

   2. _____

   _____

   _____

   3. _____

   _____

   _____

  b. Opinions

   1. _____

   _____

   _____

2. _____
_____
_____

3. _____
_____
_____

c. Feelings

1. _____
_____
_____

2. _____
_____
_____

3. _____
_____
_____

2. TOPIC: The next five years of your life
   a. Facts

1. _____
_____
_____

2. _____
_____
_____

3. _____
_____
_____

b. Opinions

1. _____
_____
_____

2. _____
_____
_____
_____

3. _____
_____
_____

c. Feelings

1. _____
_____
_____
_____

2. _____
_____
_____
_____

3. _____
_____
_____

3. TOPIC: The present state of this country's government
   a. Facts

1. _____
_____
_____
_____

2. _____
_____
_____
_____

3. _____
_____
_____

b. Opinions

1. _____
_____
_____

2. _____

_____

_____

3. _____

_____

_____

c. Feelings

1. _____

_____

_____

2. _____

_____

_____

3. _____

_____

_____

From pages 165–167:

▶ Sharpen your skill at asking open-ended question by trying the following activities, either independently or in your assertiveness-building group.

1. Write a list of five open-ended questions that you could comfortably ask in each of the following settings:

 a. Meeting a stranger at a party

  (1) _____

  _____

  (2) _____

  _____

  (3) _____

  _____

  (4) _____

  _____

  (5) _____

  _____

 b. Talking with a traveler from another part of the country

  (1) _____

  _____

  (2) _____

  _____

  (3) _____

  _____

  (4) _____

  _____

  (5) _____

  _____

 c. Being introduced to a new worker at your job

  (1) _____

  _____

  (2) _____

  _____

  (3) _____

  _____

(4) _____

_____

(5) _____

_____

d. Sitting next to a stranger on the first day of class or at a lecture series

(1) _____

_____

(2) _____

_____

(3) _____

_____

(4) _____

_____

(5) _____

_____

e. One other situation you recently experienced in which you were at a loss for conversation

(1) _____

_____

(2) _____

_____

(3) _____

_____

(4) _____

_____

(5) _____

_____

2. With two companions form a trio consisting of a questioner, responder, and observer. The questioner's role is to begin and carry on a conversation by asking only open-ended questions. The responder should only reply to these questions, not ask any questions in return. As in preceding exercises, the critic should point out both the strengths and areas of potential improvement in the questioner's behavior. Rotate the roles until each participant has filled all three parts.

3. Tune in one of the many "talk shows" or public affairs programs on television every week. Notice how the interviewer almost exclusively asks open-ended questions to encourage the guest to offer free information. Do you "interview" people—solicit their opinions, feelings, or seek information? Ask yourself how you could apply some of the skills you observed on television to these situations.

From page 179:

Events surrounding the feeling	The feeling you experienced	The manner in which you expressed the feeling	The consequences of your behavior

From page 179

Events surrounding the feeling	The feeling you experienced	The manner in which you expressed the feeling	The consequences of your behavior

From pages 203–206:

▶ Test your understanding of these methods for assertively coping with criticism. Below is a list of three complaints you have probably heard more than once in your life. For each one indicate how you might use the questioning and agreeing techniques described in the text.

As you read each comment, try to visualize a specific person from your life speaking it. Picture the place, time, and the circumstances that prompted the comment. As you write your responses, get a clear image of yourself speaking the words in an assertive manner.

SAMPLE CRITICISM: "Sometimes I think you don't take me seriously. It seems like everything I say goes in one ear and out the other."
  A. Questioning responses
    1. Ask for specifics "I'd understand what you mean better if you could give me some examples of when I seem to be ignoring you."
    2. Guess about specifics "Are you talking about times this has happened just lately, or has it been going on for a while?"
    3. Paraphase the speaker's ideas "It sounds like you're mad at me because you think I'm just humoring you sometimes so you'll stop talking. Is that it?"
    4. Ask for the consequences of your actions "Why does it matter whether I take you seriously or not?"
    5. Ask for more complaints "Is it just my not taking you seriously that's upsetting you, or is there something else too?"
  B. Agreeing responses
    1. Agree with the truth "Well, I suppose you're right. Sometimes I don't pay attention to what you say, mostly when I'm tired or mad."
    2. Agree with the odds "I suppose you're probably right. I'm sure I don't always give you my full attention."
    3. Agree in principle "You're right. The decent thing would be for me to always pay attention to you. If I was a better communicator, I'd probably do it more."
    4. Agree with the perception "I can see why you might think that I'm not listening when I say I'll do something and then don't."

STATEMENT #1: "You know, you're sure sensitive to criticism. You shouldn't be so touchy—it'll only get you in trouble."
  A. Questioning responses

    1. Ask for specifics _____

    _____

    _____

    2. Guess about specifics _____

    _____

    _____

3. Paraphrase the speaker's ideas _____

_____

_____

4. Ask for the consequences of your actions _____

_____

_____

5. Ask for more complaints _____

_____

_____

B. Agreeing responses

1. Agree with the truth _____

_____

_____

2. Agree with the odds _____

_____

_____

3. Agree in principle _____

_____

_____

4. Agree with the perception _____

_____

_____

STATEMENT #2: "You're going to have to do a better job around here. I just don't think you're trying your hardest."

A. Questioning responses

1. Ask for specifics _____

_____

_____

2. Guess about specifics _____

_____

_____

3. Paraphrase the speaker's ideas _____

_____

_____

4. Ask for the consequences of your actions _____

_____

_____

5. Ask for more complaints _____

_____

_____

B. Agreeing responses

1. Agree with the truth _____

_____

_____

2. Agree with the odds _____

_____

_____

3. Agree in principle _____

_____

_____

4. Agree with the perception _____

_____

_____

STATEMENT #3: "You've certainly been in a lousy mood lately. Sometimes you're awfully hard to live with."

A. Questioning responses

1. Ask for specifics _____

_____

_____

2. Guess about specifics _____

_____

_____

3. Paraphrase the speaker's ideas _____

_____

_____

4. Ask for the consequences of your actions _____

_____

_____

5. Ask for more complaints _____

_____

_____

B. Agreeing responses

1. Agree with the truth _____

_____

_____

2. Agree with the odds _____

_____

_____

3. Agree in principle _____

_____

_____

4. Agree with the perception _____

_____

_____

You can also practice managing criticism by trying the following exercise, based on the work of Smith (1975).

Join with a partner and decide which of you will take the role of critic. The other partner then becomes the coping recipient. The critic begins by pointing out some fault—real or imagined—about the recipient, who in turn uses one or more of the techniques described in this chapter to respond. The critic then escalates the attack by either amplifying the original complaint or finding a new one. This process goes on for a period of three or four minutes, during which the only responses the recipient can make are limited to those listed above. Upon completing this half of the role-playing, the partners switch positions and repeat the procedure.

This activity can become quite humorous as the criticisms become more and more outlandish, but the point is still clear: You can listen to and respond to the attacks of another person without becoming defensive or abusive yourself.

From pages 215–218:

▶ Check your understanding of the various styles of conflict management by examining the four communication situations below. Either by yourself or in a small group, write four responses for each: Nonassertive, directly aggressive, indirectly aggressive, and assertive. Describe the probable consequences of each.

EXAMPLE: Three weeks ago your friend borrowed an article of clothing, promising to return it soon. You haven't seen it since, and the friend hasn't mentioned it.

Nonassertive response <u>Say nothing to the friend, hoping she will remember and return the item.</u>

Probable consequences of this response <u>There's a good chance I'll never get the item back. I would probably resent the friend and avoid her in the future so I won't have to lend anything else.</u>

Directly aggressive response <u>Confront the friend and accuse her of being inconsiderate and irresponsible. Say that she probably ruined the item and is afraid to say so.</u>

Probable consequences. <u>My friend would get defensive and hurt. Even if she did intentionally keep the item, she'd never admit it when approached this way. We would probably avoid each other in the future.</u>

Indirectly aggressive response <u>Drop hints about how I loved to wear the borrowed item. Casually mention how much I hate people who don't return things. Gossip about the incident to others.</u>

Probable consequences <u>My friend would be embarrassed by my gossip. She might ignore my hints. She'll most certainly resent my roundabout approach, even if she returns the article.</u>

Assertive response <u>Confront the friend in a noncritical way and remind her that she still has the item. Ask when she'll return it, being sure to get a specific time.</u>

Probable consequences <u>The friend might be embarrassed when I bring the subject up, but since there's no attack it'll probably be okay. Since we'll have cleared up the problem, the relationship can continue.</u>

1. Someone you've just met at a party criticizes a mutual friend in a way you think is unfair.

   Nonassertive response _____

   _____

   _____

   _____

   Directly aggressive _____

   _____

   _____

   _____

   Indirectly aggressive _____

   _____

   _____

   _____

Assertive _____

_____

_____

_____

2. A fan behind you at a ballgame toots a loud air horn every time the home team makes any progress. The noise is spoiling your enjoyment of the game.

Nonassertive response _____

_____

_____

_____

Directly aggressive _____

_____

_____

_____

Indirectly aggressive _____

_____

_____

_____

Assertive _____

_____

_____

_____

3. Earlier in the day you asked the person with whom you live to stop by the store and pick up snacks for a party you are having this evening. He/she arrives home without the food, and it's too late to return to the store.

Nonassertive response _____

_____

_____

_____

Directly aggressive _____

_____

_____

_____

Indirectly aggressive _____

_____

_____

_____

Assertive _____

_____

_____

_____

4. You are explaining your political views to a friend who has asked your opinion. Now the friend obviously isn't listening: You think to yourself that since the person asked for your ideas, the least he/she can do is pay attention.

Nonassertive response _____

_____

_____

_____

Directly aggressive _____

_____

_____

_____

Indirectly aggressive _____

_____

_____

_____

Assertive _____

_____

_____

_____

Now that you understand these four types of responses, return to the personal conflicts you described on pages 209–210 and decide in which manner you handled each. Based on these examples and other incidents you can recall, how would you say you behave when your needs are unmet—nonassertively, with direct aggression, with indirect aggression, or assertively? After you have formed your own opinion, explain these concepts to one or more friends and see how they classify you. Are you satisfied with your present manner of handling conflicts? If not, consider how you can apply the methods described in this chapter to your life.

From pages 220–221:

▶ In order to manage your conflicts constructively, it is vital for you to recognize that the only time you initiate a conflict is when some need for yours is not being met. To verify this principle, describe below four incidents in which you either thought about or actually did judge or criticize another person's behavior. Describe your problem in each incident—in other words, state the need that prompted you to speak out.

EXAMPLE

Your complaint or criticism <u>I criticized my friend in an indirectly aggressive manner by mentioning that she must be quite busy since she hasn't dropped by to see my new place as she promised.</u>

Your unmet need that prompted the comment <u>I had two unmet needs here: (1) I enjoy socializing with her, and (2) I need some reassurance that my friendship is still important to her.</u>

CONFLICT #1

Your complaint or criticism _____

_____

_____

Your unmet need that prompted the comment _____

_____

_____

CONFLICT #2

Your complaint or criticism _____

_____

_____

Your unmet need that prompted the comment _____

_____

_____

CONFLICT #3

Your complaint or criticism _____

_____

_____

Your unmet need that prompted the comment _____

_____

_____

From pages 220–221

CONFLICT #4

Your complaint or criticism _____

_____

_____

Your unmet need that prompted the comment _____

_____

_____

From pages 224–227:

▶   Write an "I have a problem" response for each of the situations below. Remember to include in your answer a description of the <u>specific behavior</u> that causes or constitutes your behavior, and a clear indication of the intensity of your <u>feelings</u> on the matter. Label each of these elements in parenthesis.

SAMPLE SITUATION: For some time you have felt that an old friend is angry at you. This person hasn't suggested that you get together in a long time, and every time you try to suggest a date you get a cool response.

   Your statement <u>There's something that has been bothering me and I want to share it with you. I'm afraid that you're angry with me for some reason (feeling). I say that because you haven't invited me to get together with you for almost three months, and every time I call you say that you're busy (behavior). I'm worried that if things go on this way our friendship will be over, and I'd hate to see that (consequences)."</u>

   Situation #1: An acquaintance has lately become involved in a local fund-raising drive and has asked you several times to join in the effort by doing some door-to-door soliciting. You've politely said that you aren't interested, but the acquaintance has continued to insist that you help.

   Your statement _____

_____

_____

_____

_____

_____

Situation #2: You have enrolled in a class you find interesting. The only problem is that the instructor often disgresses from the subject at hand by telling long and (to you) uninteresting stories about his travels. You want to spend your time learning more about the stated topic.

   Your statement _____

_____

_____

_____

_____

_____

   Situation #3: For several years you have been eating at a local restaurant. The food has been good, the atmosphere pleasant, and the service friendly and attentive. Lately, however, the place has changed. The new waiters haven't seemed to care about you, the place hasn't seemed as clean as before, and the food is often mediocre. You have decided to give the restaurant one last chance, and as you are eating a tasteless stew, the owner approaches you and asks you if everything is all right.

   Your statement _____

_____

_____

_____

_____

_____

▶ Once you have completed the statements above and are satisfied that you understand how to use the "I have a problem" formula, turn to the personal conflicts you described on pages 209 and 210. In the spaces below describe how you could apply this new method if you chose to share your problem with the other person or people involved. As before, make sure you clearly identify the problem as your own and that your descriptions of the troublesome behavior, its consequences, and your resulting feelings are detailed.

Conflict #1 _____

_____

_____

_____

_____

Conflict #2 _____

_____

_____

_____

_____

Conflict #3 _____

_____

_____

_____

Conflict #4 _____

_____

_____

_____

From pages 233–234:

▶ Take another look at the conflicts you described on pages 209 and 210. For each one decide how you would like the other person to change and describe how you could make the request by hinting, demanding, and asking assertively.

SAMPLE CONFLICT

Hint "I'm glad you're here. I was beginning to wonder whether I had written the wrong date on my calendar."

Demand "You're going to have to show up on time from now on. I'm sick of waiting around for you."

Ask "From now on I'd like you to show up within a few minutes of the time we agree on."

CONFLICT 1

Hint _____

_____

_____

Demand _____

_____

_____

Ask _____

_____

_____

CONFLICT 2

Hint _____

_____

_____

Demand _____

_____

_____

Ask _____

_____

_____

CONFLICT 3

Hint _____

_____

_____

Demand _____

_____

_____

Ask _____

_____

_____

CONFLICT 4

Hint _____

_____

_____

Demand _____

_____

_____

Ask _____

_____

_____

From pages 235–236:

▶ In the following spaces describe the consequences that will follow the acceptance or the rejection of the requests you outlined on pages 233 and 234. Phrase your description in a way to demonstrate your nonthreatening attitude and genuine desire to find a solution that's satisfying for both parties.

SAMPLE CONFLICT: "If you can show up on time from now on, I know it will be better for both of us: We won't have to rush so much, and we won't fight over being late. On the other hand, I'm afraid that if we do continue to run late, I'll probably get angrier and angrier."

CONFLICT 1 _____

_____

_____

_____

_____

CONFLICT 2 _____

_____

_____

_____

_____

CONFLICT 3 _____

_____

_____

_____

_____

CONFLICT 4 _____

_____

_____

_____

_____

▶ **SELF-MODIFICATION PROGRESS CHART**

TENTATIVE INTERMEDIATE GOALS*   REINFORCERS*

1. _____   _____
2. _____   _____
3. _____   _____
4. _____   _____
5. _____   _____
6. _____   _____
7. _____   _____
8. _____   _____

Frequency of Target Behaviors Described in (c) Below

Days

Target

a.   The person or people involved _____
     _____

b.   The circumstances in which I want to behave more assertively _____
     _____

c.   The specific behavior(s) I want to increase _____
     _____

*Projects following the elements approach should use the Supplementary Progress Chart on the next page to record intermediate goals and reinforcers.

▶ **SELF-MODIFICATION PROGRESS CHART**

TENTATIVE INTERMEDIATE GOALS*   REINFORCERS*

1. _____   _____
2. _____   _____
3. _____   _____
4. _____   _____
5. _____   _____
6. _____   _____
7. _____   _____
8. _____   _____

Frequency of Target Behaviors Described in (c) Below

Days

Target

a.   The person or people involved _____

_____

b.   The circumstances in which I want to behave more assertively _____

_____

c.   The specific behavior(s) I want to increase _____

_____

*Projects following the elements approach should use the Supplementary Progress Chart on the next page to record intermediate goals and reinforcers.

▶ SELF-MODIFICATION PROGRESS CHART

TENTATIVE INTERMEDIATE GOALS*   REINFORCERS*

1. _____   _____
2. _____   _____
3. _____   _____
4. _____   _____
5. _____   _____
6. _____   _____
7. _____   _____
8. _____   _____

Frequency of Target Behaviors
Described in (c) Below

Days

Target

a.   The person or people involved _____

b.   The circumstances in which I want to behave more assertively _____

c.   The specific behavior(s) I want to increase _____

*Projects following the elements approach should use the Supplementary Progress Chart on the next page to record intermediate goals and reinforcers.

▶ **SELF–MODIFICATION PROGRESS CHART**

TENTATIVE INTERMEDIATE GOALS*   REINFORCERS*

1. _____   _____
2. _____   _____
3. _____   _____
4. _____   _____
5. _____   _____
6. _____   _____
7. _____   _____
8. _____   _____

Frequency of Target Behaviors Described in (c) Below

Days

Target

a.   The person or people involved _____

b.   The circumstances in which I want to behave more assertively _____

c.   The specific behavior(s) I want to increase _____

*Projects following the elements approach should use the Supplementary Progress Chart on the next page to record intermediate goals and reinforcers.

From page 268:

▲ SUPPLEMENTARY PROGRESS CHART
(Sample in Appendix IV)

1. Use this chart in projects with intermediate steps consisting of separate elements. (See pages 127–128.)

2. As you work on each element, describe it in the leftmost clear space above the graph, and record your progress immediately below.

3. Along with each intermediate goal, describe the reinforcer you will use to increase its frequency.

4. In addition to working on the intermediate goals listed below, remember to keep recording the frequency of your ultimate target on the Self-Modification Progress Chart. As you master each intermediate goal, you should begin to see improvement on your final target.

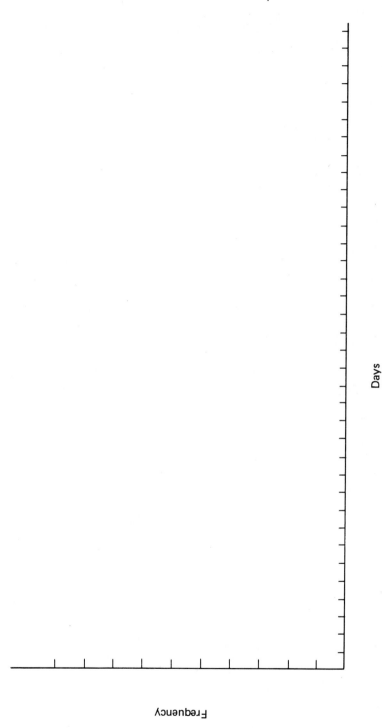

Frequency

Days

From page 268

▲ SUPPLEMENTARY PROGRESS CHART
(Sample in Appendix IV)

1. Use this chart in projects with intermediate steps consisting of separate elements. (See pages 127–128.)

2. As you work on each element, describe it in the leftmost clear space above the graph, and record your progress immediately below.

3. Along with each intermediate goal, describe the reinforcer you will use to increase its frequency.

4. In addition to working on the intermediate goals listed below, remember to keep recording the frequency of your ultimate target on the Self-Modification Progress Chart. As you master each intermediate goal, you should begin to see improvement on your final target.

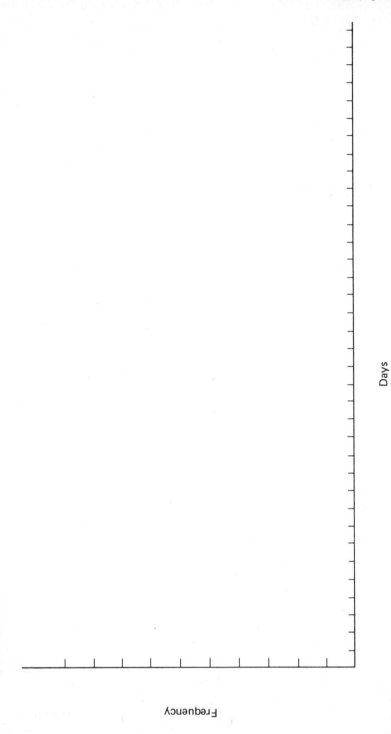

Frequency

Days